HOMICIDE IN THE UNITED STATES

THE UNIVERSITY OF NORTH CAROLINA
SOCIAL STUDY SERIES

UNDER THE GENERAL EDITORSHIP OF HOWARD W. ODUM. BOOKS MARKED WITH *
PUBLISHED IN COÖPERATION WITH THE INSTITUTE FOR RESEARCH IN SOCIAL SCIENCE.

*The University of North Carolina Press, Chapel Hill, N. C.; The
Baker and Taylor Co., New York; Oxford University Press,
London; The Maruzen Company, Tokyo; Edward Evans &
Sons, Ltd., Shanghai; D. B. Centen's Wetenschappelijke Bock-
handle, Amsterdam.*

HOMICIDE IN THE
UNITED STATES

BY

H. C. BREARLEY, Ph.D.

Professor of Sociology in the Clemson Agricultural College

CHAPEL HILL
THE UNIVERSITY OF NORTH CAROLINA PRESS
1932

TO

HOWARD W. ODUM
Teacher and Friend

PREFACE

THE DRAMA of violent death has been a favorite literary theme from the time of Homer's *Iliad* to the present day vogue of the tabloid and the detective story. Homicides have, however, far greater significance socially than as source material for writers. Yet in the United States the wider significance has received scant attention from sociologists. This monograph is an attempt to supply in part this deficiency.

A comprehensive study of all aspects of the homicide problem has not, however, been possible, mainly because of the difficulty of securing reliable data. Since the original studies reported in this volume have been made from time to time as opportunity could be obtained, they are not all based upon the same period of years. The relative scarcity of material from foreign countries is also regretted.

The author wishes to express his indebtedness to the officials of the United States Division of Vital Statistics for help in securing unpublished data, to the University of North Carolina Institute for Research in Social Science for financial aid in obtaining records and in providing for publication, to *Social Forces* and *Sociology and Social Research* for permission to use material which originally appeared in their columns, to Dr. Howard W. Odum for his encouragement and guidance through many difficulties, and to Dr. Edwin H. Sutherland, Dr. Maurice Parmelee, and Dr. Frederick L. Hoffman for assistance even greater than that indicated by numerous citations.

H. C. B.

September, 1931.
Clemson College, South Carolina.

[vii]

CONTENTS

HOMICIDE IN THE UNITED STATES

CHAPTER I

THE HOMICIDE PROBLEM

IN MATERIAL CULTURE modern man gives increasing evidence of his mastery of the forces of nature, but in the field of human relationships he has failed signally to make equal progress. This failure to achieve social well-being is revealed by the persistence, if not the actual increase, of crime and criminalistic behavior. Among the more significant manifestations of the inadequacy of social control is the prevalence of homicide, the non-accidental slaying of one person by another.[1] This crime, consequently, and other types of anti-social behavior should receive even greater attention, if human welfare is to keep pace with material progress.

In studying crime, however, the lack of reliable data proves to be a serious obstacle, as the third report of the National Commission on Law Observance and Enforcement has clearly pointed out.[2] Prison records enumerate only those offenders who are apprehended and convicted. The statistics published by police departments and court officials are often inaccurate, obscure, or otherwise unsatisfactory.[3] With a few notable exceptions such reports deal with criminals rather than with the number of offenses actually committed.

Concerning homicide, however, relatively trustworthy data can be secured from the reports of the vital statistics registration bureaus. Within the federal registration area,

---

[1] For a more detailed definition of homicide see p. 203.
[2] United Press report, April 26, 1931.
[3] *Cf.* pp. 200-03.

[3]

now comprising over 95 per cent of the population of the United States, each death is reported upon a uniform certificate which gives the cause of death, age of the deceased, and similar information. In spite of certain inaccuracies these death certificates are the source of valid data relating to the extent of one type of anti-social behavior—homicide.[4]

Not only is homicide the one offense of importance for which reliable data can be secured, it is also a crime typical of many others in that it arises from the exaggeration of the wishes of the offender and consequent minimization of the rights and desires of others. Besides, it has been observed that, except perhaps in regions of primitive culture, wherever life is unsafe, property also is likely to be endangered. According to Haynes, crime is most prevalent in towns and small cities and least frequent in rural communities, cities of over 100,000 population coming between these two.[5] This volume will present evidence that homicide follows the same relative distribution. There is the possibility, therefore, that rates of homicide may indicate the amount of crime of all types. If this is correct, the investigations to be described in this monograph will have a two-fold significance: first, as data concerning the homicide problem itself, and, second, as indices revealing the presence of anti-social attitudes and tendencies in somewhat the same way that illiteracy rates indicate ignorance and educational inefficiency.

HOMICIDE RATES

Yet in proportion to its importance, both in itself and as an index of social disorganization, the homicide problem

[4] *Cf.* pp. 12-15.   [5] *Criminology*, pp. 14-15.

has received relatively little study in the United States. Vital statistics reports give rates per 100,000 for each of the states within the registration area and for some of the larger cities. This information is rather inaccessible, however, and is little used, even by criminologists. For the general public the newspaper articles of Frederick L. Hoffman have been the chief source of knowledge.

The principal tables presented in Chapter X of this volume have been prepared in order to supply a greater amount of definite information. By an examination of Table X the reader can find the rate per 100,000 population of all cities in the registration area which had 10,000 or more inhabitants upon January 1, 1920.[6] Many will doubtless be surprised to learn that Chicago in spite of its gangster wars has a homicide rate far less than those of dozens of the smaller cities. In this case, the little information supplied the public by the newspapers proves upon further study to be somewhat distorted by the spectacular nature of the slayings. The "holier than thou" attitude of many of the less populous communities is often based upon ignorance of comparative data. Chicago's "homicide a day" may be a less deplorable record than some small city's one slaying a week.

A citizen of the United States, especially one from the South, is likely to defend the homicide record of his country by laying a large part of the blame upon the Negro. In Table XI are shown the comparative rates for white and colored persons in those cities for which the necessary data were available.[7] This topic is also treated in Chapter VI.[8]

[6] *Cf.* p. 209.
[7] *Cf.* p. 217.   [8] *Cf.* p. 97.

A previous study of homicide in South Carolina during the period 1920-1926 revealed the fact that state-wide data may conceal significant local differences. Although the average rate of homicide for the state in this period was 13.44 per 100,000 persons, within the state the rates

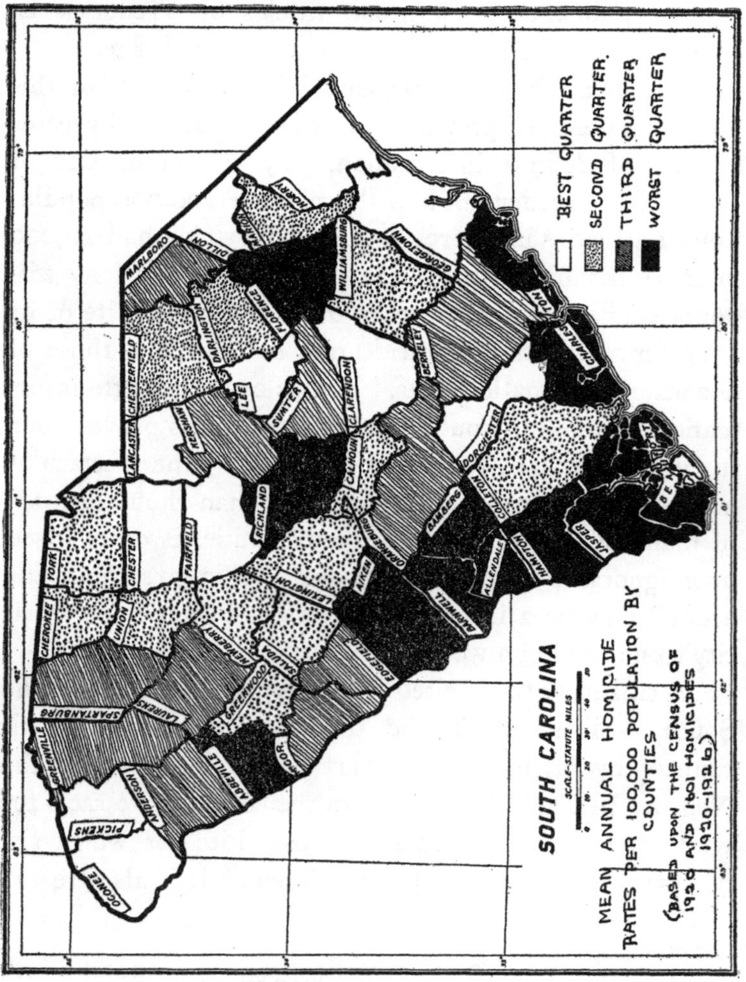

FIGURE 1. DISTRIBUTION OF HOMICIDE IN SOUTH CAROLINA, 1920-1926.

ranged from 2.02 in one county to 82.8 in one city. Figure
1 shows a homicide map of this state based upon the number of slayings in each county during the years 1920-1926
and upon the population for January 1, 1920. In preparing the data for this map the homicides for each of the
cities were included in their respective county totals. (This
is contrary to the usual practice.)

In order to discover, if possible, other important regional and local differences the homicide rate was calculated for each of the counties in the registration area states.
In these calculations the data for the cities were not placed
in the county totals, so that Table XII gives information
concerning rural areas only.[9] As will be explained elsewhere, however, the rates for rural communities are
slightly decreased by the transportation of fatally wounded
persons from the country to city hospitals. The comparative rates for city and country are also discussed at length
in Chapter VIII.[10]

The more than 3,000 calculations presented in the
three tables mentioned above were based upon unpublished records copied from the files of the United States
Division of Vital Statistics and upon the estimated number
of inhabitants upon July 1, 1920, and July 1, 1925. The
data for the two years were combined in order to give a
more reliable index than would the two years taken separately. Whenever complete information was lacking or
when the population estimates could not be made upon the
usual basis, the exceptions have been noted in the table.

The publication of these data may, perhaps, help
arouse local pride and lead to efforts to reduce the inci-

[9] *Cf.* p. 220. [10] *Cf.* p. 151.

dence of crime, especially of deeds of violence. Such information has resulted in great interest in several cities, notably in Chicago, and has appreciably assisted in increasing public support of the agencies for the prevention and reduction of crime.

OTHER STUDIES

Besides attempting to supply a greater volume of facts concerning the extent of homicide, this monograph presents studies of many other phases of this problem. If homicide is a fairly accurate index of crime, do the people of the United States really live in "the most lawless of civilized nations," as is so frequently asserted? Sir Gilbert Chesterton feelingly describes the "barbarism" of this country and tells of one state "where if a man insults you, you are expected to shoot him with a gun or you're not considered a gentleman. Call it barbarism or chivalry, it's the feudal spirit full of feud."[11] Do the facts support this distinguished visitor's conclusions?

Is the high rate of homicide in the South due to the warm climate, to the presence of the Negro, or to other causes? Does the weather influence the amount and type of crime? In some sections of the United States many persons are accustomed to carry revolvers. Is this practice likely to result in more homicides? England and Canada have justly famous police systems. How do those of the United States compare with these?

What type of person commits homicide? Is he the worst of criminals, as the penalties for murder attest? Or is he really the least anti-social of offenders, as is implied in the following description?

[11] Associated Press report, April 29, 1931.

Both before and after a murder the perpetrator thereof is usually quite an ordinary human being, personable or commonplace as the case may be, a dullard, a genius, a scholar, a gentleman or even a hero. . . . A wife doesn't poison her husband for the joy of seeing him die. She does it for his money, for a lover, to be free of his cruelty. Beyond this slight defect in her social scheme, she may be a loving mother, a good housewife and an excellent cook, except upon the day that she puts in the arsenic.[12]

Is the cause of crime individual or social? Is the offender responsible or is his community or his family? Is there evidence in support of Paul Aubrey's conclusion that the criminal's situation may properly be compared to one's contracting a contagious disease? If the bacteria are present, the susceptible individuals become ill but others escape because they do not provide a suitable medium for the growth of the disorder. Similarly with crime, the social situation or circumstances are the bacteria, while the persons deficient in character represent the susceptible individuals. Is crime, consequently, both individual and social?[13]

Does the study of the personality of the slayer lead one to sympathize with his misfortunes?[14] Does the phrase "to understand all is to forgive all" apply to a knowledge of the character of those who commit homicide? In regard to this Bjerre says, "The deeper we succeed in penetrating into the psychic life of, for example, a murderer, the more morally revolting the crime he has committed

[12] C. R. Cooper, "The Worst of Us," *Collier's*, LXXXVII, 19 ff, February 28, 1931.

[13] Bernaldo de Quiros, *Modern Theories of Criminality*, p. 60.

[14] In this volume the word *slayer* is generally used instead of the common term *murderer*, since in legal phraseology a murderer is one who commits homicide after premeditation. There seems to be no single precise word meaning one who commits homicide—planned or unplanned.

usually appears," even though "the moral condemnation is directed more and more against the evil rather than against the evildoer."[15]   Is Bjerre's comment defensible? Does the slayer, upon intimate acquaintance, attract or repel?

Such questions as those suggested above have been given extended treatment in the subsequent chapters of this volume.   To these and to the many other questions that arise, categorical answers have rarely been possible. When the evidence is equivocal or conflicting, the primary data have been given, if available, in order that the reader may make his own evaluation.

TOPICS FOR FURTHER INVESTIGATION

The studies reported in this volume have, however, been insufficient to treat of all phases of the homicide problem.   Many important topics need further investigation. Some of these have been omitted for lack of definite information, which could not be secured without great effort or expense.   For example, there is need of a thorough field survey to determine how accurate are the homicide reports now being made to state and federal bureaus of vital statistics.   What proportion of the "probably accidental" cases are really homicides?   Are homicides often concealed by inaccurate or indefinite statements upon the death certificates?

A study of inter-racial slayings would make it possible to estimate what proportion of the homicides among Negroes is due to whites.   Do Negroes kill whites more or less frequently than whites kill Negroes?   Besides, is the Negro's high homicide rate due to a racial difference or is

[15] *The Psychology of Murder*, pp. 10-11.

it because many Negroes are poor, uneducated, and unable to secure redress of wrongs except by violence?

A similar investigation is needed in order to determine more accurately the effect of immigration. Do the foreign-born really commit more homicides than do native whites who are equally handicapped financially and socially? Such a study might clarify the problem of the alien slayer.

The tables giving homicide rates for the counties of each state show striking variations, neighboring counties often differing greatly. Careful studies of these variations should be made in an attempt to explain territorial diversities. From this regional research it might be possible to discover what conditions tend to increase homicide and thus to arrive at more adequate explanations of the high homicide rates in the United States.

The principal tables in this volume have been based upon the homicidal deaths in the years 1920 and 1925. When the 1930 records are available, they can, it is hoped, be included with the previous data and will provide rates which should be more trustworthy and conclusive. This continuation and extension of city and county data should increase their reliability and their usefulness in studying the causes of homicide and other anti-social behavior.

CHAPTER II

THE EXTENT OF HOMICIDE IN THE UNITED STATES

IN 1928, in the United States death registration area, there were 10,050 homicides reported. (At this time the registration area comprised 95.4 per cent of the estimated population of the nation and 80.8 per cent of the land area.) This figure probably represents an appreciable minimization of the extent of this problem, even when the total is estimated to be about 10,512 in order to compensate for the 4.6 per cent of the population not included in the registration area. Frederick L. Hoffman, who has made many painstaking investigations into the statistics of homicide, estimates the annual death rate from this cause at approximately 12,000 persons.[1] This estimate does not appear to be greatly exaggerated when one takes into consideration the numerous evidences that slayings are often reported in such a way as to conceal the actual nature of the deed.

The basis of all mortality statistics is the death certificate filed with the local registrars. This certificate is usually prepared within a few hours after the subject's death in order that the undertaker may secure permission to move the body for burial. The attending physician is responsible for the statement concerning the primary and secondary causes of the death. When violence is suspected, a coroner's investigation is held. This may, however, do little to clarify the record, since the inquests are

---

[1] "Murder and the Death Penalty," *Current History*, XXVIII, 408-10.

often hasty and superficial. Unless the evidence is un-equivocal, the jurors hesitate to charge that a felonious crime has been committed. Later, when further inquiry has revealed the fact of homicide, no change is made in the death certificate already sent to the state and federal bureaus of vital statistics. Consequently, both attending physicians and coroners' juries tend to choose the less blameworthy classifications whenever there is a choice of terms in reporting violent deaths. In this way the jurors avoid injury to persons who might be innocent and the physicians reduce their chances of being called to testify in court. Many certificates, therefore, that might be re-ported as homicides are actually stated to be accidents. Other terms used to smooth over the situation temporarily are "probably an accident," "gunshot wound of unknown origin," "unknown cause, violent death," "fractured skull," etc. In such cases, letters of inquiry from the bureaus of vital statistics often remain unanswered. In defense of this practice physicians state that they are quite willing to certify the *medical* situation, as death from gun-shot wound or blow on the skull, but that they wish to avoid statements of a *legal* nature, such as "homicide" or "suicide." Accordingly, when reporting violent deaths, they attempt to avert criticism and antagonism by min-imizing the gravity of the situation whenever the facts are not generally known or clearly established.

A second source of error is that undoubtedly some slayings are successfully concealed. The newspapers occa-sionally report the finding of an unidentified skeleton and thus controvert the familiar proverb, "Murder will out." Some, at least, of the persons who mysteriously disappear every year must be victims of "foul play." In the United States registration area in 1922 there were 65,283 deaths reported to be due to accidents, including 2,514 deaths from the accidental discharge of firearms. In discussing these figures Hoffman says, "How many of these were homicides can not be known or even safely conjectured, but it requires no extended study of so called 'accidental deaths' to justify the conclusion that in quite a number of cases [further investigation] would, in all probability, have revealed the fact of murder."[2] When two unaccompanied persons engage in a fatal affray, it is often possible for the survivor, if undisturbed for some minutes, to arrange the corpse and conceal the circumstantial evidence in such a way as to support his claim of suicide or accident. For example, in a recent notable trial in South Carolina a man was convicted of having beaten and strangled his wife and of then placing her dead body in an outhouse and pouring poison into her mouth from a bottle left clasped in her hand. His report that his wife had disappeared was believed by the neighbors, who joined him in his search for her. When the body was found, it was assumed to be a suicide. Only the later discovery of blood stains led to an investigation that resulted in the arrest of the husband. How many such attempts at concealment are successful can only be conjectured. Besides, it is possible that some homicides are reported under classifications other than those of suicide and accident. In many deaths there is no attending physician to certify the cause. The registrar of deaths accepts the word of the parents or relatives. Concealment is, therefore, relatively easy. Criminal neglect

[2] *The Homicide Problem,* p. 3.

equivalent to murder or manslaughter may sometimes appear as "lack of care," under which rubric there were reported in 1927 the deaths of 153 children.[3]

An investigation in four counties of South Carolina revealed that the official homicide reports did not include all such cases known to county officials and others. This inquiry, although too restricted in area to be accepted as conclusive, showed that the homicide rate for one county should be increased 9.4 per cent, another 16.7 per cent, and the other two 50 per cent each. This evidence, even though based upon an inadequate sample, gives support to the conclusion that official mortality statistics probably understate the extent of homicide. The validity of homicide records is, consequently, an important topic for further research.

An examination of the possible sources of error, therefore, supports Hoffman's conclusion that the number of slayings in the United States is probably not less than 12,000 a year. This means that in four years there are as many homicides in this country as there were battle deaths among its soldiers during the World War.

THE TREND OF HOMICIDE RATES IN THE UNITED STATES

An examination of the homicide rates for the United States death registration area apparently shows a steady increase. These rates per 100,000 of estimated population for the years 1906-1929 are as follows:[4]

1906.....5.0	1908.....6.4	1910.....5.9	1912.....6.6
1907.....6.3	1909.....5.6	1911.....6.6	1913.....7.2

---

[3] *Mortality Statistics 1927*, p. 20.

[4] F. L. Hoffman, *The Homicide Problem*, p. 13; U. S. Bureau of the Census, *Mortality Statistics*; and reports of the U. S. Division of Vital Statistics for 1928 and 1929.

1914.....7.4	1918.....6.8	1922.....8.4	1926.....8.8
1915.....7.0	1919.....7.5	1923.....8.1	1927.....8.7
1916.....7.1	1920.....7.1	1924.....8.5	1928.....8.8
1917.....7.7	1921.....8.5	1925.....8.6	1929.....8.5

These figures seem to indicate that in the United States human life is steadily becoming less secure. The rates before 1906 are usually considered to be unreliable, but they support the trend of the data presented above, the average for the ten year period ending in 1909 being only 4.3 per 100,000 population.[5] Since, however, the states included in the registration area have changed materially since 1906, the homicide rates for the entire area cannot properly be compared. Hoffman, accordingly, has secured the records for 28 large cities in the United States during the years 1900-1924. These data can be contrasted directly, since they represent a uniform area. This inquiry shows that for these 28 cities, having a total population in 1924 of 21,445,413 persons, the homicide rate per 100,000 estimated population steadily increased from 5.1 in 1900 to 10.3 in 1924.[6] In other words, for these cities the homicide rate doubled in a quarter of a century.

On the contrary, Sutherland reports that for those states which were in the registration area in 1905 the average annual homicide rates have been as follows:

1905-1909...........2.22	1915-1919...........2.66
1910-1914...........2.83	1920-1922...........2.86

This, again, is a strictly comparable area, consisting principally of the New England states. Moreover, Sutherland found that in 1912 there were 61 cities of 100,000

[5] F. L. Hoffman, *The Homicide Problem*, p. 13.
[6] *Ibid.*, p. 96.

or more inhabitants in the death registration area.   In 1922, of these cities 29 had lower homicide rates than in 1912; while 29 had higher rates; and 3 had the same. Besides, in 1912 there were 23 states in the registration area.   In 1922, one of these 23 states had the same homicide rate; 11 had higher rates; and 11 had lower ones.[7] Sutherland's investigation, therefore, shows that for comparable areas the homicide rate has not appreciably increased in recent years.   This result is in direct conflict with the report made by Hoffman for the 28 cities.   Of the two investigations, however, that by Sutherland is statistically more reliable since it covered a larger number of cities in addition to valid state-wide data.

Other factors, moreover, cast doubt upon the conclusion that the homicide rate is steadily increasing.   The table presented above showing rates for the entire registration area should be interpreted in the light of additional information.   It is possible that in later years the vital statistics records are more accurate and complete, some cases being unreported in former years because of the public's relative unfamiliarity with the registration system. A more important factor, however, is the composition of the death registration area.   In general, the registration of deaths began in the New England states and has gradually spread westward and southward.   The recently added states have appreciably higher rates of homicide than do the original states.   It is possible, of course, that homicide has actually become more frequent in the United States during the last twenty or thirty years; but, if this

[7] "Murder and the Death Penalty," *Journal of the American Institute of Criminal Law and Criminology*, XV, 522-29.

is true, the increase is, doubtless, much smaller than is evidenced by the rates, as given above, for the registration area during the period 1906-1929.

STATE AND REGIONAL DIFFERENCES IN HOMICIDE RATES

Homicide rates for the entire United States death registration area conceal state and regional differences of great significance. For example, for the nine year period, 1919-1927, the rate for the registration area in continental United States was 8.26 per 100,000 of estimated population. For the same nine years the state-wide figures varied from a low of 1.43 in Vermont to a high of 29.55 in Florida. In order to examine similar variations, Table I has been prepared. In it are given the records for each state for the ten year period, 1918-1927, whenever the state has been in the death registration area for that time. If the ten year figures are not available, the mean (average) rates refer only to the years presented in the table. All the data have been secured from the United States Bureau of the Census' annual *Mortality Statistics* reports.

Figure 2 and Figure 3 have been prepared in order to show in graphic form the mean homicide rates already presented in Table I. The states are divided into four groups: the worst, second, third, and best quarters according to the mean or average homicide rate for the period 1918-1927. If the individual state was not in the registration area for this entire period, it is represented by the average of the years for which data are available. Figure 2 is based upon the homicide rates for all classes of the population. It shows that the South and her northern neighbors, Missouri, Illinois, Ohio, and West Virginia,

TABLE I. HOMICIDES PER 100,000 ESTIMATED POPULATION 1918-1927

	1927	1926	1925	1924	1923	1922	1921	1920	1919	1918	Mean (Unweighted)
Registration Area	8.7	8.8	8.6	8.5	8.1	8.4	8.5	7.1	7.5	6.8	8.10
White	5.3	5.2	5.4	5.3	5.1	5.6	6.2	5.0	5.3	4.8	5.32
Colored	43.8	45.4	42.5	40.1	38.5	34.7	33.7	29.6	30.5	30.5	36.93
Registration States	8.4	8.5	8.3	8.2	7.9	8.0	8.1	6.8	7.1	6.4	7.77
Urban	10.3	10.3	10.5	10.1	9.6	9.1	9.1	8.2	8.8	8.2	9.42
Rural	6.8	6.8	6.4	6.5	6.4	7.0	7.2	5.4	5.7	4.8	6.30
Registration Cities in Non Reg. States	26.0	25.0	25.3	26.5	23.4	31.7	30.7	27.0	26.6	22.0	26.42
All Reg. Cities	10.8	10.8	11.0	10.7	10.0	9.8	9.9	8.8	9.5	8.8	10.01
Alabama	20.6	20.1	17.2	....	....	....	....	....	....	....	19.30
White	9.9	8.3	7.4	....	....	....	....	....	....	....	8.53
Colored	40.6	41.7	34.3	....	....	....	....	....	....	....	38.87
Arizona	10.5	14.2	....	....	....	....	....	....	....	....	12.35
Arkansas	16.4	....	....	....	....	....	....	....	....	....	16.4
White	8.7	....	....	....	....	....	....	....	....	....	8.7
Colored	38.2	....	....	....	....	....	....	....	....	....	38.2
California	8.8	8.6	7.9	9.6	9.1	10.3	11.6	8.2	9.4	9.4	9.29
Colorado	5.5	6.6	8.1	10.0	9.2	11.7	11.8	9.2	10.6	7.5	9.02
Connecticut	2.1	2.7	3.5	3.5	3.0	2.9	2.9	3.9	5.0	3.8	3.33
Delaware	9.9	8.3	3.8	7.3	3.9	9.2	7.1	4.0	7.7	....	6.80
Florida	35.6	50.0	35.9	28.9	30.0	22.7	24.9	20.2	17.8	....	29.55
White	14.4	20.5	15.4	12.6	11.3	9.3	14.1	8.8	8.6	....	12.77
Colored	81.7	113.5	79.6	62.8	69.2	50.0	46.5	42.5	35.2	....	64.55
Georgia	....	....	....	18.3	17.2	18.9	....	....	....	....	18.13
White	....	....	....	8.3	7.2	8.6	....	....	....	....	8.03
Colored	....	....	....	32.9	31.9	33.8	....	....	....	....	32.87
Idaho	2.8	2.9	3.9	5.0	3.4	3.0	....	....	....	....	3.50
Illinois	10.4	10.4	10.9	10.5	9.3	9.8	8.8	7.4	8.5	6.6	9.26
Indiana	6.3	5.8	6.6	7.3	6.1	5.7	6.4	4.7	4.7	4.1	5.77
Iowa	2.4	2.4	2.7	2.7	2.1	....	....	....	....	....	2.46
Kansas	4.4	5.7	5.2	5.5	6.8	7.2	7.5	4.7	6.7	5.9	5.96
Kentucky	16.8	14.5	15.7	14.3	14.2	11.6	16.2	9.0	7.8	10.1	13.02
White	11.6	9.7	10.6	9.3	9.8	8.4	12.2	6.6	5.1	6.6	8.99
Colored	73.5	65.9	67.6	64.7	57.8	42.3	53.4	31.5	32.4	41.7	53.08
Louisiana	21.6	21.0	23.3	19.2	18.2	17.7	18.8	14.1	17.0	19.1	19.00
White	10.1	10.4	10.4	8.6	8.2	9.2	11.4	6.9	7.2	10.7	9.31
Colored	42.4	39.8	45.3	36.9	34.7	31.5	30.6	25.4	32.2	32.0	35.08
Maine	1.9	1.1	2.2	1.5	1.7	1.7	2.2	1.4	1.6	1.3	1.66
Maryland	7.1	6.8	7.5	7.8	6.3	7.5	7.8	4.8	5.4	6.6	6.76
White	3.4	3.3	4.0	4.5	3.3	4.8	5.1	2.4	2.8	3.6	3.72
Colored	26.5	25.1	25.5	24.7	21.7	20.6	21.1	16.7	18.0	21.4	22.13
Massachusetts	2.0	2.0	2.7	2.7	2.7	2.6	2.8	2.1	2.8	2.3	2.47
Michigan	8.3	10.5	7.5	7.3	6.3	4.4	4.8	5.5	4.3	3.0	6.19
Minnesota	2.4	2.1	3.6	3.1	2.8	3.6	4.4	3.1	3.2	2.9	3.12
Mississippi	24.2	25.6	21.7	16.8	17.4	19.6	21.1	19.8	19.0	....	20.57
White	9.5	12.1	9.8	8.0	8.8	7.6	11.1	6.8	6.7	....	8.93
Colored	37.6	38.0	32.6	24.9	25.2	30.5	30.5	31.7	30.2	....	31.24

TABLE I *(Continued)*

	1927	1926	1925	1924	1923	1922	1921	1920	1919	1918	*Mean (Unweighted)*
Missouri................	10.7	11.6	12.3	13.2	12.3	11.4	10.1	7.9	9.7	10.1	10.93
Montana...............	5.2	6.5	7.6	5.9	4.3	7.1	7.1	8.2	8.0	11.1	7.10
Nebraska..............	3.4	2.6	3.9	4.3	4.0	4.5	4.9	4.1	....	....	3.96
New Hampshire........	0.7	0.9	1.3	1.6	2.7	1.6	2.2	1.8	1.1	0.9	1.48
New Jersey............	4.3	4.5	5.1	5.0	5.3	4.7	5.2	4.2	4.6	4.8	4.77
New York..............	5.6	4.8	5.1	5.4	4.3	4.9	4.9	4.6	4.6	4.0	4.82
North Carolina........	9.7	10.0	9.2	10.4	9.9	9.2	8.6	9.8	8.5	7.6	9.29
White..............	4.3	5.2	4.5	4.8	4.5	5.1	5.5	4.8	3.8	4.5	4.70
Colored.............	22.8	21.7	20.5	23.9	22.9	18.9	15.8	21.2	19.3	14.6	20.16
North Dakota..........	1.7	1.9	2.0	2.2	....	....	....	....	....	....	1.95
Ohio..................	8.2	8.3	7.8	6.8	7.7	7.2	7.8	6.9	7.3	8.5	7.65
Oregon................	3.8	4.3	4.1	3.5	3.9	5.9	7.7	4.1	4.9	4.0	4.62
Pennsylvania..........	5.7	5.5	6.0	6.2	7.0	6.0	6.3	5.6	6.0	6.5	6.08
Rhode Island..........	2.6	3.0	1.8	1.9	3.5	2.3	3.1	1.8	3.3	2.4	2.57
South Carolina........	11.1	12.4	12.0	12.2	11.1	14.1	17.1	15.2	13.7	10.4	12.93
White..............	5.9	5.1	7.8	6.0	5.6	8.4	11.3	9.4	8.3	5.5	7.33
Colored.............	16.6	20.1	16.3	18.4	16.4	19.7	22.7	20.8	18.9	14.9	18.48
Tennessee.............	17.4	17.5	17.3	18.5	17.8	17.3	16.7	13.8	15.1	11.3	16.27
White..............	8.5	7.8	8.9	10.8	10.5	10.7	11.4	7.0	8.8	6.9	9.13
Colored.............	60.0	63.1	55.4	52.5	49.8	45.9	39.5	42.4	41.3	29.2	47.91
Utah..................	2.5	3.9	5.6	5.8	5.5	6.0	5.2	5.1	4.5	1.8	4.59
Vermont..............	0.9	2.3	0.6	0.6	1.4	1.1	1.7	2.3	2.0	2.0	1.49
Virginia...............	10.6	8.7	10.0	9.8	10.3	11.1	13.3	11.2	9.8	11.4	10.62
White..............	7.2	5.4	5.9	5.6	5.6	6.9	9.0	7.5	5.7	6.3	6.51
Colored.............	19.4	17.2	20.1	20.0	21.8	21.3	23.8	19.9	19.4	23.0	20.59
Washington............	4.2	3.4	5.5	6.2	4.7	5.2	5.9	5.1	7.5	4.2	5.19
West Virginia..........	13.5	12.2	12.1	....	....	....	....	....	....	....	12.60
Wisconsin.............	2.5	2.5	2.2	1.8	2.2	1.8	2.2	1.7	1.9	1.9	2.07
Wyoming..............	9.1	13.6	10.5	12.9	13.7	16.9	....	....	....	....	12.78

After the material for this volume was in the hands of the publisher the homicide rates for 1928 and 1929 have been made available through the courtesy of the U. S. Division of Vital Statistics. These rates are as follows:

AREA	1928	1929	AREA	1928	1929
Registration Area..........	8.8	8.5	Missouri................	11.1	9.7
Alabama.................	21.2	19.5	Montana...............	8.2	11.1
Arizona.................	12.9	15.6	Nebraska..............	3.7	3.0
Arkansas................	15.5	15.4	Nevada................	....	20.0
California...............	7.2	6.1	New Hampshire........	1.3	1.5
Colorado................	6.0	8.7	New Jersey............	4.5	4.5
Connecticut.............	2.7	2.6	New Mexico............	....	12.2
Delaware................	5.9	6.7	New York..............	5.0	5.3
Florida..................	26.8	25.8	North Carolina........	10.0	10.5
Georgia.................	18.2	18.3	North Dakota.........	1.0	1.2
Idaho...................	5.0	3.6	Ohio..................	8.2	8.3
Illinois.................	10.5	8.9	Oklahoma.............	10.8	10.4
Indiana.................	7.0	7.0	Oregon................	4.5	3.5
Iowa...................	2.3	2.6	Pennsylvania..........	5.7	5.2
Kansas.................	5.5	6.2	Rhode Island..........	2.7	2.3
Kentucky...............	17.7	16.7	South Carolina........	13.4	14.1
Louisiana...............	19.8	16.6	Tennessee.............	18.1	16.7
Maine..................	1.6	1.0	Utah..................	4.0	4.6
Maryland...............	7.6	8.1	Vermont..............	1.4	1.4
Massachusetts...........	1.9	1.7	Virginia...............	10.7	10.1
Michigan...............	7.0	8.2	Washington............	4.7	5.2
Minnesota..............	2.8	2.2	West Virginia..........	12.8	10.3
Mississippi..............	22.8	23.2	Wisconsin.............	2.1	2.3
			Wyoming..............	8.2	8.5

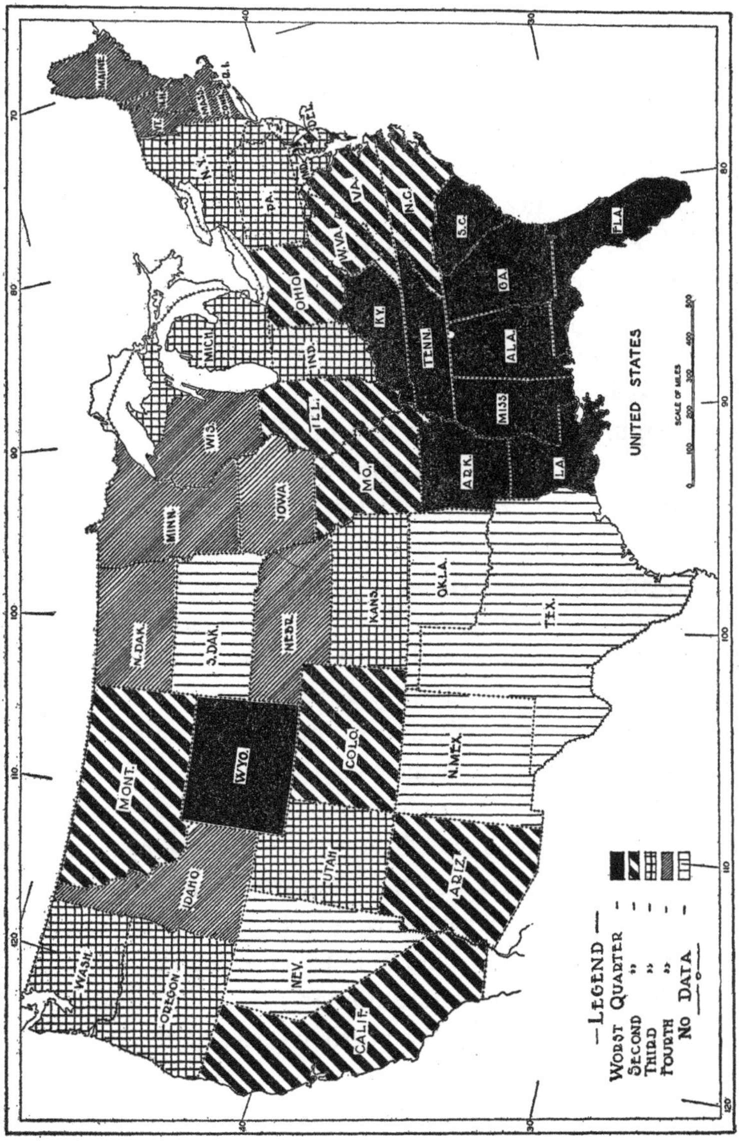

FIGURE 2. DISTRIBUTION OF HOMICIDE IN THE UNITED STATES, 1918-1927.

— LEGEND —
WORST QUARTER - - -
SECOND   ,,   - - -
THIRD   ,,   - - -
FOURTH   ,,   - - -
NO DATA   - - -

UNITED STATES

SCALE OF MILES
0   100   200   300   400   500

make up one of the two great homicide regions, the other being in the Far West.   Unfortunately, no data are available for the states of Texas and Oklahoma, but their few cities with acceptable death registration bureaus report such high homicide rates that it is quite probable that the Southwest is as much inclined to killing as is the Southeast.

For fear that Figure 2 represents the South unfairly because of the concentration of the colored population there, Figure 3 has been prepared to show homicide rates based upon whites only, wherever the official reports show such a classification.   The data for Figure 3 are the same as for Figure 2 except that the rates are for only white homicidal deaths in the following states: Alabama, Arkansas, Florida, Georgia, Kentucky, Louisiana, Maryland, Mississippi, North Carolina, South Carolina, Tennessee, and Virginia.   This division is somewhat in favor of the standing of the states named above, since some Negroes and other colored persons live in the remaining 31 states and increase their rates slightly above what they would be if only whites were considered in making the calculations. Nevertheless, the South again makes an unfavorable showing, although several states improve their *relative* position, notably North Carolina.   Figure 3 portrays once more the two homicide centers, one reaching from Florida to Michigan and the other consisting of the Rocky Mountain states and California, Idaho and Utah excepted.   It also shows the two regions where human life is most safe, the New England states and the northern part of the Middle West.

The four regions described above present a most interesting problem to the student of human geography.

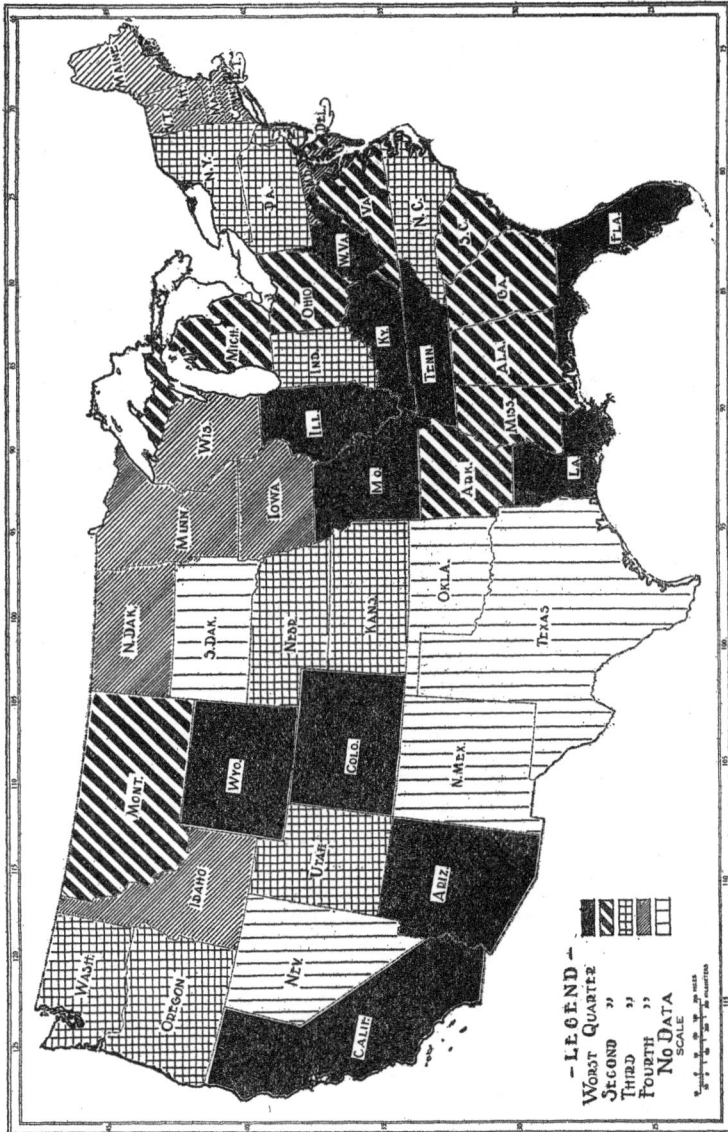

FIGURE 3. DISTRIBUTION OF WHITE HOMICIDAL DEATHS IN THE UNITED STATES, 1918-1927.

New England may have low homicide rates because it has been settled longer than other parts of the country and it is farthest removed from the strife of frontier conditions. But, on the other hand, it has had in recent years a large influx of foreign-born, many of whom are from southern and eastern Europe. Yet if the date of settlement explains the situation in New England, it fails to help in giving the reason for the excellent record of the upper Middle West, for that region has become heavily populated only in recent decades, largely as a result of heavy immigration from Germany and Scandinavia. Of course, there is the possibility that immigrants are superior in the qualities of citizenship to those who settled the original thirteen colonies and whose descendants spread over the remainder of the nation.

In New England, it is true, there is a larger proportion of women in the population than there is in the Rocky Mountain and Pacific states. This would tend to lower the homicide rates in New England. This difference in the ratio of sexes is not sufficient, however, to explain the much greater disparity in homicide rates. Moreover, even if New England makes a better record because of an excess of females, its population is so much more dense that homicide rates there should be higher, since urban communities usually have a greater proportion of slayings than do contiguous rural areas. Accordingly, whatever advantage in homicide record New England secures because of its smaller percentage of males is probably more than counterbalanced by its greater density of population.

The West, however, is ready to explain that the high homicide rates prevailing there are due to the frontier conditions of the recent past and their survival in present-day culture patterns. This defense is not adequate, although it doubtless is partially correct.[8] The South, also, proclaims its vindication, pleading in extenuation the presence of the Negro. This plea is supported by a part of the evidence but cannot be accepted without reservation.[9]

The rates presented in Tables X and XII of Chapter X show clearly, however, that state and regional records may be unfair to many urban and rural communities where homicide is extremely infrequent. Within a state having as a whole an unfavorable record there may be cities and counties exceptionally free from slayings. The explanation of such differences is an important problem for further study.

NEWSPAPER REPORTS OF HOMICIDE

The daily newspapers are literally filled with stories of criminal behavior, especially with accounts of sensational homicides. Joseph L. Holmes measured the amount of space devoted to crime in twelve New York dailies for the period of November 8 to December 7 or 8, 1926. According to his tabulation, "the total number of items of crime news published by the 12 papers during one month when statistics of crime indicate that crime is at a minimum, was 4,712. The total amount of space devoted to these items during that same month was 89,622.00 inches. Allowing 50 words to the inch this makes a total of 4,481,100 words. If this crime news were printed in book form it would make nearly six volumes of 300 pages each."[10]

[8] *Cf.* pp. 47-50.   [9] *Cf.* ch. vi.
[10] *Crime and the Press,* pp. 12-32.

On the contrary, a careful examination of the files of the Columbia, S. C., *State* revealed accounts of the commission or trial of only 321 homicides in South Carolina during the three year period from August 1, 1925, through July 31, 1928. Yet during this time, by conservative estimate the actual number of homicides committed in the state was at least 650. Since the average number of slayings in this state for the eleven years 1916-1926 was 222.36 per annum, this estimate of 650 is not likely to be too high. Consequently, this daily newspaper published at the state capital mentioned only about one half of the homicides reported to the registrars of vital statistics. This newspaper, moreover, although somewhat conservative about featuring crime news, makes a special effort to secure reports from all sections of the state in which it is published.

If these two investigations are typical, they indicate that newspapers spend much space upon a few sensational crimes, especially upon the more spectacular homicides, and yet mention in their columns only a small proportion of the total number of slayings. The reader of the daily paper may, therefore, safely estimate that the actual number of homicides in the state where his paper is issued is greatly in excess of those described in its files.

HOMICIDE AND OTHER CAUSES OF DEATH

Numerically, homicide is by no means a negligible cause of death in the United States; it outranks several dreaded diseases. *Mortality Statistics*, Table 5, gives for the registration area in continental United States the number of deaths from each of the principal causes. For 1927 a part of this record is as follows: homicide 9,470; typhoid and paratyphoid 5,905; malaria 2,875; diphtheria 8,426; smallpox 145; scarlet fever 2,440; meningitis 1,705; erysipelas 2,567; rheumatism 4,177; and bronchitis 5,851. Accordingly, in 1927 homicide claimed more victims than diphtheria or than typhoid, paratyphoid, and malarial fevers combined. It was almost as deadly as rheumatism and bronchitis combined or as meningitis, smallpox, scarlet fever, erysipelas, and malaria combined.

HOMICIDE IN OTHER COUNTRIES

Comparisons between two regions of the United States do not portray the homicide situation in perspective, since all rates are relatively high; but the contrast between the records of this country and those of other civilized nations is quite clearly marked. For the years 1907-1911, the homicide rate per 100,000 population was 5.5 for New York, 0.9 for London, and 2.0 for Berlin.[11] According to Dr. Warren Stearns the mean rates for the period 1911-1921 were for Australia 1.88 per 100,000, for Sweden 1.32, for England and Wales 0.76, for Quebec 0.54, for Ontario 0.53, for Scotland 0.40, for Switzerland 0.18, and for the United States 7.2.[12] For 1922 the rate for the United States was 8.4, while for England and Wales it was 0.5 and for Japan it was 0.8. For 1923 the corresponding figures were for the Commonwealth of Australia 1.6, for Scotland 0.2, for Ontario, Canada, 1.6, for England and Wales 0.6, and for the United States 8.1.[13] Later statistics show the same relationship. In 141 Amer-

[11] F. L. Hoffman, *The Homicide Problem*, p. 25.
[12] Quoted in the Columbia, S. C., *State*, August 24, 1925.
[13] F. L. Hoffman, *The Homicide Problem*, p. 2.

ican cities the rate for 1928 was 10.4 and for 1929 it was 10.5, while for 13 Canadian cities the corresponding figure was 1.7 for 1928 and for England and Wales it was 0.5.[14]

The array of statistics presented above shows clearly that in the United States one's life is far less safe than in most of the European nations. In only one region has there been noted a rate higher than in this country. An Associated Press report for February 18, 1928, gives the slayings in Sardinia for 1924 as 16.2 per 100,000 inhabitants, for Sicily as 24.1, and for Calabria as 22.0. These Italian provinces, the birth-place of the Mafia and the home of the vendetta, alone save the United States from the position of being the most murderous of the territorial units which have trustworthy homicide records.

THE REDUCTION OF HOMICIDE

In this volume no general recommendations are made for controlling the incidence of homicide. An examination of the subsequent chapters will show how complex is the homicide problem and how varied and involved are its relationships to other phenomena. To lay out a plan, therefore, for the reduction of the rate of homicide would be almost equivalent to formulating a program for the betterment of society. In view of the difficulty of such a task, accordingly, no specific suggestions are offered except those which are implied in the results of certain of the investigations.

[14] "More Murders," *Literary Digest*, CV, 13, April 5, 1930.

CHAPTER III

EXPLANATIONS OF THE HIGH RATE OF HOMICIDE IN THE UNITED STATES

THE GREAT DIVERGENCE between the homicide rates of the United States and those of other civilized nations has led to many attempts at explanation. For a large number of these reasons or hypotheses little evidence has been offered. For others, some superficial difference between this country and Europe has been noted and magnified into an all-sufficient cause. Most of these theories, doubtless, contain at least a small element of truth, but their validity is greatly lessened by their oversimplification of an exceedingly complex problem. A few representative explanations are presented, more for purposes of illustration than in the attempt to summarize the many theses which have been advanced.

WEALTH

The vast increase in material wealth in the United States during the past few decades is believed by many to have resulted in an increase of crime of all kinds through the multiplication of temptations. Hoffman says, "Our enormous increase in wealth is in itself one of the underlying causes of the murder tendency. Temptation to murder, as well as to less violent crimes, increases on every hand."[1] Arthur Pound, an amazed observer of England's lack of crime during a general strike, reports that for England and Wales the prison population decreased from 167,000 in 1914 to 58,000 in 1924, while the commit-

[1] "Our 12,000 Killings in 1926,"*Literary Digest*, XCIV, 12-13, July 2, 1927.

ments per 100,000 diminished from 500 in 1914 to 120 in 1924. Nevertheless, he justifies the record of the United States, saying:

Our crime wave coincides with an economic golden age which manifests itself otherwise in industrial expansion, crowding inventions, huge building programs, and intense interests in material achievements. I argue that we have more crime *per capita* than the British for the same reason that we have more automobiles, more telephones, more ton-miles of freight moving, and more horse-power of electrical energy *per capita*. In other words, a good deal of our crime, certainly the major part of our money crimes which multiply most rapidly, flows from our "go-getting" spirit, while much of the British innocence from crime may be traced to the quite evident lack of that spirit. . . . Crime is anti-social action and must be suppressed, of course, by public authority. But it is action, nevertheless! A society like ours which produces much crime and is properly shocked by it is far from being beyond hope.[2]

If these statements are correct, the highest homicide rates should generally be found where there is great wealth and development of industry. On the contrary, the relatively unindustrialized South and Far West have many more slayings than does the East. The per capita tangible wealth is lowest in the South, where the homicide rates are the highest. In 1922 every southern state had a per capita wealth below that of the national average of $2,918.[3] An examination of the homicide rate and the per capita wealth of each of the states indicates that the relationship between the two is negligible.

[2] "The Sunny Side of Crime," *Independent*, CXVI, 708-10.
[3] U. S. Department of Commerce, *Statistical Abstract of the United States 1929*, p. 296.

THE AFTERMATH OF WAR

Shortly after the close of the World War there was a marked increase in sensational murders committed by mere youths, such as the notable Hickman and Loeb and Leopold cases. By many these slayings were attributed to the disorganization following in the wake of war. For example, Dr. A. A. Brill, a psychiatrist, presented in an interview the theory that such homicides were due primarily to the failure to develop the proper inhibitions in those who were children during the period of the war. "Emotions," he says, "have not changed, do not change. Every child is a little criminal! He becomes law abiding only when we have grafted inhibitions—do nots—upon his impressionable mind." During the war years parents were unable to create an aversion to slaying in the minds of their children, especially in the minds of those who were emotionally undeveloped or infantile. "The boys who are killing now were seven, eight, nine and ten then. They waged mimic wars with tin soldiers and they chose for hero-worship the man who had brought down fifteen enemy planes, who had bayoneted twenty foemen in a bull rush across to the waiting trench. One inhibition was swept away . . . when a nation which held murder in horror suddenly broke out in sturdy anthems of praise for killers and killing." Dr. Brill believes, furthermore, that "the psychological effects of the World War will not wear off for at least another fifty years."[4]

This effect of war conditions seems to have influenced soldiers, as well as the children at home. In 1923 about one-fourth of the prisoners in the Wisconsin penitentiary

[4] Milton Mackaye, "Youthful Killers," *Outlook*, CLI, 3-6.

and reformatory were ex-soldiers. A study made by two former army officers reported that this situation was due in large part to soldiers' becoming accustomed to "take" whatever they wished from supply depots, "salvage dumps," and elsewhere. When they returned to the United States, the stupid or untrained ones were unable to realize that conditions had changed. "Nothing in war," the investigators concluded, "is uplifting, at least not for the humbler participants."[5]

This explanation of the increase of crime after 1920 has, perhaps, an element of truth, especially with reference to crimes against property. An examination of the most reliable homicide data for the past quarter of a century indicates, however, that within comparable areas there has been very little increase in homicide since the beginning of the World War.[6] It is probable, therefore, that only a small part of the obloquy is due to the personal and social disorganization incident to war. Besides, the glorification of slaying appears to have caused little harm to the youths of other participants in the conflict—England, France, and Germany—although this may be due to the fact that in these nations the sorrow and suffering of war may have counteracted the effect of praises for the blood-stained victors.

THE MOTION PICTURE

Upon the motion picture has been laid the blame for the increase of certain spectacular types of crime, notably homicide and highway robbery. For example, Roger W. Babson, a statistician, says, "Such studies as I have made

[5] F. L. Holmes, "Making Criminals out of Soldiers," *Nation*, CXXI, 114-15.
[6] *Cf.* pp. 16-18.

lead directly to the movies as the basic cause of the crime waves of today. . . . It is evident that the movies are the greatest force today in molding character for good or evil."[7] In reply, Frederick L. Hoffman, another statistician, states, "Every industry or effort is liable to misuse but, considering the vast amount of good done by the motion picture, I feel that the amount of harm and its relation to homicidal tendencies may safely be considered negligible."[8]

As is to be expected in such matters, there is much opinion but little evidence concerning the rôle of the movies in the causation of crime. Healy and Bronner conclude that only one per cent of their 4000 cases of juvenile delinquents were motivated to misconduct through the influence of the motion picture.[9] Burt reports "a passion for the cinema" in 7 per cent of the male juvenile delinquents studied by him and in only 1.4 per cent of the girls.[10] Blanchard thinks that the movies appear to the child as merely a part of his world of phantasy, as "make-believe," and are, therefore, dissociated from his sense of reality and unimportant as a source of motivation. She states, "In five years of daily contacts with more than a thousand problem children in different parts of the country, the author is unable to recall more than five cases in which the motion picture was intimately related to the causation of conduct disorders."[11] Joseph L. Holmes re-edited a seven reel picture so as to make it a portrayal of

[7] Quoted in editorial in the Columbia, S. C., *State*, June 28, 1929.
[8] *Ibid.*
[9] *Delinquents and Criminals: Their Making and Unmaking*, p. 281.
[10] Phyllis Blanchard, *The Child and Society*, p. 301.
[11] *Ibid.*, p. 202.

assassination, false accusation, and suicide. This was shown
to about 500 school children from the fourth through the
eighth grades. The children were then asked to answer
40 questions about the picture and to write an essay or
theme telling the story. "Of all the children none indicated the least sympathy for the various evil characters
portrayed." The fact most frequently reported was that
the villain was punished by being put in prison. This
somewhat inadequate experiment was supplemented by a
questionnaire sent to 616 law enforcement officers. Only
111 replied to the question concerning the relationship between the motion picture and crime. Of these replies, 57
said that the movies do not increase crime, 29 affirmed that
they do, and 25 answers were evasive or irrelevant.[12] The
opinion of these officers was, therefore, divided, although
the majority of those replying thought the movie harmless.

Without giving the evidence upon which his conclusions are based Maxim Gorki, the Russian novelist, presents the following indictment of the motion picture as a
promoter of crime:

With astonishing success the cinema assists these two [news-
papers and detective stories] by producing crime films. The zoö-
logical emotions of some are roused; the imagination of others is
corrupted; and the rest of society is rendered insensible to the facts
of crime; its feeling of revulsion is numbed. All this is done
merely to provide entertainment for people who are bored;
whereas more than likely the cinema augments and intensifies the
ennui of people who, in the manner of drums, are empty inside
and produce a sound only after receiving a shock from without.[13]

[12] *Crime and the Press*, pp. 80-89.
[13] "About Murderers," *Dial*, LXXXV, 201-10.

In contrast, however, to the four investigations described above, Alice M. Mitchell's *Children and Movies* presents very different results based upon a study of 10,000 juveniles, boy and girl scouts being contrasted with delinquents.[14] She found that delinquents preferred movies to athletics more often than did the scouts. Both groups preferred movies to reading, but the preference was greater among the delinquents. Moreover, the delinquents were more interested in romantic and "wild west" pictures than were the scouts. The last conclusion would be of great significance, it seems, if a causal relationship could be clearly established. It is possible that the movies create phantasies that result in crime, yet it may be that previous delinquencies tend to develop a preference for pictures that portray anti-social behavior.

Until further investigations are made, it will be difficult to determine with accuracy whether or not the prevalence of "gun-play" and murder in motion pictures increases the homicide rate of the United States. At any rate, the popularity of blood-thirsty heroes does reveal the careless and even flippant attitude of the public towards the taking of human life.

NEWSPAPERS AND OTHER PUBLICATIONS

Critics of the motion picture usually also condemn newspapers and "cheap" literature, especially "yellow journals," tabloids, pornographic writings, and detective stories. Gorki believes that murderers are as a rule emotionally unstable, infantile personalities who are often either extraordinarily suggestible or vain and eager for

[14] *Social Forces*, IX, 127.

notoriety of any kind. Consequently, he says, "there is no doubt that newspaper gossip, sensational detective stories, and films, representing the agility and daring of murderers, develop in the unstabilized population, which thirsts for sensations, an unwholesome curiosity about criminals and contribute to the growth of criminality."[15] In illustration he tells of a murderer who took great delight in referring to great writers by their given names, as "Feodor" for Dostoevsky. "He mentioned Shakespeare, speaking of him too in a friendly intimate way as William." Finally, he offered Gorki the carefully preserved clippings describing his crime and trial, saying, "Perhaps you would care to make use of them? Murder because of jealousy's a subject that would make you a fine novel." Such incidents, according to Gorki, clearly indicate that "it would be wiser and more hygienic to create an atmosphere of silence and unconsciousness around murderers— an atmosphere in which there would be no place for active interest in their acts and personalities." This conclusion is supported by others. For example, Venn says, "The movies and cheap fiction may have a hand in lowering the moral consciousness of youth, but even the most perverted of youths would not be affected by these unless there were some foundation for them in the morning papers."[16]

The amount of newspaper space devoted to crime has apparently been steadily increasing and has, in recent years, reached noteworthy proportions. According to Speed and Holmes, the crime news in the New York *World* increased from less than a column on Sunday, April

[15] "About Murderers," *Dial*, LXXXV, 201-10.
[16] "Murder," *Independent*, CXIII, 361-2.

17, 1881, to 6 columns on Sunday, April 16, 1893, and to a mean of 349.05 inches or 14.54 per cent of its total space for the days of the month from November 8 to December 8, 1926. Yet while the *World* was averaging 14.54 per cent of its space in crime news, the New York *Daily News*, a morning tabloid, was devoting 33.11 per cent of its columns to the doings of criminals. During this month, November 8 to December 8, 1926, twelve New York daily papers contained 4,712 items dealing with crime, covering a space of 89,622 inches and containing about 4,480,000 words.[17] During the Hall-Mills murder trial at Somerville, New Jersey, in 1926, two hundred correspondents and fifty photographers came for the trial. One newspaper had sixteen reporters at the scene, another had thirteen. Twenty-eight operators manned the portable electric switchboard set up in the basement of the court house, and sixty leased wires carried bulletins to the newspapers of the country. At the end of twenty-four days of the trial there had been sent by wire 12,000,000 words, enough, according to the Associated Press, to fill 960 pages of solid reading matter—"words enough, if put into book form, to make a shelf of novels twenty-two feet long."[18]

As an example of the evil effects of newspaper publicity for crime Holmes cites the epidemic of attempts at kidnapping following the abduction and murder of Marion Parker by Edward Hickman in Los Angeles in December, 1927. The danger became so great that the superintendent of schools of New York City felt it advisable to

---

[17] *Crime and the Press*, pp. 13-32.
[18] Charles Merz, "Bigger and Better Murders," *Harper's*, CLV, 338-43.

issue instructions to teachers to exercise caution in permitting children to leave school at the request of persons not
known to be their parents. In at least four of these crimes
or attempted crimes there was a definite statement that
the Hickman case had been an inciting cause. Of these the
most significant, perhaps, was the slaying of a little girl in
Michigan under circumstances closely resembling the murder of Marion Parker. Some of the questions and answers
in the confession of Hotelling, the slayer, are as follows:

Q. Did you read about the crime in Los Angeles?

A. Yes, sir. I thought it was terrible. I could not sleep that
night. It had been on my mind and I could not get rid of it. I
think about it—think about it and think about it.

Q. About the little child in California?

A. Yes. . . .

Q. What do you think is the cause of that?

A. I think that reading about the crime in California is to
blame.

Q. Do you think that crime had any bearing on your committing this crime?

A. I do; it preyed on my mind and I could not get it off my
mind.[19]

How newspapers affect the potential criminal has been
explained by W. I. Thomas in his analysis of "yellow
journalism:"

The condition of morality, as well as of mental life, in a community depends on the prevailing copies. A people is profoundly
influenced by whatever is persistently brought to its attention. A
good illustration of this is that an article of commerce—a food, a
luxury, a medicine, a stimulant—can always be sold in immense
quantities if it be persistently and widely advertised. In the same

[19] J. L. Holmes, *Crime and the Press*, pp. 63-65.

way the yellow journal by an advertisement of crime, vice, and vulgarity, on a scale unexampled in commercial advertising and in a way that amounts to approval and even applause, becomes one of the forces making for immorality.[20]

Law enforcement officers are, however, far from unanimous in support of the logically defensible position taken by Thomas. In New York state Holmes asked 616 judges, district attorneys, police captains, and other officials dealing with delinquents, "Do you consider that the methods used by the newspapers of securing and presenting crime news are in any way a factor in the present crime situation?" Only 111 replied. Of these, 42 believed the newspaper to be harmful, 46 thought they were not, and 23 were evasive or irrelevant in their answers.[21] This result is merely evidence of the divided state of public opinion concerning this matter. In problems of such complexity the conclusions of the law enforcement officer are doubtless no more dependable than those of the man in the street.

Stories and novels which idealize criminalistic heroes and heroines are believed by many to be quite as harmful as newspapers and motion pictures. The Jesse James stories and the Diamond Dick novels have been succeeded by cheap magazines featuring confessions of crime and misconduct. Suggestive erotic literature tends to induce sex excitement and immorality.

In summarizing his discussion of the evil effects of newspapers, movies, and questionable literature Sutherland says,

[20] Edwin H. Sutherland, *Criminology*, p. 166.
[21] *Crime and the Press*, pp. 45-52.

Public opinion in pre-literate society made it practically impossible to commit crime. Public opinion in present society not only puts no such impassable barriers around the individual, but gives him glorified examples, makes him believe that crime is customary, breaks down the legal influences. It is probable that the principal reason for the difference in frequencies of crime in the United States and Canada or England is this public opinion.[22]

The rôle of public opinion is indisputable, but at present, unfortunately, it is still impossible to state with accuracy how large a part in the creation of this anti-social public opinion is played by the movies, the newspapers, and "cheap" literature. This part may be a very great or a relatively insignificant one. The evidence is scanty and inconclusive.

THE IMMIGRANT

The immigrant is often assumed to be the source of much crime, especially acts of violence such as homicide. In particular, suspicion is directed towards the "new" immigration from southern and eastern Europe, beginning about 1890 after the "old" or Teutonic tide had waned. Odum says, "The United States Census reports of 1910 indicate that the proportion of the foreign-born among our criminal classes is greater than that of the native-born in all but two kinds of crime—forgery and juvenile offenses. . . . The foreign-born are guilty of three times the number of assaults, and twice the number of such offenses as lesser homicide, drunkenness, disorderly conduct."[23] H. H. Laughlin's *Analysis of America's Melting Pot* supports this conclusion, stating that if 100, the average of all groups, is taken as the basis of comparison, the rate of

---

[22] *Criminology*, p. 167.
[23] *Man's Quest for Social Guidance*, p. 220.

commitment to state and federal penal institutions for persons born in the Balkan States would be 294, for those born in southern and eastern Europe it would be 141, and for those from northwestern Europe it would be 38.[24]

These statements, however, neglect to add that the typical immigrant is a male adult dwelling in a city, and that in the United States males have higher crime rates than females, adults than children, and city-dwellers than rural. If these factors are taken into consideration, the record of the immigrant may not be abnormal, especially if it be recalled that he is more liable to arrest and conviction than is the native-born. Sutherland presents evidence that for the states of New York and Massachusetts the foreign-born have lower crime rates than do the native whites, when corrections are made for differences in age and sex.[25]

An analysis of the census of prisoners in 1923 suggests that "the native-born commit more serious crimes than the foreign-born—a conclusion contrary to the popular opinion that foreigners commit more serious crimes, even if they do not engage in crime more frequently."[26] An exception to this seems to be found in examining the records of the Italian immigrants, especially those from southern Italy, who have a high incidence of homicide. In Massachusetts in 1920 out of 21 persons committed to the state prison for homicide, 13 were Italian immigrants, although this racial group made up only 3 per cent of the total population of the state.[27] Nevertheless, a study made at

[24] Edwin H. Sutherland, *Criminology*, p. 99.
[25] *Ibid.*, p. 98.
[26] Fred E. Haynes, *Criminology*, p. 75.
[27] Edwin H. Sutherland, *Criminology*, p. 100.

the Western Penitentiary of Pennsylvania indicates that many good things can be said for the Italian immigrant: he is a good prisoner, he is rarely a professional criminal, he is eager to learn, he usually commits a felony only under emotional stress. Haynes says, "Taking it all in all, the Italian as a criminal is far less dangerous than the native white."[28]

Additional evidence in favor of the immigrant is given by the distribution of homicides in the United States. The East, with a heavy concentration of foreign-born, has a far better homicide record than either the West or the South, in which immigrants are much less numerous.[29] In general, the testimony against the immigrant is not convincing. The belief that he is prone to murder must have other bases. Perhaps it is due to his higher *conviction* rate, to prejudice against strangers, to hasty generalization from literary portrayal of dark visaged villains, or to the desire for a scape goat—especially an alien one.

INCREASE OF MENTAL DISORDER

The rapid increase of insanity and lesser mental disorder in the United States has been pointed out as a possible cause of the mounting homicide rate.[30] The prevalence of emotional instability and irrational conduct would inevitably, it seems, increase the probability of violent personal encounters with fatal results. The incidence of insanity appears to be steadily increasing. Ogburn and Winston say, "Whatever the interpretation may mean, it seems to be a fact that the chances of a white person 15 years old in such a state as New York or Massachusetts

---

[28] *Criminology*, pp. 77-78.   [29] *Cf.* p. 21.
[30] F. L. Hoffman, *The Homicide Problem*, p. 10.

being committed to a hospital for mental diseases during the course of a lifetime (the mortality and commitment rates remaining the same as in 1920) are about 1 in 20, and that very probably the chances of developing a psychosis or severe incapacitating neurosis, whether sent to a hospital or not, are somewhere near 1 in 10."[31]

The explanation of mental ill health serves, however, merely to transfer the inquiry to the cause of the psychological disorders. Man appears to be mentally unadjusted to the American type of culture or civilization. A favorite explanation is that the use of automatic machinery and "high pressure" methods results in such a thwarting of natural impulses that both the laborer and his employer are "apt to seek relief in stimulants, and to crave thrills temporarily blotting out the discontent that overlays their lives."[32] This thrill-hunting, which has been called "the American malady," may or may not be due to the boredom resulting from mechanized industry and "the strenuous life," but it probably does provide an element in the national life which predisposes toward crime.

TYPE OF EDUCATION

The American public school system with its methods of mass education and its emphasis upon efficiency and materialistic success has been accused of failure to do its proper share in the reduction of crime. In the classroom and on the athletic field the competitive spirit is encouraged at the expense of the coöperative attitude. Individualism is

[31] "The Frequency and Probability of Insanity," *American Journal of Sociology,* XXXIV, 822-31.

[32] Arthur Pound, "The Iron Man and the Mind," *Atlantic Monthly,* CXXIX, 179-89; and Ralph W. Sockman, "Morals in a Machine Age," *Harper's,* CLXII, 365-374.

stimulated. The classes are usually too large to permit the teacher to give individual instruction or to attempt to aid problem children to adjust themselves to the requirements of organized society. In particular, training for good citizenship and altruistic behavior is neglected. In describing the personality of murderers Hoffman has observed, "One trait common to most of them is the want of a character qualified to deal with the stern realities of modern life. The question is properly raised whether fundamentally our system of education is not seriously at fault in overemphasizing mental development and purely material aims and purposes."[33]

Evidence for or against this conclusion is difficult to secure or to evaluate. In the South, where educational efficiency is low, homicide is most prevalent. Yet it is possible that the Southern schools have less materialistic aims than do the schools of the East and the West. According to the Ayres index, used for indicating the efficiency of state school systems, in 1918 the relative educational indices were: for the Western states 64.24; for the North Atlantic states 58.94; for the North Central states 56.66; for the South Central states 35.83; and for the South Atlantic states 34.76.[34] A comparison of the indices for the individual states and their relative homicide rates fails to indicate any clear-cut relationship. In general, the southern states have the worst records both in homicide and in educational efficiency, but homicide is more prevalent in the West than in the East, although, if the Ayres index is assumed to be valid, the school systems of the West are superior to those of the East.

[33] "U. S. Redder Than Russia," *Literary Digest*, XCVII, 12, April 21, 1928.
[34] Leonard P. Ayres, *An Index Number for State School Systems*, p. 28.

The evidence presented above, unfortunately, is of little aid in determining whether or not the public school system is doing its full duty in crime prevention. Only one type of education, with relatively few significant variations, prevails in the United States. Comparisons are, consequently, of small value. Efficiency in education as measured by the Ayres index is based upon such concrete data as percentage of attendance and per capita costs. Such items are susceptible of more than one interpretation; they may mean lack of interest or lack of financial resources. Until further investigations are made, especially in Europe where diverse types of education prevail, no categorical answer can be given to the question concerning the failure of the American public schools to develop high character and ideals of citizenship.

FAMILY DISORGANIZATION

If divorce rates are correctly interpreted as indices of the extent of family disorganization, home life in the United States is far more unstable than in Europe. This difference may partly explain the greater incidence of crime in the United States. In 1919 Great Britain had one divorce granted for every 96 marriages performed; in 1920 in France there was one divorce to every 21 marriages, in Germany one to 24, and in Sweden one to 33; in 1921 in Canada, a nation very much akin to the United States, there was one divorce to every 161 marriages, while in the United States there was in 1922 one divorce for every 7.6 marriages.[85] The effect of this instability is to decrease the chances that the children of such marriages will be adequately trained for social responsibilities. In

[85] C. A. Ellwood, *Sociology and Modern Social Problems*, p. 149.

1909 Ellwood found that, of 7,575 children in 34 state reform schools, 29.6 per cent came from families in which there had been divorce or desertion, although at that time divorces were in the ratio of less than one for every 12 marriages and although broken homes have relatively few children.[36] It has been estimated that in California about 80 per cent of the child delinquents are "divorce orphans."[37] Even in institutions of higher learning, "the boys who, on the side of morals and conduct, do least well in college are the sons of divorced parents. . . . It appeared that, in the long run, cases of troubles occurred in this group three or four times more frequently than in groups of the same size composed of boys whose home conditions might be classed as normal."[38] Apparently domestic discord is an important cause of increased crime and, consequently, of homicide.

PROHIBITION

The Eighteenth Amendment to the Constitution and the Volstead Act are thought by some to be largely responsible for an increase in homicide in the United States. The Association Against the Prohibition Amendment has issued a pamphlet entitled *Reforming America with a Shotgun*, which asserts that by November, 1929, more than 1000 persons had lost their lives in the enforcement of these laws. This estimate is based upon official records showing that up to October 15, 1929, a total of 184 citizens and 79 officers had been slain through the activ-

[36] *Ibid.*, pp. 149-50, 152, and 167.
[37] R. S. Miller, "Divorce and Child Crime," *Ladies Home Journal*, XLIV, 26, March, 1927.
[38] "Confessions of a Dean: Sons of Divorce," *Saturday Evening Post*, CCII, 25, January 11, 1930.

ities of Federal enforcement agents. The Association says that more than 700 additional deaths have been caused by the work of state and local officers. In addition, anti-prohibitionists believe that the Eighteenth Amendment is answerable for a large part of the slayings committed by rivals for the control of the illicit liquor traffic.

On the contrary, the advocates of prohibition point out that these 1000 deaths represent only about one per cent of the total of 100,000 or more homicides that have occurred since the enactment of the Volstead law. They believe that prohibition has actually reduced homicide by partly eliminating the open saloon, cheap whiskey, and public drinking.

In such highly controversial matters impartial evidence is difficult to secure. The United States was far from being free from homicide before the enactment of prohibition laws. The "beer barons" and "bootleg kings" might have turned their attention to other types of crime if there had been no opportunity to exploit the liquor traffic. Perhaps prohibition has increased the amount of homicide; perhaps it has not.

HISTORICAL BACKGROUND

The conditions under which the United States were settled have been held responsible for the prevalence of crimes of violence in this country. Many of the early settlers left Europe under a cloud of judicial disfavor; the disorganization of frontier life did not encourage respect for authority; the Revolutionary War developed the doctrine of the "right of revolution"; the expansion of the West made a hero of the desperado. Arthur Pound

has forcefully portrayed the effect such conditions have
had upon the enforcement of law:

American crime is a cross between Original Sin and the Frontier Spirit. . . . One reason that the British who stayed at home
bred a peaceful posterity is that they lacked a frontier; one reason
that we are more lawless is the simple fact that America had a
frontier from 1607 to 1890.

As the frontier moved west, it rolled along its load of deviltry
—horse stealing, cattle rustling, murders, gang feuds, lynchings,
gambling, stage-coach stick-ups, train robberies, and bank robberies. Either the law or the vigilantes got most of these sinners in
the end; yet scores of them, like Billy the Kid, the James brothers,
and John Oakhurst, live on in history, folklore and literature,
sublimated into heroes by a populace which forgives anything except listlessness, and sees in every desperate act some smattering
of the admirable. That our geographical frontier has passed sig-
nifies nothing as yet; our great cities, the present hot beds of crime,
are the frontiers for a host of new Americans, offering to their
released energies and stimulated wants as many immunities and
opportunities as the West used to offer its "bad men." . . .

Civilization is a taming process. The British are tamer than
Americans; likewise more civilized. . . . The bandit is just as
much a part of our social picture as the dole is of theirs.[39]

This state of affairs has developed the feeling in this
country that laws are obeyed only by the weak and the
submissive. According to William E. Dodd, "There has
been a habit of lawlessness in the United States from
earliest days, a habit which has influenced immigrants on
their arrival, which has warped the minds of the young,
which has swayed the officers of the law, and which gravely

[39] Arthur Pound, "The Sunny Side of Crime," *Independent*, CXVI, 708-10.

threatens the existing social order."[40]   This attitude has resulted in a veritable "cult of resistance to law."

How the modern city has become a new kind of frontier is described by the Birmingham, Alabama, *News* in its apology for the high homicide rate of that city:

This is in many respects a pioneer city. In less than a generation it has changed from a small town to a great metropolis. . . . The presence of uprooted folk, finding themselves in a strange environment, of industrial transients, constantly on the move, has made for a certain flux. The city's life is not yet crystallized—we have not yet found our soul—the process of stabilization checked by accessions of populations and interests, has not yet given Birmingham the character and form which is described by the term "settled down."[41]

The historical background is evidently of importance, but its importance is difficult to appraise. There is a tendency for cities and communities to follow the patterns set by the early inhabitants. If, then, the first settlers were lawless and unrestrained individualists, it might be expected that these same tendencies would persist. For example, the homicide rate in South Carolina is apparently lower for those localities which were originally colonized by *group* migrations. In contrast to those regions first settled by individuals of diverse European origins, these communities with a history of group colonization seem to be more law abiding. This may be due to the superiority of the original inhabitants or to the fact that social control and public opinion were transplanted from the former home in Europe. On the contrary, the

[40] "Our Ingrowing Habit of Lawlessness," *Century*, CXVI, 691-98.
[41] "Our 12,000 Killings in 1926," *Literary Digest*, XCIV, 12-13, July 2, 1927.

communities settled by individuals from many homelands were under the necessity of developing new means of social control and of creating a public opinion to support the enforcement of law.   If this principle holds true for states other than South Carolina, it may assist in explaining some of the wide variations in homicide rates.

The results of frontier life on "free" land and in the great cities of the twentieth century have often been emphasized to the neglect of two other historical bases for lawlessness.   The Revolutionary War and the break with English courts may be of some importance.   Besides, Reconstruction in the South resulted in the almost complete destruction of the power and prestige of the courts.   The corrupt or impotent judiciary was disregarded, and reliance was placed upon violence, even for defense against aggression.   This background may possibly explain in part the high homicide rates in the southern states.

The appeal to history has, perhaps, been overemphasized, since it is a rather comforting explanation of the prevalence of lawlessness.   Against this tendency Venn makes vigorous protest:

We are a young country; Australia, Canada, and South Africa are still younger and their murder rates are tiny fractions of ours. We have a multitude of races living in close contact; the greatest number of races, in what is certainly the closest contact, live in New York City—and New York's rate is lower than the average for the rest of the country.[42]

These statements by Venn are supported by conclusive evidence and leave little ground for complacency.

[42] "Murder," *Independent*, CXIII, 361-2.

CULTURE PATTERNS

Homicide rates in the United States are very probably increased by the strength of certain culture patterns or "folkways" which either predispose or incite to deeds of violence. Crime may be due to the strength of public opinion, as well as to its weakness. A homicide is often an indication of the presence of a social group with *mores* or with social standards which are antagonistic to the rules and customs of the larger society. Such a homicide may be unwillingly committed in order to secure the approval of friends and associates. Under such circumstances the slayer is merely the agent of others, and the act has its chief significance in the fact that it indicates a lack of social solidarity, the ideals of conduct of the face-to-face group being in conflict with the laws of the state and nation.

Among these anti-social folkways is the so-called "unwritten law," especially valid in the South, which almost requires that a man slay another who disrupts his home by seduction or adultery. In one community the pressure of public opinion in such a case was so powerful that the timid husband was forced to feign insanity in order to avoid doing his "duty." In another, S. was informed by an anonymous telephone call that his wife was guilty of misconduct with a neighbor. For about five weeks he brooded over the matter. Finally, he told a friend, "I have traced the S. family as far back as I know and have never seen a murderer. I hate to be the first one, but I see no way out of it." Within a few days he met the "invader" of his home and slew him.[43] Both these

[43] Columbia, S. C., *State*, July 6, 1930.

cases illustrate how homicides may be reluctantly committed in the effort to maintain or to secure group approval.

In some regions of the United States there are important survivals of the *code duello*. The South, especially, takes pride in the tradition of the "gentleman," ready to risk his life in defense of his "honor." Odum lists twenty-two formal duels in which Southern men of prominence in public affairs were principals.[44] Even today the descendants of the plantation owners and aristocrats enjoy "a certain braggadocio about the fighting South," prompt to revenge an "insult" by a personal attack upon the offender.[45] When the son of Colonel C., while engaged in shooting out the street lights of a nearby town, was arrested by an officer of the law and placed in jail until he could give bond for his appearance in court to answer a charge of disorderly conduct, the outraged father demanded that the boy return and slay the policeman in order to vindicate the honor of the family. When the son hesitated, the father threatened to take the matter into his own hands. The boy then departed upon his mission of vengeance, and shortly two more homicide victims were carried to their graves.

Another anti-social folkway requires that certain "fighting words," such as "liar" and "bastard," be answered by an immediate assault upon the one who pronounced the malediction. This, perhaps, is a survival of primitive man's fear of the curse or taboo. How this tradition may lead to homicide is clearly shown in the case of P.

[44] *An American Epoch*, pp. 70-71.
[45] *Ibid.*, p. 70.

At the age of twenty-five P. had committed his third man-slaughter. One night, while perhaps under the influence of alcohol, he had exhibited to a fellow traveler his skill with a revolver by using as a target a fire some distance away and had slain an old man who was seated beside the fire, warming his hands. For this offense P. served a short prison term. After his discharge from the state penitentiary he secured a position as guard for a "chain gang" engaged in highway construction. One of the prisoners escaped. P. pursued him with blood hounds. The prisoner was overtaken when his chains became entangled in some underbrush. Immediately P. ran up and with a load of heavy shot literally "blew out" the fugitive's brains.

Later P. and several companions were occupants of a car which was parked beside the highway about midnight. An electrical engineer, who had been called to assist in repairing the lighting system of a nearby town after its injury by a storm, drove his car into that of P. According to P., the engineer got out of his car and exclaimed, "You, s— o— b—! What are you doing here without a light on your car?" P. promptly attacked the engineer and in the affray killed him with his pistol. P. then drove home, leaving the body of the slain man lying beside the road. When the sheriff arrived several hours later, he found P. fast asleep.

At the trial of P. the defense proved that he and the engineer were almost unacquainted with each other and that premeditated murder should, therefore, be excluded from the charges. The prosecution presented evidence that P. did not first make a personal attack upon the engineer, as claimed by the defense, but that immediately upon hearing the insulting words he drew his revolver and fired, the bullet striking the engineer in the top of his head, as he was stooping down to examine the injury to the radiator of his car. The defense, however, offered another explanation of the position of the fatal wound, alleging that it was inflicted as the engineer crouched beside his car preparatory to firing upon P. after having been worsted in the fight.

P. was sentenced to life imprisonment. (He has now been released after serving seven years.) While awaiting removal to the state penitentiary, he talked freely about the injustice done him. "If I had it to do again tomorrow, I'd kill him again! Suppose you were with your best girl and a fellow would call you a s— o— b—. Don't you know you wouldn't be any man, if you didn't make him take it back or kill him?"

This story illustrates not only the conviction that an abusive epithet is equivalent to the first blow in a personal attack but also the low esteem in which human life is held in some communities. Wherever the taking of a man's life arouses little indignation, there one may expect to find many slayings and few convictions therefor. In the United States a violent death, whether accidental or homicidal, evokes little comment, unless the circumstances be extraordinary or the persons involved very prominent. In certain localities, especially in the West and the South, human life ranks so low in the scale of social values that homicide is almost inevitable whenever a personal difficulty arises.

On an isolated country road in a southern state two white men, each driving a one horse wagon, met each other. One of them, Welch, gives in a sworn statement his version of what happened:

"When I got right near to him he told me to stop and we both stopped the horses. Then Truett said he wanted to know the truth about what I had done about his dog. I told him I had killed the dog in my hen nest. Truett said that was a damn lie, that the dog did not suck eggs and looked like he was going to get off the wagon and I shot him twice then. He said to cut that out and started to drive on and said don't shoot any more, you have done killed me. Then I jumped off my wagon towards his wagon and shot him four more times."

Both Welch and Truett were poverty-stricken young farmers, each with a wife and two small children. According to the newspaper report, "The families are said to have insufficient clothing and with one family head dead and the other in jail their condition now is worse than formerly.

Welch following his confession did not seem to realize the seriousness of his offense. He asked Sheriff Gamble how much the thing would cost him. When the sheriff told him he would probably be given the death penalty if he was convicted of first degree murder, Welch broke down and cried."[46]

These men, and perhaps the community in which they live, are, indeed, far from civilization, if it is true that "civilization means, above all, an unwillingness to inflict unnecessary pain."[47] In this incident, the slayer's failure to realize the importance of his offense, as shown by his query as to the probable expense of the affair, indicates an almost barbaric indifference to violent death.

C. H., a Southern Highlander, fired his revolver at a distant wagon filled with Negroes and hit a woman. Later he was informed that one of his best friends had reported the facts of the case to the county sheriff who was making an investigation. C. H. sought the supposed "traitor" and shot him down without a word of warning. Then he found out that the slain man, the father of six small children, was absolutely innocent; the sheriff had learned from other sources that C. H. had done the shooting.

C. H. was tried for murder and sentenced to be executed. In the courtroom he showed no sign of regret except that he had erroneously killed the wrong man. He expressed the wish that he could get out of jail long enough to shoot the slanderer who had caused him to slay his friend.

[46] Quoted in an editorial in the Columbia, S. C., *State*, May 22, 1929.
[47] Harold J. Laski, "The Dangers of Obedience," *Harper's*, CLIX, 5.

During his successful efforts to escape the electric chair C. H. said to the psychologist who had been sent to give him an intelligence test, "Until they brought me to G. [the county seat] I never heard anybody say it wasn't all right to shoot a man that done you wrong."

Such disregard for the value of human life is not confined to backward rural areas; it is equally characteristic of strongly-knit minorities dwelling in cities. The lightness of heart with which the urban gangster prepares to "bump off" a rival or "take him for a ride" indicates the presence of a scale of values in striking conflict with that of the majority.

If, therefore, an attempt is made to understand why the homicide rates of the United States are so much higher than those for other civilized countries, emphasis should be laid upon the presence in this country of influential folkways or culture patterns, most of them survivals of more barbarous days, when human life was little esteemed.[48]

[48] For other explanations of the high rate of homicide in the United States see chapters vi, vii, and viii.

CHAPTER IV

THE SLAYING

THE IMPORTANCE of the dramatic incidents surrounding a homicide is generally given undue emphasis in newspaper accounts of the tragedy. In reality, these incidents merely portray what happened, while their significance can be revealed only by a careful study of the background causes of the difficulty and of the personality traits of the slayer. Nevertheless, these incidents, often superficial in themselves, may give important clues to the nature of the fundamental causes of homicide.

Of 100 murderers in the state of Massachusetts, Dr. Stearns found that 21 committed the homicide while engaged in some other crime, 33 as the outcome of a quarrel over a woman, 9 in disputes concerning money, and 30 in "miscellaneous quarrels."[1] It is probable that many of the 21 slayings incident to other crimes occurred during robberies. In the United States, murders during "hold-ups" are quite frequent, Sutherland reporting that 36.2 per cent of the homicide victims in Chicago during 1920 were slain while resisting burglary or robbery.[2] In general, Dr. Stearns' results are in agreement with those of other investigators, even though his subjects had a high percentage of mental abnormality, 9 of them being definitely insane, 8 exhibiting gross personality disorders, and 3 being feeble-minded.

The *Illinois Crime Survey* (page 610) gives a detailed

[1] Quoted in the Columbia, S. C., *State*, August 25, 1925.
[2] *Criminology*, p. 65.

classification of 760 *murders* reported in Cook County, Illinois, during the years 1926 and 1927. This includes those in the city of Chicago. Exclusive of 49 deaths due to automobile accidents in which the driver was violating the law, the remaining 711 cases were distributed as follows: 130 "gang killings"; 28 abortions; 47 infanticides; 54 homicides due to jealousy; 55 domestic quarrels in which 13 husbands and 42 wives were slain; 20 slayings of law enforcement officers; 43 murders from unknown motives; 1 girl thrown from an automobile; 3 victims of morons; 1 killed by father, not insane; 2 killed by mother, not insane; 2 victims of rape; 2 innocent bystanders; 71 victims of "hold-ups"; and 201 deaths from altercations and brawls. This rather unsatisfactory classification refers only to cases in which murder was correctly or incorrectly charged against the offender. In addition to those listed above, there were 62 manslaughters; 134 justifiable homicides; and 89 persons killed by police officers.

In South Carolina an analysis of 401 accounts of homicides showed results not unlike those of Dr. Stearns. The reports consisted of 321 summaries of newspaper articles describing slayings, supplemented by 80 additional records furnished by students and county officials. Of the 401 cases, 154 reports were indefinite or incomplete. Of the 257 cases giving information concerning the situation that led to the slaying, 99 were described as being due to sex and family problems; 50 to matters of property, including a number of robberies and of affrays among parties of gamblers; 35 to attempted arrests for offenses other than violation of the prohibition laws; and 62 to the

enforcement of the prohibition laws and to drunkenness
as a primary cause, exclusive of numerous other cases
where the use of alcohol was a contributing factor. Besides, there were 11 miscellaneous cases, including 5
prisoners killed by their guards and several infanticides.

In England, however, the percentage of murders due
to passion is relatively greater and the proportion of
those committed for gain is much less. Calvert says, "In
an official analysis covering all the convicted murderers
in England over a thirty year period it has been shown
that 29 per cent of the murders were due to drink, quarrels, and violent rage, 30 per cent to jealousy, intrigue,
and revenge, 10 per cent to extreme poverty and sexual
passion, and less than 10 per cent to robbery or other
mercenary motives. . . . Murder has become in England
a crime which is nearly always committed without a ra-
tional consideration of consequences, either under the dom-
ination of violent passion or in certain cases by abnormal
people like most poisoners, with such an unbalanced sense
of their ability to escape detection as not to consider the
result of discovery. 'Hold-ups' and murders for robbery
in England are rare, because the chances of discovery, conviction, and punishment have become too great."[3] This
rarity of murder for economic gain may not be due to certainty of punishment, as Calvert believes, but it is in
marked contrast to the situation in the United States, where
such slayings are quite frequent.

ALCOHOL

Many investigators have reported that the use of alcohol is an important inciting cause of homicide. Dr. Stearns

[3] "Murder and the Death Penalty," *Nation*, CXXIX, 406.

found that of the 100 murderers studied by him 20 were
intoxicated at the time of the murder and 14 others had
been drinking. In Ukrainia an investigation of 216 homicides showed that, of those prompted by the "hooligan
motive," 73.8 per cent were intoxicated when the crime
was committed and, of the murderers classed as "weaklings in conflict," 24.8 per cent were intoxicated.[4]   In
England Sullivan found that of 200 cases of homicide
60 per cent were due to alcoholism.[5]   In South Carolina,
as reported above, alcohol is an important factor, both directly and indirectly.

That alcohol is closely associated with homicide and
other acts of violence is to be expected because of its
psychological effects. Since it is a slight narcotic, it re-
leases the individual from his repressions and increases his
emotionality. In particular, the sexual passions are
aroused, and murder because of jealousy often results.
Besides, the heightened emotionality due to the effect of
alcohol makes mature social behavior more difficult to
achieve, and the disturbed intellectual functions may result in errors of reasoning and judgment. These conditions may lead directly or indirectly to altercations and
homicides. In addition, the problem of alcohol is also
indirectly responsible for many slayings resulting from attempts to enforce the prohibition laws of the United
States.

TRIVIAL GROUNDS FOR THE ALTERCATION

Even the casual newspaper reader is often cognizant of
the frequency of homicides due to altercations which have

---

[4] *Social Science Abstracts*, II, p. 947.
[5] *Encyclopaedia of the Social Sciences*, I, 626.

arisen from exceedingly trivial differences of opinion or conflicts of interests. These apparently frivolous slayings may, of course, receive a disproportionate amount of newspaper space because of their greater news value, but even when deduction is made for this, their number is evidently large. In many such cases, however, the triviality is more apparent than genuine, the insignificant incidents leading to homicide only because of previous enmity, alcoholic excess, or some other important ground for disagreement. Nevertheless, in the Ukrainian study already described strangers constituted 50 per cent of the victims. Even if this proportion does not hold true in the United States, still previous enmity cannot enter into all of these slayings over trifles. The following newspaper report illustrates how even strangers are not safe from attack, especially when, as is likely in this case, drunkenness is a factor in the altercation.[6]

William Wilson, former magistrate at Honey Hill, Berkeley county, was found guilty today of manslaughter in the case resulting from the death of Dave Finklea, Negro, early in May. He was sentenced to serve ten years.

Wilson, together with A. K. Crawford, was indicted for the slaying of Finklea at Gamble's filling station, May 7. Wilson, it was alleged, drove up to the filling station and with no other reason than he voiced when he said, "Nigger, I don't like your looks," so far as was shown, shot and killed Finklea.

Crawford was found not guilty.

The jury deliberated two and a half hours.

Other stories of similar slayings are frequently found in the newspapers. An uncle hunts up his nephew and

---

[6] Columbia, S. C., *State*, June 15, 1928.

kills him because of a quarrel about the sum of 25 cents. A man in a drunken stupor shoots his best friend. A beggar kills a stranger who refuses to give him a small sum of money. Two trustees of a public school are slain in a dispute over the election of a teacher. That such cases as these are fairly frequent can be easily demonstrated by an examination of newspaper files or court records. After presenting a similar list of homicides from trifling initial causes, Hoffman comments, "Such cases as these re-emphasize earlier conclusions that the problem of crime and punishment is much more profound and difficult of solution than is apparently the case."[7]

Yet even when homicide arises from grave conflict, the act usually results in making bad matters worse. In cases of marital infidelity, homicide is apparently a less satisfactory solution than legal separation or divorce. When the dispute is over the possession of property, the value is often negligible when compared with the shock of the tragedy, the cost of legal defense, etc. Except in genuine cases of self-defense, homicide is usually a tragically inadequate method of resolving a conflict. This supports the hypothesis, elsewhere advanced, that the majority of slayers are infantile personalities lacking in emotional control.[8]

LEGAL CLASSIFICATION OF HOMICIDES

With reference to the circumstances surrounding the deed, a homicide may be either justifiable or felonious. A justifiable homicide is one for which the slayer is not liable to receive punishment, as when a house-holder kills a burglar who is attempting to rob his dwelling. Felonious

---

[7] *The Homicide Problem*, p. 36.   [8] *Cf.* p. 93.

homicides are of two types: murder and manslaughter. The distinguishing characteristic of murder is that the slayer "premeditates" or plans his deed. In manslaughter, however, the act is committed by one who responds to the impulse of the moment and is overcome by sudden rage. (In those states where felonious homicides are divided into three classes—murder in the first degree, murder in the second degree, and manslaughter—only the first class is premeditated and, accordingly, as a rule punishable by execution or life imprisonment.)

Of the total number of homicides it is not known exactly what proportion is due to murder, to manslaughter, or to justifiable homicide. In Washington, D. C., for the period of 1914-1918 justifiable or excusable homicides comprised 32 per cent of the total; in 1920 in Detroit they were 26.6 per cent, and in Chicago 31.5 per cent.[9] In Cook County, Illinois, in 1926 and 1927 there were 760 murders, 62 manslaughters, 134 justifiable homicides, and 89 slayings by police officers, all of whom were later exonerated.[10] After excluding 49 automobile deaths from the total, justifiable homicides, including slayings by the police, make up 22.4 per cent of all the cases. If these studies are typical of the facts elsewhere, it may be safely concluded that justifiable homicides comprise from one-fourth to one-third of the total number of slayings.

The distinction between felonious and justifiable homicide is, however, of much less importance than is generally believed to be true. In reality, a justifiable homicide is almost, if not quite, as accurate an indication of the pres-

[9] Edwin H. Sutherland, *Criminology*, p. 38.
[10] *Illinois Crime Survey*, p. 601.

ence of anti-social behavior as a premeditated murder is. In a murder it is the slayer who is guilty of anti-social conduct, while in a justifiable homicide it is the slain who has been so reprehensible in his behavior that the slayer is excusable for putting him to death. It is possible that the legal distinction between premeditated murder and impulsive manslaughter is of little sociological signifi-cance, for the difference may be due chiefly to the per-sonality type of the slayer, the murderer having a pre-dominance of intellectual difficulties and the man-slayer having a pronounced lack of emotional control.

"GANG SLAYINGS"

A type of homicide that has attracted much attention is the so-called "gang execution." Such murders are gen-erally confined to large cities and are in marked contrast to the usual murder, which is characteristically an affair between individuals. These "gangsters" or "racketeers" are frequently engaged in occupations which are either illegal or disreputable. In particular, they often control the city's gambling dens, liquor businesses, vice resorts, and similar enterprises. Besides, they may carry on black-mail and other types of extortion. In Chicago in 1927 "over ninety legitimate businesses" were "dominated by gangsters," largely through contributions extorted upon some pretext.[11]

When these gangs of freebooters come in conflict with each other, there can normally be no appeal to the courts. Consequently, they "fight it out." Rival leaders seek to destroy their competitors. When one slaying occurs, re-

---

[11] *Ibid.*, p. 639; and John Gunther, "The High Cost of Hoodlums," *Harper's*, CLIX, 529-40.

prisals follow, beginning a chain of murder that ends only with the surrender or extermination of one of the gangs. The spectacular nature of these "executions" is increased by the weapon employed—sub-caliber machine guns and bombs, in many cases—and by the participants' apparent immunity from punishment. In Chicago during 1926 and 1927 there were 130 slayings by gangsters, yet the *Illinois Crime Survey* reports, "There have been no convictions in gang murders in Chicago during the period covered by this analysis—1926 and 1927."[12] This immunity from punishment is apparently due in part to collusion between "politicians" and "racketeers" and to the "rule of silence" required by the "underworld code of ethics."

These gang slayings are not of great importance statistically, for they represent only a small proportion of the total number of homicides. Even in Chicago, where they are alleged to be most numerous, they did not account for one seventh of the slayings during 1926 and 1927. Their significance depends more upon the boldness with which they are committed, the freedom of the slayers from arrest, the spectacular methods employed, and the inability of the police to cope with the situation. In many ways these "gangsters" correspond to the "robber barons" of the Middle Ages, exacting tribute from the defenseless public and engaging in bitter wars with one another.

HOMICIDE AND OFFICERS OF THE LAW

In many parts of the United States an officer of the law is rarely thought of as a guardian of the peace, a representative of the public. If he is slain in the discharge

[12] *Ibid.*, pp. 594 and 610.

of his duties, no one is aroused except his fellow officers and his family and friends. This attitude results in frequent slayings of policemen and in small punishment to the slayers.

Of 739 homicides in Atlanta, Birmingham, Memphis, and New Orleans during the years 1921 and 1922 police officers were involved in 6.6 per cent of the total, furnishing the victim in one case out of seven.[13] In Cook County, Illinois, including the city of Chicago, 20 officers were slain during the years 1926 and 1927.[14] In South Carolina from August 1, 1925, through July 31, 1928, one newspaper published accounts of the slaying of 11 officers of the law on duty, 5 of them at the hands of Negro men and 6 by white men. According to the census of 1920 there were in South Carolina at that time only 740 policemen, sheriffs, constables, detectives, etc.[15] If this number had not been increased by the period 1925-1928, and if the newspaper referred to above published accounts of all of the actual slayings of officers, the annual homicide rate for this occupation in this state was 495.5 deaths per 100,000 persons, one of the highest homicide rates ever published, approximately 40 times greater than the rate for the general population of South Carolina.

This attitude that the policeman is an unimportant, if not a menial, servant and that he is a "fair mark" for the slayer is in striking contrast with the situation in Europe, where the policeman is often considered a respected public official, the defender of law and order. In Lon-

---

[13] J. J. Durrett and W. G. Stromquist, "Preventing Violent Death," *Survey*, LIV, 435-38.

[14] *Illinois Crime Survey*, p. 610.

[15] *The Fourteenth Census of the United States*, IV, p. 124.

don, for example, the officers do not usually carry revolvers while on duty, yet "the killing of a London policeman is practically unheard of."[16]

The treatment accorded the policeman is also in marked contrast with that given the soldier. When a man is slain upon the field of battle, he is honored as a hero, and his family is pensioned. But when a policeman is killed by a desperado, he is quickly forgotten, his wife and children may soon be in want, and his slayer often escapes with little or no punishment.

This high homicide rate among law enforcement officers not only reduces their zeal in the pursuit of desperate criminals and lowers the quality of the men available for such positions, but it also increases markedly the number of persons slain by the police. As one patrolman put it, "When I go out to my 'beat' in the morning and see those badges up there in memory of those of us who have been killed on duty, I think about my wife and children. Could you blame me if I should shoot to kill if I should see a 'mean one' reach for his gun?"

The number of persons slain by officers of the law is, consequently, by no means insignificant. In Chicago during 1926 and 1927 a total of 89 persons were reported as having been killed by the police.[17] In New York City there were 152 killings by policemen during the period 1922-1928, an average of 21.7 persons each year.[18] In South Carolina a single daily newspaper reported during a three year period 33 deaths at the hands of officers of the law. Of the victims, 23 were Negro men and 10 were white men.

[16] O. G. Villard, "Official Lawlessness," *Harper's*, CLV, 605-14.
[17] *Illinois Crime Survey*, p. 601.   [18] *World's Almanac 1930*, p. 568.

This readiness of police officers to fire upon persons who resist arrest is deplorable, but it seems almost necessary for self preservation.   When an American officer who was cleaning his revolver was asked what would happen if the policemen in his city should go unarmed, as in London, his reply was, "If it was known, there wouldn't be one of us alive by night."   This evident exaggeration indicates, nevertheless, the attitude of the officer and his opinion of the attitude of the general public.   Slayings of and by the police are likely to continue, therefore, until these attitudes are changed.   This, in turn, seems to depend upon an improvement in the quality of the men employed as officers, more adequate salaries and pensions, prompt punishment of their assailants, the removal of graft and corruption from police departments, and the establishment of the conception of an officer as an honorable official charged with the defense of the rights of the citizen.

FIREARMS AND HOMICIDE

In the United States, slayers use firearms more frequently than in any other country for which records are available.   From 1920 through 1926 there were 63,906 homicides reported from the vital statistics registration area.   Of these 45,666 were committed with firearms, a total of 71.46 per cent.   In contrast, during 1923 only 10.4 per cent of the slayings in England were the result of shootings, while in Australia the proportion was 17 per cent, and in Japan it was only 1.3 per cent.[19]   Of 216 murderers with non-mercenary motives in Ukrainia only

---

[19] F. L. Hoffman, *The Homicide Problem*, p. 4.

one third used firearms, hatchets and clubs being more frequently employed.[20]

The proportion of slayings in which firearms are used is apparently increasing. For example, according to Hoffman, during the years 1910-1913 firearms were used in slaying 62.8 per cent of the males and 52.2 per cent of the females. Hoffman also presents a table showing a steady increase in the proportion of homicidal deaths due to firearms from the year 1910 through 1921.[21] Although a part of this increase is due to the inclusion of several southern states in the registration area rather than to the increased use of firearms in the states covered by the earlier reports, the general tendency is apparently toward a greater proportion of homicides committed with firearms.

The percentage of homicidal deaths caused by firearms varies appreciably for certain groups. During the years 1924-1926, in the United States registration area this percentage was 74.5 for homicides in rural territory, while for urban districts it was 67.1 per cent. This was perhaps due to the country dweller's experience and skill in the use of firearms or to his greater tendency to carry weapons, especially concealed ones. Contrary to common belief, the Negro was more often slain with firearms than was the white, 72.3 per cent of the Negro homicidal deaths being caused by firearms, while only 68.3 per cent of the slayings among the whites were due to this means. For Negro females the percentage of firearms slayings was 63.2, while for the white females it was only 46.8.

The mortality statistics of the United States Division of Vital Statistics describes the means by which homicides

[20] *Social Science Abstracts*, II, p. 947.
[21] *The Homicide Problem*, pp. 29 and 70.

are committed as (1) those in which firearms were used, (2) those slain with cutting or piercing instruments, and (3) those due to other means, such as poison, bludgeons, etc. From these reports it is possible to find the percentage of cases in which firearms were used by dividing the total number of homicides into the number of slayings in which guns and revolvers were used. For the three years, 1924-1926, these percentages have been calculated and are presented in Table II, together with the unweighted average homicide rate for each state for the same three years.

TABLE II. RATE OF HOMICIDE AND USE OF FIREARMS

STATE	Mean Homicide Rate 1924–26	Percentage of Firearms 1924–26	STATE	Mean Homicide Rate 1924–26	Percentage of Firearms 1924–26
Florida	38.27	73.48	Indiana	6.57	71.71
Mississippi	21.37	77.89	Delaware	6.47	54.35
Louisiana	21.17	71.76	Pennsylvania	5.90	68.25
Alabama[1]	18.65	72.07	Kansas	5.47	72.30
Georgia[2]	18.30	75.23	New York	5.10	56.57
Tennessee	17.77	76.56	Utah	5.10	68.42
Kentucky	14.83	86.01	Washington	5.03	74.34
Arizona[3]	14.20	74.60	New Jersey	4.87	52.77
Missouri	12.37	72.12	Oregon	3.97	73.53
Wyoming	12.33	79.76	Idaho	3.93	76.27
South Carolina	12.20	78.60	Nebraska	3.60	74.32
West Virginia[1]	12.15	80.60	Connecticut	3.23	33.77
Illinois	10.60	71.45	Minnesota	2.93	61.74
North Carolina	9.87	74.97	Iowa	2.60	67.20
Virginia	9.50	74.43	Massachusetts	2.47	46.71
California	8.70	68.30	Rhode Island	2.23	56.52
Michigan	8.43	67.81	Wisconsin	2.17	62.37
Colorado	8.23	72.05	North Dakota	2.03	58.97
Ohio	7.63	63.67	Maine	1.60	52.63
Maryland	7.37	60.17	New Hampshire	1.27	41.18
Montana	6.67	76.69	Vermont	1.17	41.67

[1] Data for 1925 and 1926 only.
[2] Data for 1924 only.   [3] Data for 1926 only.

Even a casual examination of this table will reveal a tendency for the lower homicide rates to be associated with a smaller percentage of firearms slayings. To measure this more accurately than by mere inspection, the coefficient of correlation between these two factors was calculated by the Pearsonian method. The numerical relationship was found to be +.61 with a probable error of ±.07, indicating a high relationship between the two. For fear that this coefficient might be raised by the inclusion of Negro homicides, a second calculation was made by the rank-difference method, using data for whites only both for homicides and for firearms slayings. This coefficient was found to be +.67 with a probable error of ±.06.[22] These results indicate quite clearly that, so far as this method of analysis is applicable to the data, there is a fairly close relationship between the high homicide rate and a large percentage of firearms slayings. If one knows the percentage of homicides committed with firearms, he can with fair success predict whether the homicide rate for that state is relatively high or low. This conclusion is in accord with the observation made by William Tallack in 1896, "The districts where there are most murders are those where private citizens habitually carry weapons."[23]

CONCEALED WEAPONS

The consensus of opinion is that these slayings by means of firearms are committed far more frequently

[22] These coefficients of correlation, as well as the others presented elsewhere in this volume, are based upon the assumption of a linear relationship between the factors involved. Inspection of the regression lines indicates that the calculation of correlation ratios in order to test for curvilinear relationship would not have appreciably increased the coefficients. See H. E. Garrett, *Statistics in Psychology and Education*, pp. 203-11.   [23] *Penological and Preventive Principles*, p. 258.

with revolvers than with rifles or other guns. "The pistol is the curse of America, and they are almost as plentiful as lead pencils in this country, good citizens and bad citizens possessing them. . . . There are more people shot to death or wounded by pistols in the United States in one year than in all of the rest of the world besides."[24] Another writer states, "Nearly seven thousand are killed by pistols in this country every year; in England and Wales there are sixteen."[25] Although reliable data cannot be secured in support of these rather extreme statements, the opinions expressed are, doubtless, far nearer right than wrong.

Since many homicides are not premeditated murders but are various types of manslaughter carried out "in sudden heat and passion," it is evident that the custom of carrying concealed firearms would naturally tend to increase the number of slayings. For committing a homicide of this type three things are necessary: the emotional urge to destroy, the opportunity to attack the offender, and a suitable weapon.[26] If any one of these is missing, the slaying does not take place. If, then, the men of a community are always armed with revolvers, one of the three essentials is ever present, and a homicide takes place whenever the rage is sufficient and the opportunity is suitable. In hundreds of cases, perhaps, if the would-be slayer did not have upon his person a deadly weapon, he would delay his attempt at vengeance and often would, upon reflection, resort to less violent methods of securing

---

[24] William McAdoo, "Crime and Punishment: A Symposium," *Scientific Monthly*, XXIV, 415-47.

[25] F. E. Venn, "Murder," *Independent*, CXIII, 361-2.

[26] J. R. Oliver, *Foursquare*, p. 65.

justice. Consequently, a high rate of homicide should be expected wherever the carrying of a revolver is considered a symbol of manhood—as in some southern and western communities. In such communities, especially in those lying within what has been lightly called "the Smith and Wesson line," many a man without his pistol would feel himself as emasculated as would a Sikh without his sacred dagger. In one of these states the attorney general writes in his annual report:

The record shows to the world that during the previous twelve months 243 of our fellow-citizens were put to death at the hands of our own fellow-citizens. . . . I am sure that each of you can assign certainly as one cause the deplorable custom of carrying pistols, a custom carried to such an extent that our state may be regarded as an armed camp in time of peace. Our young men and boys, white and black, rich and poor, seem to think that their outfit is not complete without a pistol; some of our older men show a bad example, and I regret to say some public officials have on occasions been found armed in violation of law. Pistols are carried, not as protection at night on some lonely road or in some remote part of the country during the day or in some dangerous neighborhood, but at public meetings, on the streets, at social gatherings, even at dances, even at daily labor and following the plow, and I add also even at church and prayer-meeting.[27]

In contrast to this striking description of conditions actually prevailing in this state, there should be quoted a section from its criminal code dealing with concealed weapons:

It shall be unlawful for any one to carry about the person, whether concealed or not, any pistol less than twenty inches long and three pounds in weight, and it shall be unlawful for any per-

[27] Quoted by F. L. Hoffman, *The Homicide Problem*, p. 31.

son, firm, or corporation to manufacture, sell or offer for sale, lease, rent, barter, exchange, or transport for sale into this state, any pistol of less length and weight. Any violation of this section shall be punished by a fine of not more than one hundred ($100) dollars or imprisonment for not more than thirty (30) days.

Evidently the law and the *mores* are at variance, and, as usual, the *mores* prove to be the stronger.

REGULATION OF CONCEALED WEAPONS

Although revolvers are seldom used for sport and are often purchased for slaying human beings, their sale and manufacture are practically unregulated except in a few states. Even though strict regulations are carried upon the statute books, they are either easily evaded or are rendered inoperative because of the strength of public opinion to the contrary. Yet even when one state does attempt to suppress the open sale of revolvers, the dealers in other states and mail order houses assist in evading the law. The extent of the mail orders for revolvers can be judged by Mr. Julius Rosenwald's statement that his firm, Sears, Roebuck and Co., was doing a $3,000,000 business in them when it decided to discontinue the sales for the good of the country.[28] In one publication, offered for sale on nearly every news stand, Hoffman noted seven advertisements of revolvers, ranging in price from $6.25 to $9.75.[29] Yet if these prices are too high, the weapons can be secured otherwise, for, according to Judge McAdoo, "Down in Texas and some other states, the Negroes rent the pistols and pay for them on the installment plan."[30]

---

[28] Associated Press report, October 26, 1930.
[29] *The Homicide Problem*, p. 4.
[30] "Crime and Punishment: A Symposium," *Scientific Monthly*, XXIV, 418.

Such sales policies, supported by the strength of custom, result in so great a demand that the large domestic production is insufficient and heavy importations are made from Europe, especially from Spain, "whose entire output of these murderous weapons finds its way to this market."[31]

Not only is the adult in the United States a carrier of concealed weapons; he often insists upon purchasing similar equipment for his children. The sale of toy revolvers is enormous. Small boys armed with such toys play gunman and robber. They lurk in ambush and in sport hold up pedestrians. These activities are, of course, quite harmless in themselves, but the idea back of them is far from harmless. Older boys and youths armed with small caliber rifles and pistols often busy themselves killing song birds and household pets, meanwhile endangering the lives of bystanders and becoming accustomed to the reckless use of firearms. Further training of the same nature is provided by moving pictures featuring "gun-play"—a term significant in its levity. These practices indicate quite clearly the attitude of the people of the United States towards revolvers and their users.

This practice of carrying concealed weapons is, moreover, in marked contrast to the situation in most European countries, where the possession of revolvers is subject to stringent governmental regulation and where criminals arrested with unlicensed firearms on their persons are almost certain to receive additional penalties. In Canada, where the rate of homicide is about one sixth of what it is in the United States, both public opinion and law limit

[31] *Ibid.,* p. 417.

the ownership of concealed weapons, and heavy sentences are given burglars or robbers who are so armed when placed under arrest.[32]   In England, "any one found in possession of firearms with intent to endanger life may be sent to penal servitude for twenty years."[33]   In many countries even officers of the law go unarmed. As has already been pointed out, the situation is quite different in the United States.

The practice of carrying concealed firearms is, it seems evident, of great importance if the high rate of homicide in the United States is to be materially decreased. It cannot be gainsaid that a large number of such crimes are due to the "pistol toter, who has been banking on his gun, more since the close of the World War than ever before."[34]   Whether the relationship between homicide and concealed weapons is to be explained by the purchase of revolvers by those with homicidal tendencies or by the greater chance of unpremeditated manslaughter by those who carry pistols in accordance with custom, the relationship does exist, none the less, and the prevalence of such weapons undoubtedly increases the average citizen's danger of violent death. To many persons, moreover, the possession of firearms gives a false sense of security and encourages recklessness and arrogance. Those most experienced in such matters generally agree that it is almost suicidal for the average householder to attempt to use a firearm against a professional burglar or robber. Besides, among the young and the emotionally infantile, the pos-

[32] William Banks, "Canada's Effective Criminal Law System," *Current History*, XXVIII, 405-07.

[33] F. L. Hoffman, *The Homicide Problem*, p. 58.

[34] Quoted in editorial in the Columbia, S. C., *State*, September 4, 1930.

session of a weapon engenders a "devil may care" attitude that is provocative of altercations. Then the ready weapon may come into death-dealing use. It seems justifiable to conclude, therefore, that the rate of homicide in the United States will probably remain higher than in Europe until there is marked improvement in the regulation of the sale and possession of concealed firearms, and until the measures for governmental control are heartily supported by custom and public opinion.

CHAPTER V

THE SLAIN AND THE SLAYER

E XCEPT for the facts revealed by the mortality records very little definite information is available concerning the victims of homicide. It is generally assumed, however, that the victim and the offender belong to the same group, with regard to color, age, and nationality.[1] How reliable this assumption is has not been carefully investigated, but at least concerning color it is open to doubt, for there is some evidence that whites slay Negroes more often than Negroes slay whites.[2]

AGE OF VICTIM

With respect to age of the victim it has been found that "for both sexes and races the ages of greatest frequency of death by homicide are from 25 to 30 years."[3] Hoffman gives the following percentages for the different age groups of homicide victims in the United States registration area for the period, 1908-1912:[4]

Age Group	Males	Females
Under 5	3.7	12.0
5-19	7.2	14.7
20-29	33.8	32.6
30-39	28.1	21.3
40-49	15.9	11.2
50-59	7.3	5.0
60-69	2.9	1.7
70-79	0.9	1.2
80 and over	0.2	0.3
Total known ages	100.0	100.0

[1] Edwin H. Sutherland, *Criminology*, p. 64.
[2] *Cf.* p. 100.
[3] Edwin H. Sutherland, *Criminology*, p. 64.
[4] F. L. Hoffman, *The Homicide Problem*, p. 23.

This percentage table is corroborated by Hoffman's later studies. For the year 1920 the homicide rates per 100,-000 persons were as follows:[5]

		RATES PER 100,000	
Ages	*Males*	*Females*	*Both Sexes*
Under 1 year	2.3	2.2	2.2
5-14 years	0.9	0.5	0.7
15-44 years	17.3	4.4	10.9
45-64 years	10.5	1.4	6.2
65 and over	4.8	1.2	3.0
All ages	10.7	2.7	6.8

About 73 per cent of the total number of homicide victims were in the age group 15 to 44. Hoffman estimates that more than 8,000 persons are killed annually in the United States in this age group, "the period when human life has its highest economic value and when willful destruction involves the greatest loss to the community." For four cities the average ages at death for homicide victims were:[6]

Memphis, 1924-1928 .... 31.7 years
Birmingham, 1927-1929 .... 31.6 years
New Orleans, 1920-1926 .... 31.3 years
Boston, 1920-1926 .... 31.6 years

A similar study for the period, 1920-1924, in South Carolina arrived at a higher average age at the time of death. These results for homicide victims as compared with the average ages of the general population living in the state on January 1, 1920 were:

	HOMICIDE VICTIMS		GENERAL POPULATION	
	Mean	*Median*	*Mean*	*Median*
Whites	36.7	36.0	24.7	20.5
Negroes	31.5	29.0	22.7	18.1
Both races	33.0	30.6	23.7	19.2

[5] *Ibid.,* p. 3.
[6] F. L. Hoffman, "The Homicide Record for 1929," *Spectator,* March 22, 1930.

Of those who were slain during this period, about 75 per cent exceeded the mean age of the general population and about 90 per cent exceeded the median age of the general population. This indicates quite clearly that the victims of homicide are, for the most part, mature persons. Although the Negroes slain are younger than the whites, this does not necessarily indicate an important racial difference in juvenile homicide, since the average age of the total Negro population is much lower than the average age of the total white population.

INFANTICIDE

In the United States, infanticide, the slaying of children less than one year of age, is relatively rare in proportion to the total number of homicides. In England in 1916, 33 per cent of the total number of homicides were infanticides, while for the same year in the United States the percentage was only 2.[7] For the three years, 1924-1926, there were in the United States registration area states 464 infanticides, only 1.86 per cent of the total. Part of the unfavorable record of England is, of course, due to the relative rarity of adult homicide in that country. Adherents of the Malthusian doctrines concerning population will see in the data presented above an illustration of the principle that social problems are aggravated whenever the number of inhabitants press closely upon the means of subsistence. In England, therefore, population pressure may induce unwilling parents to destroy their offspring more frequently than in the United States, where food and land are still relatively abundant. The difference may, however, be due to other conditions, such

[7] Edwin H. Sutherland, *Criminology*, p. 39.

as the amount of illegitimacy, extent of birth control measures, the comparative expense of rearing a child, etc.[8]

SEX OF VICTIMS

Like infanticide, the slaying of women is much less
frequent in the United States than in England. During
the period 1924-1926, there were in the United States
registration area states 24,949 homicides. In 4,874 of
these, females were the victims, 19.5 per cent of the total.
Slightly more than four times more males than females
were homicide victims. In England, however, women
are more often slain than are men. Although nine out
of every ten murders are committed by men, "two out of
every three persons murdered are women."[9] Of the
women slain by men 42 per cent are their wives and 38
per cent their mistresses or sweethearts.[10]

This remarkable contrast in the incidence of homicide among women is probably due in large part to the
nature of the types of homicide prevalent in the two countries. In England the homicide rates are extremely low
and punishment is so sure that premeditated murder is
relatively rare. Crimes of passion and rage are, however, little affected by public opinion or the certainty of
punishment. Consequently, in England the murders are
predominantly those due to "sudden fury." In such cases
women are very often the victims. In the United States,
on the contrary, many homicides are mercenary, committed in carrying out a burglary or highway robbery.
Under such circumstances men are more liable to be slain.

[8] For a comparison of white and Negro infanticide see chapter VI.
[9] Roy E. Calvert, "Murder and the Death Penalty," *Nation*, CXXIX, 405-07.
[10] *Ibid.*

THE SLAYER

If, as is generally assumed, the slayer corresponds closely to the slain as regards both age and race, he is on the average not far from thirty years of age. Approximately 90 per cent of the slayers are males. Those who commit homicide do not usually possess a high educational status. Of 19,080 persons committed to state and federal prisons during the first six months of 1923, the median school grade completed by those sentenced for homicide was only the fifth grade. This was lower than for any other group except for those sentenced for felonious assault, who had completed only the fourth grade, as a median. The males convicted for homicide were nearly twice as illiterate as the average of the total number of males. Again, only those committed for felonious assault have a worse record.[11] This low educational status of those serving prison sentences for having committed homicide may, however, be due not to any causal relationship but to such factors as the large number of Negroes among the prisoners, to the greater ability of the educated to escape punishment, or to some other less evident factor.

DEGENERACY AND THE MURDERER

The school of criminology founded by Lombroso has for many years emphasized the physiological degeneracy of the "real" criminal, the person who commits an offense because of his own nature rather than for any concatenation of "accidental" circumstances. When the large group of "pseudo-criminals" is excluded, the true crim-

[11] U. S. Bureau of the Census, *The Prisoner's Antecedents*, p. 21.

inal will, according to the followers of Lombroso, be found to exhibit "stigmata" of degeneracy. For example, Di Tullio's recent study of 400 confessed murderers "showed 137 epileptics, 174 cases of constitutional neurasthenia, psychic degeneration in 45 cases, moral inferiority in 35 cases, paranoidism 6 times, schizoidism 4 times, and mild insanity 6 times."[12] This, according to Di Tullio, indicates that the true murderer is constitutionally or biologically defective and lends support to the doctrines of Lombroso.

Investigations by Goring and many others have, however, cast grave doubt upon the belief that the true criminal is "born" and carries physical indications of reversion to a more primitive type of man. The followers of Lombroso would find it difficult to explain upon any basis of biological degeneracy why Wyoming should have three times as many homicides as Idaho, or New York twice as many as Massachusetts. The constitutional defective probably contributes more than his share of murderers, since such a person finds the problems of life difficult to solve, but many of the physically degenerate are citizens of exceptional worth.

While studies of the native intelligence of criminals do not agree in all points, they show that the prisoner is not much below the average of the general population. For example, Murchison shows that of 3,368 prisoners at Fort Leavenworth, 30.6 per cent had grades above C upon the army Alpha intelligence test, while a sample of 94,004 World War soldiers had only 27.3 per cent above the grade of C. When the same test was administered to

<hr>

[12] *Social Science Abstracts*, II, p. 946.

84   HOMICIDE IN THE UNITED STATES

white male prisoners in the state penitentiaries of Illinois,
Ohio, Indiana, New Jersey, and Maryland, the 521 cases
committed for physical injury showed 35 per cent above a
C grade. In Ohio, Illinois, and Indiana, 221 cases of murder in the first degree showed medians of six grades of
school, of 32 years in age, and of a score of 58 upon the
Alpha test. In one prison, moreover, on an intelligence
test "the average score of the criminals was just 75 per
cent higher than the average score of the guards."[13]

A study of 1,916 prisoners at the Western Penitentiary
of Pennsylvania during 1924-1925 resulted, however, in
a lower average of intelligence, as measured by the Stan-
ford revision of the Binet-Simon test. While the normal
intelligence quotient ranges from 90 to 110, the median
quotients for these prisoners were as follows:[14]

CRIME	Median Intelligence Quotient	CRIME	Median Intelligence Quotient
Embezzlers	103.75	Arson	75.0
Robbers	84.3	Rape	72.8
Forgers	83.75	Sodomy	72.1
Burglars	81.75	Homicides	70.9
Larceny	78.3	Felonious assault	68.3

According to this investigation, those sentenced for homicide are in the group usually considered as "borderline"
to mental defect, since their median score falls in the 70
to 80 class. It should be noted that at this prison the intelligence of offenders against property is superior to that
of offenders against the person. This is probably due in
part, at least, to the presence in the latter group of a larger

[13] Carl Murchison, "Criminal Intelligence," *Journal of the American Institute of Criminal Law and Criminology*, XV, 239-316 and 435-94.
[14] Fred E. Haynes, *Criminology*, pp. 64-70.

proportion of the truly "feeble-minded"—imbeciles and morons.

From the studies presented above it is, perhaps, safe to conclude that while physiological and mental defects do not necessarily lead to crimes of violence, their presence in sub-normal persons makes life adjustments more difficult and homicide at their hands proportionately more frequent.

THE SLAYER'S PREVIOUS RECORD IN CRIME

Additional evidence in support of the conclusion that the slayer is not typically a moral degenerate is found in examining his previous record in crime. Of all persons committed in 1926 to state and federal prisons, 55.6 per cent were first offenders, but of those committed during the same period upon charges involving homicide 70.8 per cent were reported as first offenders. Comprising the total of 29.2 per cent of the slayers who were "repeaters" or recidivists, 7.6 per cent had never before been in a prison or reformatory but had been in jail once, 2.1 had been in jail twice, and only 0.9 per cent had been in jail three or more times; while 13.5 per cent had been in prison or reformatory once, 3.6 per cent twice, and only 1.5 per cent three or more times.[15] Yet, since punishment for homicide is still based more upon the act than upon the character of the accused, the sentences of the recidivists did not appreciably exceed those of the first offenders. When life sentences were arbitrarily assumed to be forty years in length—although actually far less—the average maximum sentence for the slayers described above was 23.49 years for the first offenders and 23.93 years for the

[15] U. S. Bureau of the Census, *Prisoners 1926*, pp. 27-9.

recidivists.[16] Judges and juries treated both groups about alike, since the first offenders averaged less than six months shorter sentences than did those who were "repeaters."

This relative freedom of slayers from previous criminal records is also illustrated by Dr. Warren Stearns' careful study of 100 murderers committed to the Charlestown, Massachusetts, prison between 1919 and 1923. Half of them had not even been under arrest previous to the slaying for which they had been imprisoned. Of the 50 per cent who had been under arrest, 27 had been arrested more than once and 23 only once, most of them for minor misdemeanors such as violating automobile regulations.[17] The typical slayer is not, therefore, a person who has been "hardened" by years of anti-social behavior—he is far more likely to be a first offender.

THE SLAYER'S PRISON RECORD

The behavior of those sent to prison for homicide reveals that the average slayer is not always "a brutal desperado, repeatedly in the hands of the police, gradually passing from one stage of criminality to another until at last he puts upon himself the brand of Cain." On the contrary, "prison wardens without exception report that the prisoners on life terms are almost always the best behaved prisoners they have."[18] For the Maryland state penitentiary Oliver reports, "In ours, as in most other prisons, the murderers are the pleasantest class to deal with. Indeed, murderers are, in a sense, not criminals at

---

[16] Ibid.
[17] Quoted in the Columbia, S. C., State, August 25, 1925.
[18] Edwin H. Sutherland, Criminology, p. 374.

all. For by a criminal we usually mean a man whose life is, more or less, devoted to evading the law."[19] In the "chain gang" camps in the southern states the "trusties" or honor prisoners are very often murderers; in fact, the guards usually consider the man guilty of homicide to be more reliable than one convicted of crimes against property. At one time in Aiken County, South Carolina, there was a small chain gang composed entirely of honor men who were serving life sentences for murder. These men were unguarded but worked under the orders of an employed foreman.

This favorable picture of the man-slayer describes, of course, only the average or typical prisoner. There are many exceptions. The "gangster" slays as an incidental but necessary part of his occupation and suffers little remorse, murder being a distasteful but unavoidable part of his "business." Besides, there is the fortunately rare "killer type" to whom a human life means almost nothing and who shoots an enemy as calmly as he would kill rabbits or quail. These two types are, naturally, extraordinarily dangerous prisoners and are nearly always a serious problem for guards and wardens.

PERSONALITY TYPES

The personality traits of the murderer have in recent years received much attention from the adherents of what might well be called the psychiatric school of criminology. Almost every psychiatrist with experience among criminals has proposed a classification of murderers in accordance with their psychological characteristics. Several of these will be presented.

[19] *Foursquare*, p. 56.

According to Schlapp and Smith, "Studies have shown that all murderers fall into one of four groups: First, those afflicted with obvious insanity—dementia, paranoia, mania, etc.; second, those suffering from mental deficiency, the more or less gravely feeble-minded of all ranks; third, the epileptics; fourth, the emotional defectives, including the group disordered by extrinsic poisons, drugs, etc."[20]

This excellent classification resembles that given by J. R. Oliver. Acording to Oliver, some slayers are prompted by "a momentary blinding passion," others are more dominated by intelligence and act with premeditation. In some cases the slayer is like a cornered animal, blindly attacking those around him. An unusual combination of circumstances leads others to become murderers. Finally, there are the few "killers," who slay "with less emotional reaction than if they were killing an annoying fly."[21]

The All-Ukrainian Cabinet for Research in Criminality and the Criminal has recently made a detailed "bio-sociological analysis" of 216 murderers, 197 men and 19 women, who killed their victims for reasons other than economic gain. Of the 216, more than 70 per cent, 153 in number, fell into the category designated as "weaklings in conflict," those who "resolve a mental conflict by the panacea of annihilation." These persons have usually been involved in family or sex difficulties, and their slayings are brought on by such situations as jealousy over unfaithfulness, fear of ridicule because of the desertion of a mate, the desire to get rid of a husband or wife in order to secure another lover, etc. The outstanding characteristic

---

[20] *The New Criminology*, p. 234.   [21] *Foursquare*, p. 51.

of this group was the presence of fear in the form of an emotional complex. In the group described as prompted by the "hooligan-motive," or rowdyism, were placed 17.1 per cent of the murderers. Of these, 73.8 per cent committed murder while intoxicated, in contrast to only 24.8 per cent of the "weaklings in conflict," and they often slew persons who were strangers. The group committing murder in order to protect fellow criminals comprised 5.1 per cent of the total, and those "jointly liable" because of complicity in the deed furnished only 2.3 per cent. Two additional conclusions from this study are of interest: "Of the whole group 43 per cent were victims of mental disorder ranging from psychopathy to traumatic conditions," and "fear of an enemy plus a sense of insecurity are the highest factors in producing criminality."[22]

The conclusion that crime of all kinds, especially homicide, is often due to a feeling of insecurity when faced by difficulty, is supported by many other observers. For example, Bjerre says, "The determining factor in all crime is *weakness*. . . . This weakness, or general unfitness, is found among murderers in various forms, which, superficially regarded, most certainly do not appear to possess any psychological affinity, but which are all, at bottom, means of escape from the realities of life, with which the socially unfit are unable to cope."[23]

In many cases this feeling of insecurity exhibits itself in braggadocio or exhibitionism, which is really motivated by the hope, often unconscious, of deceiving the public by a "brave show" of courage and audacity. The gangster

[22] *Social Science Abstracts*, II, p. 947.
[23] *The Psychology of Murder*, pp. 4-5.

seems to be predominantly of this type. As Maynard comments, "The greatest incentive to the machine-gun type of crime is a childish vanity. The little fellows want to be known as big shots. To achieve this they must attract attention. . . . To that end they are willing to risk anything. Their crimes are committed with great excitement and ballyhoo and much carnage. They read of their exploits in the newspapers, and gloat over the more gaudy accounts." Maynard also describes a battle he once witnessed between two rival gang leaders.

"Ev had been the ring leader of our old gang. It greatly wounded his vanity to see himself stripped of his glory and influence in the neighborhood." Finally Ev began to make threats against Amati, the rival leader. At last they met at the neighborhood "fence" and "dive." Amati overheard Ev defying his rival and challenged him. Ev immediately drew his revolver and opened fire. "Amati laughed. He was taking his time, letting Ev waste his ammunition. Amati was enjoying the situation, waiting for a chance to plug Ev with one shot. It wasn't bravery that made him stand there under Ev's fire. It was egoism, his desire to dramatize the moment, to hog the spotlight."[24]

Gorki tells a similar story about an old rag and junk dealer who many years before had murdered with a mowing knife his uncle's entire family of five persons because they teased him. Because of his simplicity, actual and assumed, he had served only 23 years in prison. The old man was very proud of his extraordinary past and was flattered by the questions of the curious. One day he said, "Before the crime I lived as a shadow, then the devil

[24] Lawrence M. Maynard, "Murder in the Making," *American Mercury*, XVII, 129-35.

struck me, and I became conspicuous to myself as well as to others."[24]

Vanity and exhibitionism are, however, inadequate explanations, for many vain and boastful persons are never even suspected of crime. This inadequacy is, in part, removed by the theory advanced by R. G. Gordon. Both homicide and suicide are, according to Gordon, due to a failure to adjust to the demands of social life. Persons who are in harmony with life develop psychoneuroses, such as "shell-shock," in time of great stress. Those who are out of harmony with life tend to develop psychoses, such as dementia precox, when they are subjected to grave emotional conflict. It is in the latter group that suicides and homicides are found.[26] This theory makes its contribution in emphasizing that there are usually two types of factors in the causation of homicide: first, personality difficulties, and, second, certain social situations, especially those arousing powerful emotions. Nervous and mental instability resulting in exceptional weakness of emotional control appears to be one of the most characteristic personality traits of the slayer. Whenever such a person comes into a situation which arouses extraordinary rage or fear, he loses control of himself and may commit homicide if the circumstances make it possible.

Another type of slayer is the person who has a strong sadistic trend and who, consequently, derives pleasure from the infliction of pain. The famous murder of Bobby Franks by Loeb and Leopold seems to have been of this variety. The slayers confessed that they greatly enjoyed

[25] Maxim Gorki, "About Murderers," *Dial*, LXXXV, 201-10.
[26] *Social Science Abstracts*, I, p. 1546.

the "thrill" of murdering the little boy. In February, 1930, a young man only twenty-five years old admitted having killed eight men with poison and a ninth with a revolver. He informed the authorities that he poisoned his victims because he wanted to observe the effects of the drugs and because the deaths of human beings gave him "a funny sort of mental satisfaction." If sadism is a relatively rare tendency, this type of slayer is not often found. If, however, there are concealed sadistic tendencies in many persons, such tendencies may, even when not apparent to either the slayer or the observer, become under favorable circumstances an important factor in the causation of crimes of violence.

Epileptics, perhaps because of their irritability, are especially liable to commit homicide. De Quiros quotes Burlureaux as saying:

When an inexplicable crime, completely out of harmony with the culprit's antecedents who is not insane, is committed with unusual rapidity, ferocity, or multiplicity of extraordinary aggressions, foreign to the usual mechanism of crime and complicity; when the culprit has lost all remembrance and seems a stranger to the act, or when he has a vague consciousness of the deed and speaks of it with indifference as if another had committed it; then it is necessary to look for epilepsy.[27]

Others have emphasized "psychic epilepsy," in which the sufferer does not fall into a convulsion, as in *grand mal*, but undergoes a change of personality accompanied by or arising from emotional stress. In such a state a person may commit crimes quite out of accord with his usual behavior and may afterwards be wholly unable to account for his

---

[27] Quoted in Bernaldo de Quiros, *Modern Theories of Criminality*, p. 16.

own acts. This should, of course, be distinguished from hysterical, purposive forgetting about the crime because of fear of the consequences. The epileptic, then, tends to commit more than his proportion of homicide, especially of the impulsive, unpremeditated type.

The attitude of slayers towards their deed throws some light upon their personalities. In general, it can be said that those who commit homicide may be divided into the tender-minded and the tough-minded. The former express great regret because of their acts and sometimes spend years in endeavoring to help the families of their victims. For example, when an elderly man committed suicide by shooting himself, the account of his death contained this explanation, "Mr. A. worried over the fact that he killed a Negro 40 years ago and this is thought to have caused the act." On the other hand, the hardened "killer type" rarely condemns himself for his conduct. During the period, 1922-1928, Tersiev studied 130 murderers who were serving sentence in Moscow, Russia. Of these 27 were considered to be untrustworthy. Of the 103 others, 90 condemned their acts—69 unconditionally disapproved of their deeds, 21 disapproved with reservations. Only 13 justified their conduct.[28] If this proportion holds true in the United States, it indicates that the tender-minded far outnumber the tough-minded. Besides, it gives further evidence to show that the average slayer is not a heartless brute.

THE SOCIOLOGICAL AGE OF THE SLAYER

These studies of the murderer's personality traits seem to agree only in the conclusion that certain types of per-

[28] *Social Science Abstracts*, II, pp. 1661-62.

sons are unusually liable to commit homicide when prov-
ocations arise.   Other investigations, however, emphasize
the importance of certain environmental conditions, such
as the presence of a culture pattern which minimizes the
value of human life.   These two points of view, the psychiatric and the sociological, can be reconciled, perhaps, by
means of the concept *sociological age.*

As individuals grow from infancy to adulthood, they
normally pass through several fairly definite stages of
social behavior.   At one period they may be exhibitionistic;
at another, sadistic; at a third, lacking in emotional control.   In early childhood the egoistic drives or urges seem
to predominate; later more altruistic motives have a place.
This change from egoism to altruism is, in reality, the result of learning adequate methods of adjusting one's self
to the demands of others.   This process of socialization,
the development of "social-mindedness," is largely a by-
product of social contact and interaction.   Rewards and
punishments slowly train the child to respect the property
and persons of others.   When one has learned to adjust
his egocentric wishes in order to meet the requirements of
his social milieu, he may be said to have reached sociological maturity.

Many persons, however, fail to "grow up" in their
social relationships.   They are essentially infantile personalities, meeting the stresses and strains of social life with
the conduct or the attitude of a child.   For example, in a
boy three or four years old a "temper tantrum" is not abnormal, but in a man of forty years such behavior would
indicate a lack of maturity, an infantilism.   Often these
immature personalities are of exceptional mental or phys-

ical strength, yet they have failed to reach an acceptable stage of emotional development. These failures seem to arise from two sources. First, the child may live in an environment which retards his growth, as when he is "spoiled" by indulgent parents or encouraged in anti-social behavior by his "gang." Second, the child may be unable to develop adequate social conduct because of feeblemindedness, hyperemotionality arising from epilepsy, or some other defect. If either of these types of difficulties are of sufficient importance, the child will probably not attain a developmental level that will secure social approval; he will fail to "grow up" sociologically.

A person's sociological age depends, accordingly, not upon his physical or mental development but upon his relative maturity in dealing with his associates, especially upon his emotional control in social situations. If under stress the individual acts towards others as a small child would, his sociological age is low. If, however, he behaves as mature adults should, his sociological age is much higher. Those persons who are exceptionally mature in their social behavior may be classed as superior in respect to sociological age.

If in the future it should become possible to learn a person's approximate sociological age in somewhat the same way that his mental age can now be roughly estimated from an intelligence test, it might be of inestimable value in revealing potential criminals. Such a development would be a fulfillment of the dream of Lombroso, who vainly hoped to achieve this result by a study of those "stigmata" indicating biological degeneracy.

The "true" criminal is, according to this theory, a person of low sociological age who in situations of grave stress is unable to behave as the laws demand. On the other hand, the "accidental" criminal is one who *usually* conducts himself in a mature way but who resorts to infantile behavior when he is confronted by extraordinary difficulties.

One who commits homicide is, then, characteristically a "weakling in conflict." Due to his low sociological age, such a person is unable to solve his problem except by the destruction of the one who thwarts him. In some respects, the slayer corresponds to a child who smashes an offending toy. When the killing is "premeditated," it is called murder; when it is due to an inability to control a suddenly aroused emotion, it is classed as non-negligent manslaughter; but both types have as a common factor the slayer's infantile behavior, his inability to adjust to social conflict.[29]

[29] After preparing this description of the concept *sociological age*, the author has learned of the previous formulation of a similar hypothesis by C. M. Case in "Social Imbecility and Social Age," *Sociology and Social Research*, XII, 218-42. See also P. H. Furfey, "Developmental Age," *American Journal of Psychiatry*, VIII, 149-57.

CHAPTER VI

THE NEGRO AND HOMICIDE

THE HOMICIDE rate for colored persons is almost seven times more than it is for whites. For the decade, 1918-1927, the mean annual homicide rate for the vital statistics registration area in continental United States was 5.32 deaths among the whites for each 100,000 persons, while for the colored races it was 36.93 deaths per 100,-000 population.[1] In urban areas the number of colored persons slain is frequently extraordinarily large, as an examination of Table XI will show.[2] For example, in the year 1925 the homicide rate for colored persons dwelling in Cincinnati, Ohio, was 189.66 per 100,000 population; for East St. Louis, Illinois, it was 228.92; and for Miami, Florida, the corresponding figure was 276.29. Even in Chicago, notable for gang warfare, for 1925 the rate for colored persons was 102.80, while for whites it was only 10.79.

Unfortunately, the data given for *colored persons* are not precisely accurate when applied to the American Negro, but, for general purposes, they are quite representative, although the term *colored* includes Negroes, Indians, Chinese, Japanese, and "other colored persons." In the first place, Negroes constituted approximately 96 per cent of the 10,889,705 persons of color in the United States on January 1, 1920. Besides, if the years 1923 and 1924 are typical, the 426,574 persons other than Negroes included in the total given above have a homicide

[1] *Cf.* p. 19.   [2] *Cf.* p. 217.

rate less than that of the Negroes. For these two years in the registration states the homicide rates per 100,000 estimated population were as follows:[3]

Year	Total	White	Colored	Negro	Indian	Chinese	Japanese
1923 ...	7.8	5.0	38.2	39.1	12.2	18.8	17.5
1924 ...	8.1	5.3	39.6	39.8	22.2	87.4	22.7

Except for the Chinese in 1924, perhaps because of "tong" warfare, the Negroes exceeded all other groups of colored persons for whom data are available. It seems evident, therefore, that the data for colored persons can justly be considered representative of the facts concerning the Negro and homicide.

Homicide, accordingly, is an important cause of death among Negroes. Although the homicide death rate among industrial policyholders of the Metropolitan Insurance Company is lower than among the general population, only tuberculosis and pneumonia outrank homicide as a cause of death among young adult Negro males insured by this company.[4] Moreover, this marked prevalence of homicide among the Negroes is found both North and South and in urban as well as rural areas.

The homicide rates presented in Table III are based upon the reports of the United States Division of Vital Statistics for the years 1920 and 1925 and upon the sum of the estimated populations for these same years. This table indicates that a relatively low white homicide rate is often associated with a lower rate for Negroes, but that the Negro rate is consistently higher than that for whites.

[3] *Mortality Statistics 1923*, p. 79; and *Mortality Statistics 1924*, p. 80.
[4] Edwin H. Sutherland, "Murder and the Death Penalty," *Journal of the American Institute of Criminal Law and Criminology*, XV, 524; and the *Statistical Bulletin* of the Metropolitan Life Insurance Co., VII, 1-4.

In fact, only one Negro rate based upon more than 4 deaths, that for the state of Delaware, is lower than the highest white rate, that of Florida.

TABLE III. HOMICIDES PER 100,000 POPULATION,
1920 AND 1925 COMBINED
(Data in italics are based upon less than 5 deaths)

STATES	TOTAL		URBAN		RURAL	
	White	Colored	White	Colored	White	Colored
Alabama([1])	7.42	34.35	15.39	81.05	5.81	23.48
California	7.11	27.55	6.79	35.64	7.53	19.47
Colorado	7.67	67.91	8.04	66.58	7.44	70.19
Connecticut	3.50	14.43	4.00	15.06	2.01	*11.55*
Delaware	2.99	9.83	2.85	*13.29*	3.15	*7.80*
Florida	12.54	62.92	16.80	102.44	10.91	49.13
Idaho([1])	3.59	*33.33*	2.47	0.00	3.68	*38.46*
Illinois	7.16	72.38	9.12	76.24	4.38	53.40
Indiana	3.87	65.09	6.22	72.57	2.27	22.67
Iowa([1])	2.25	60.30	4.41	61.22	1.47	*57.69*
Kansas	3.76	36.89	7.81	51.86	2.53	10.59
Kentucky	8.65	49.11	9.62	72.13	8.44	38.54
Louisiana	8.73	35.35	14.36	77.97	6.03	23.56
Maine	1.80	0.00	2.24	0.00	1.63	0.00
Maryland	3.22	21.16	3.55	32.82	2.76	10.38
Massachusetts	2.27	12.78	2.48	12.26	1.40	*16.72*
Michigan	4.73	88.91	7.29	99.75	1.85	24.04
Minnesota	3.05	44.65	5.28	69.57	1.88	*20.63*
Mississippi	8.30	32.15	17.04	82.19	7.37	28.74
Missouri	6.87	66.94	12.43	81.76	3.26	33.87
Montana	7.58	20.84	15.24	*98.46*	5.64	*11.66*
Nebraska	3.26	58.47	8.03	68.98	1.94	*29.76*
New Hampshire	1.57	0.00	1.50	0.00	1.61	0.00
New Jersey	4.06	20.90	4.41	24.10	3.43	14.26
New York	4.35	28.71	5.04	30.89	2.06	12.93
North Carolina	4.68	20.82	8.81	50.49	4.07	15.37
North Dakota([1])	2.04	0.00	*5.74*	0.00	1.71	0.00
Ohio	5.10	70.16	7.28	81.83	2.40	30.13
Oregon	3.88	*15.06*	4.01	*20.59*	3.79	*11.87*
Pennsylvania	4.35	46.71	5.28	47.12	3.42	45.21
Rhode Island	1.50	*18.28*	1.82	*20.86*	0.00	0.00
South Carolina	8.58	18.52	20.84	57.88	6.80	14.98
Tennessee	7.98	48.82	14.93	103.20	6.50	24.68
Utah	4.67	44.49	5.92	*48.52*	3.97	43.06
Vermont	1.42	0.00	0.00	0.00	1.65	0.00
Virginia	6.67	20.00	9.20	37.68	5.87	13.21
Washington	4.75	26.06	5.47	41.27	4.11	12.38
West Virginia([1])	6.90	90.55	12.14	88.08	5.73	91.13
Wisconsin	1.79	28.37	2.80	87.77	1.20	0.00
Wyoming([1])	9.30	*93.75*	14.88	*333.33*	8.32	*38.46*

([1]) Rate based upon data for 1925 only.

The gross number of slayings of Negroes is correspondingly large. For the years 1924, 1925, and 1926 combined there were in states included within the vital statistics registration area a total of 10,619 Negro deaths from homicide as compared with 14,330 white deaths of similar nature. This record is further emphasized by the fact that in 1920 the Negro made up only 9.89 per cent of the total population of the United States. Besides, several states with large proportions of Negroes in their populations were not included in the totals reported above. If Alabama and Georgia had been in the registration area for three years instead of for only one each, and if Arkansas and Texas had been represented at all, the results would have been even more unfavorable to the Negro.

INTERRACIAL SLAYINGS

The Negro's high homicide rate may, however, be somewhat increased by an excess of white interracial slayings. If, obviously, the Negro is more often slain by whites than he, himself, slays a white victim, his homicide death rate is not an accurate index of his tendency to commit deeds of violence. Little evidence upon this point is available, for the death certificates upon which all homicide rates are based give information concerning the slain only. Criminologists usually assume, however, that in homicide cases "The victim and the offender generally belong to the same group, with reference to color, nationality, and age."[5] This statement should not, it seems, be construed too rigidly, for apparently the Negro is more likely to be the victim than the offender in a homicide case involving both white and colored persons.

[5] Edwin H. Sutherland, *Criminology*, p. 64.

An illustration of the tendency for Negroes to suffer disproportionately in interracial homicides is found in New York City. During the year 1925 there were 68 colored persons slain, but for the same year only 48 persons were slain by Negroes.[6] This excess of 20 homicides due to other than Negro slayers may be slightly decreased by the inclusion of Chinese and Japanese in the number of colored persons. In Washington, D. C., of the 87 Negroes slain during the years, 1915-1919, only 80 were killed by other Negroes, and in Chicago, 1921-1922, of the 41 Negro homicides only 33 were at the hands of other Negroes.[7] In Chicago during the years, 1926-1927, white men killed 14.08 per cent of the colored men, but colored men were responsible for only 11.86 per cent of the white men who were homicide victims.[8] In Memphis, Tennessee, during 1923 the whites killed 7 Negroes, while only 2 whites were slain by Negroes.[9] In South Carolina of a total of 89 interracial homicides, 32 whites were killed by Negroes and 57 Negroes were slain by white persons, although the last figure includes 30 deaths of Negroes at the hands of officers of the law. Besides, from August 1, 1925, through July 31, 1928, one newspaper in South Carolina reported 23 Negroes killed by law enforcement officers, while 5 of the officers were themselves slain by Negroes. (These figures are included in the total reported above.) This tendency of officers to be quick to shoot a Negro who resists arrest or attempts to escape is

[6] *World's Almanac 1930*, p. 568; and data secured from the files of the U. S. Division of Vital Statistics.

[7] Edwin H. Sutherland, *Criminology*, p. 64.

[8] *Illinois Crime Survey*, p. 625.

[9] F. L. Hoffman, *The Homicide Problem*, p. 81.

also shown by the fact that although Negroes constituted only about 5 per cent of the population of Chicago, 1926-1927, they provided about 30 per cent of the victims in slayings by officers of the law.[10]

The information presented above, meager as it is, indicates that the whites may be partly responsible for the large number of homicidal deaths among American Negroes. This is not surprising since neither the courts nor public opinion are consistently severe in condemnation of a white slayer of a Negro. For such a slayer a long prison sentence is exceptional and a death sentence almost unheard of. In particular, officers of the law in both South Carolina and Chicago seem ready to use their weapons against a Negro. These conditions, of course, may or may not be typical of the United States. Before definite conclusions can be drawn a more thorough-going study of interracial slayings is needed.

An interesting commentary upon the subject of interracial homicide is provided by the records of two communities almost wholly controlled by Negroes. In Mound Bayou, Mississippi, an all-Negro town, "only one arrest has been made during the past six years, and for more than twenty years the town has not had a murder." St. Helena Island, off the coast of South Carolina, also inhabited almost exclusively by Negroes, has likewise been remarkably free from crimes of violence. Perhaps these communities are not typical, but there is the possibility that they indicate that the Negro may adjust himself to the demands of civilization more satisfactorily where he is relatively freer from the white man's control.

[10] *Illinois Crime Survey*, p. 606.

THE PRESENCE OF THE NEGRO AND HOMICIDE

A high homicide rate, it is quite generally assumed, is to be expected wherever there is a large percentage of Negroes in the population. An examination of Table III lends support to this conclusion. It is possible, however, that statewide rates may obscure significant local and regional differences. To test this possibility a special study was made of the states of South Carolina and Mississippi, in both of which the Negroes exceeded the whites at the census of 1920. In South Carolina in 1920 there were 14 counties in which Negroes comprised two-thirds or more of the total population. Of these, 5 were in the worst quarter of the counties with respect to homicide during the years 1920-1926, while 4 were in the second quarter, one was in the third, and 4 were in the best quarter. This result seems to sustain the contention of the Negro philosopher, "Negroes behave mighty well wherever they live among good white folks." In Mississippi, however, the results of a similar study were less favorable to the Negro. Of the 24 counties in which Negroes in 1920 made up two thirds or more of the total population, 13 were in the worst quarter of the counties with respect to homicide for the years 1920 and 1925 combined, 6 were in the second quarter, 3 were in the third, and only 2 were in the best quarter.

Since the results described above proved somewhat contradictory, a further analysis of the problem was attempted by the use of Pearsonian coefficients of correlation. For the 46 counties of South Carolina between the homicide rate for the years, 1920-1926, and the percentage of Negroes in the 1920 population, the coefficient of correlation was only $+ .257$ with a probable error of $\pm .09$. Since, however, the Negroes lived largely in the rural districts, where homicide rates are usually lower than in urban communities, it was thought that the factor of density of population was, perhaps, obscuring the true relationship between the presence of the Negro and a relatively high rate of homicide. Consequently, a coefficient of partial correlation was computed between the homicide rates of the counties and their percentages of Negroes, with the factor of density of population held mathematically constant. This procedure raised the coefficient to $+ .374$, indicating a small degree of relationship.

A similar result was secured from a second study of the same nature, using 90 cities (all those available except a few with incomplete data) from the southern states of Alabama, Georgia, Florida, Kentucky, Louisiana, North Carolina, South Carolina, Tennessee, and Texas. In these cities of 10,000 or more inhabitants the percentage of Negroes was correlated with the homicide rate based upon the years 1920 and 1925 combined. This coefficient proved to be $+ .36$ with a probable error of $\pm .06$.

The two studies described above apparently indicate a small relationship between high rates of homicide and the existence of large percentages of Negroes in the population. Other evidence presented in this chapter suggests the possibility, however, that the small size of these coefficients may be due, at least in part, to the interference of other factors, such as a general disregard for human life in the southern states.

That many slayings do not necessarily mean that Negroes are present in large numbers is also shown by the data for the 3 cities and the 3 southern counties having the highest homicide rates for the years 1920 and 1925 combined. The annual rate per 100,000 population was for Vicksburg, Mississippi, 96.84; for Miami, Florida, 95.46; and for Florence, South Carolina, 82.07. Yet the percentage of Negroes in these cities on January 1, 1920, was 51 for Vicksburg, 31 for Miami, and 43 for Florence. The 3 highest corresponding homicide rates for southern rural areas were 77.60 in Harlan County, Kentucky; 71.27 in Baker County, Florida; and 51.36 in Morehouse Parish, Louisiana. Negroes, however, made up only 9.2 per cent of the population of Harlan County in 1920; 25.3 per cent of Baker County; and 68.0 per cent of Morehouse Parish. In these 6 cities and counties, therefore, extraordinarily high homicide rates do not mean that the percentage of Negroes is exceptional, since all 6 are within the southern states.

The studies summarized above indicate a definite positive relationship between the presence of the Negro and a high homicide rate. It should be noted, however, that this relationship seems to be less than is generally believed or than a casual reading of Table III would lead one to think. This error in the interpretation of homicide rates is due, at least in part, to the fact that the Negro is predominantly an inhabitant of the southern states, where homicide is prevalent among both races.

AGE AND SEX

Negroes differ somewhat from whites in the age and sex distributions of their homicide victims. As a group, Negroes who are slain are younger than white homicide victims. In New Orleans, for example, during the period, 1920-1926, the mean age of white homicidal deaths was 34.6 years, while for Negroes it was only 29.8 years.[11] In South Carolina during the years, 1920-1924, the mean age of the white homicide victims was 36.7 years, while for the Negro victims it was 31.5 years, a difference of 5.2 years. In this state, however, the mean age of all whites in the total population on January 1, 1920, was 24.7 years, while for the entire Negro population it was 22.7 years. Consequently, although the average white person in the total population was only 2 years older than the average Negro, the average white homicide victim was 5.2 years older than the average Negro victim. This indicates that the Negro, in the South at least, is more likely to be slain at an early age than is the white person.

Infanticide seems to be *relatively* much rarer among Negroes than among whites. In Chicago, 1926-1927, although the Negroes provided the victims in more than one third of the total slayings, they did not have a single infanticide, all 47 deaths of this type being among the whites.[12] In the states in the United States vital statistics registration area there were in the years, 1924-1926, among the whites 410 homicides in which the victim was less than one year old, while among the Negroes there were only 54 such deaths. Negroes, accordingly, were the victims in 11.6 per cent of the total infanticides, although they made up only 9.89 per cent of the population of the United States in 1920 and probably constitute an even smaller percentage of the total number of persons included

[11] F. L. Hoffman, "Murder and the Death Penalty," *Current History*, XXVIII, 408-10.
[12] *Illinois Crime Survey*, p. 604.

in the vital statistics registration area. Numerically, there-fore, infanticide is more prevalent among the Negroes. But, on the other hand, there was among the whites one infanticide to every 34.95 homicides, while among the Negroes there was only one infanticide to every 196.65 homicides. For the three years studied 2.86 per cent of all white homicide victims were less than one year old, but only 0.51 per cent of the Negro homicide victims were under one year of age. Consequently, although infan-ticides are slightly more numerous among the Negroes, they are in proportion to total homicides only about one sixth as prevalent as among the whites. This relatively lower rate of infanticide may be due to the Negro's less stern condemnation of illegitimacy, to his love of children, or to the fact that the birth of a child does not usually result in very grave financial responsibilities for Negro parents. It has been generally observed that in spite of his poverty the Negro is so willing to increase his family, either by birth or by adoption, that he makes relatively little demand upon orphanage facilities. This attitude would naturally result in less infanticide.

For the period, 1924-1926, females made up a smaller proportion of the Negro than of the white homicides. For these years there was one female slain among the Negroes for every 4.5 males, while among the whites there was one to every 3.86 males. The ratio of Negro males to white males slain was one to 1.31, while for females it was one Negro for every 1.53 whites. This result indicates that a Negro woman is less likely to be slain, considering the high homicide rate for her race, than is a white woman. In other words, if the three years studied are typical and if the relative homicide rates for the two races be taken into account, a Negro woman is somewhat safer from homicide than is a white woman. There is the possibility that the relative danger to women increases when the homicide rate is low. In England, for example, where very few persons are killed, two out of every three victims are women, but in the United States with a much higher homicide rate the proportion is one female to approximately four male victims.[13]

Little evidence is available to show whether white or Negro women are more liable to become slayers. Of 407 persons who committed homicide in South Carolina, where the two races were at the time of the study approximately equal in numbers, 20 were Negro and 13 were white females, while there were 141 Negro and 220 white males and 13 unknown offenders included in the total. Since most of these cases were secured from the files of newspapers, the ratio between the sexes of each race should be approximately the same. Since the Negro women exceeded the white women while the Negro males did not equal the white males in number, it might be correctly assumed that Negro women, in South Carolina at least, are more likely to slay an adversary than are white women. This conclusion is rather credible in view of the Negro woman's greater freedom of life, physical vigor, and familiarity with weapons. Nevertheless, this inference may, like so many other "common sense observations" concerning racial differences, prove upon further investigation to be erroneous.

[13] Roy E. Calvert, "Murder and the Death Penalty," *Nation*, CXXIX, 405-07.

THE NEGRO AND FIREARMS

Contrary to popular belief, the Negro seldom uses a razor in committing homicide. For the years, 1924-1926, Negro homicide victims were slain with firearms in 72.7 per cent of the cases, while for the same period whites were slain with firearms in only 68.3 per cent of the cases. For these years in the vital statistics registration area in continental United States firearms were used in 70.2 per cent of the total number of homicides among all races. A significant sex difference appears in the following percentages for the use of firearms, 1924-1926: for white male homicidal deaths 73.85; for white females 46.8; for Negro males 74.8; and for Negro females 63.2. Negro women, it seems, are far more frequently slain with firearms than are white women. This may be because Negro women are more likely to injure or slay their assailants. Any one, then, who plans to attack a Negro woman will prefer to use a firearm in order to avoid risk of a successful counter attack. Perhaps the Negro once was accustomed to use a razor as a murderous weapon—as many comedians and story writers are fond of assuming—but the evidence indicates quite clearly that this is no longer true. In fact, Negro homicide victims are more often slain with firearms than are the white victims, and this difference is especially marked between Negro and white females.

PUNISHMENT

The Negro is punished for homicide more frequently and perhaps more severely than is the white. In South Carolina, for example, during the years, 1920-1926, the reports of the attorney general show that, of the persons accused of murder or manslaughter, those who were Negroes were found guilty in 64.1 per cent of the verdicts, while the white persons accused were convicted in only 31.7 per cent of the cases. In all homicide trials during this period, 51.5 per cent of those tried were convicted. In this state, moreover, during the years 1915-1927 only 7 white persons suffered capital punishment, while 53 Negroes were executed. One white person was put to death for every 101 white homicides and one Negro for every 38 Negro homicides.[14] In North Carolina, where Negroes make up about one third of the population, three fourths of the persons who suffer capital punishment are Negroes.[15]

Further evidence that the Negro is more severely punished than is the white person is presented by the 1910 census of prisoners. At this time Negroes constituted only 10.69 per cent of the total population of the United States but they received 56.0 per cent of the grave homicide sentences and 49.1 per cent of the lesser homicide sentences in the United States. In the South the Negroes provided 74.4 per cent of those sentenced for grave homicide during the year 1910 and 67.6 per cent of those committed for lesser homicides.[16] During the same year the average sentence for those punished by imprisonment without fine and by definite sentences was 5.2 months for the whites and 17.4 months for the Negroes.[17] This longer average sentence for the Negroes is probably due in part to their

[14] G. Croft Williams in the Columbia, S. C., *State*, August 2, 1930.
[15] C. S. Johnson and Others, *Negro in American Civilization*, p. 327.
[16] E. B. Reuter, *American Race Problem*, pp. 351-3.
[17] Edwin H. Sutherland, *Criminology*, p. 105.

excess of punishments for homicide—such sentences usually being longer than for other offenses.

The 1926 census of prisoners also indicates the greater chances of punishment's being inflicted upon the Negro. Of 161 females received by state and federal prisons upon charges of homicide, 124 were Negroes, 35 were whites, and 2 belonged to other races. Of 2,391 male commitments for homicide, 1,029 were Negroes, 1,280 were whites, and 82 were from other races.[18] In other words, nearly half of those sent to prison for committing homicide were Negroes. Although precise information is not available since several southern states are not within the vital statistics registration area, it is probable that the Negro is responsible for not more than two fifths of the total number of homicides committed in the United States. The evidence presented above shows that he is more frequently and more severely punished than is the white slayer.

Why is the Negro slayer more liable to be punished? Many factors, doubtless, contribute to this result. Among these are: the Negro's low economic status which prevents his securing "good" criminal attorneys for his defense, race prejudice by white jurors and court officials, and, perhaps, the greater depravity of his slayings.

EXPLANATIONS OF THE NEGRO'S HIGH HOMICIDE RATE

Many attempts have been made to find a satisfactory explanation of the high rate of homicide prevailing among Negroes. These range from the more credible ones to those based upon prejudice or hasty generalization, as McCord's conclusion that "the average Negro is a child

---

[18] U. S. Bureau of the Census, *Prisoners 1926,* p. 32.

in every essential element of character, exhibiting those characteristics that indicate a tendency to lawless impulse and weak inhibition."[19]

There is some evidence, however, that the Negro is lacking in the power to control himself in accordance with the requirements of others. McFadden and Dashiell report that, as measured by the Downey Will-Temperament Test, whites have over Negroes "a clear superiority in the matter of controlled, deliberate, careful persons."[20] This conclusion is supported by Crane's study of 100 whites and 100 Negroes with regard to scores made upon an individual intelligence test, strength of impulse as measured by withdrawal of the hand from beneath a falling weight, and "self-control" as indicated by the inhibition of the actual withdrawal movement, although accompanied by flinching, disturbances in breathing, etc. "He found among the white subjects fewer withdrawals of the hand but a greater *tendency* to withdraw it, as indicated by muscle twitch and breathing. He concluded that the behavior differences between the two races were due not so much to intelligence or to strength of impulses as to difference in the power of inhibition."[21]

Evidence of similar import is given by the *Illinois Crime Survey*. In Chicago during 1926 the Negro 5 per cent of the city's total population contributed the victims in 27.63 per cent of the premeditated murders, 40.91 per cent of the manslaughters, and 44.26 per cent of the justifiable homicides. For the Negro the impulsive type of slaying predominated, although for the city as a whole

[19] C. S. Johnson and Others, *Negro in American Civilization*, p. 311.
[20] A. T. Poffenberger, *Applied Psychology*, p. 39.
[21] *Ibid.*, p. 40.

there were in 1926 a total of 380 murders, 44 manslaughters, and 61 justifiable homicides.[22] For the entire population, accordingly, murder was more than eight times more frequent than manslaughter, but for the Negro group manslaughter was *relatively* more frequent than premeditated murder. This statement is based upon the assumption that in a majority of the cases involving Negroes the slayers and the slain belonged to the same race.

This lack of self-control is, according to Parmelee, "a widespread trait in the criminal world." Its significance has been shown by the Character Education Inquiry, which found, for example, that for three groups of school children the coefficient of correlation between honesty and inhibition was $+ .487$. This power of self control, moreover, within any one community seems to rise or fall with the socio-economic status of the family, although it is not generally associated with such status independently of community background.[23] If these results can be properly applied to the Negro, they indicate that if he actually does lack self-control this lack would naturally increase his rate of crime and that this lack, perhaps, arises from his low social and economic status in the community. It seems more probable, however, that this possible deficiency in power of inhibition may be merely the end result of a culture pattern which emphasizes the value of self-expression rather than that of self-control.

His historical background may also help to explain the Negro's attitude toward the taking of human life. In central Africa, his ancestral home, both birth and death

[22] Pp. 601-606.
[23] Hugh Hartshorne, "Sociological Implications of the Character Education Inquiry," *American Journal of Sociology*, XXVI, 251-62.

rates were high, and violent death was frequent and often unpunished, especially if the victim were a slave. A lack of regard for the person and personality of others seems to have been almost characteristic of central African culture. When the Negro was brought to America as a slave, his owners did little to encourage high esteem for the sanctity of life. On the contrary, they often treated the Negro as if he were only a relatively valuable domestic animal, disciplining him by corporal punishment, using his wives and daughters as concubines, and increasing the instability of his family by the sale or exchange of its members. This background may influence the traditions and attitudes of the Negro of today and decrease his regard for the sacredness of human life.

Parmelee has a theory that can easily be applied to the solution of the problem under discussion. He finds that "excessive heat, especially a change from a moderate to a hot temperature, stimulates the emotions and tends to increase irritability, thus leading to acts of violence." Climatic conditions, furthermore, give rise to important variations in the processes of the autonomic nervous system which largely controls the emotions. Then, he thinks, "It is possible that races tend to become more or less adapted to their climatic conditions by means of permanent changes in these physiological processes, thus giving rise to permanent variations in their emotional traits."[24] According to this theory, because of his thousands of years in Africa the Negro would inherit an excessive emotionality because of his ancestors' selective adaptation to the warm climate. Today, although transplanted to a temperate region, he

---

[24] *Criminology*, pp. 43-53 and 140.

by heredity has the emotionality and irritability of his for-
bears dwelling in the torrid zone. These traits would
inevitably tend to increase his rate of homicide. Unfortunately, however, this ingenious theory lacks support. In
the first place, changes in temperature may have no permanent effects upon the endocrine glands and the processes
of the autonomic nervous system. Besides, even when
crimes against the person are associated with warm
weather, the two may not be directly causally related.

One of the best statements concerning the excessive
criminality of the Negro is given by Reuter. His arguments apply to homicide as well as to criminality in general. According to him,

The same forces [that cause white delinquency] are at work
among the Negroes. But in many cases at least the causes are
more active among them than among other groups, especially the
native elements of our population. Their education and training
is less; their poverty is greater and consequently their housing and
living conditions are more deplorable; there is less provision made
for caring for colored defectives; they are in a more or less unstable condition because they have but lately been given freedom
and many of them, especially in the cities and the North, are in a
new and strange environment; they are discriminated against socially and industrially; they are often abused by the police; and
sometimes, at least, not fairly treated by the courts.[25]

Finally, there is the possibility that the high homicide
rate of the Negro may be more apparent than real. If
interracial slayings were eliminated, and a careful study
made of comparable groups of whites and Negroes having
the same economic, educational, and social status and the
same inability to secure justice except by a resort to deeds

[25] *American Race Problem*, p. 363.

of violence, there is the possibility that approximately equal homicide rates might be found for the two races. In that event there would be no strictly racial differences to explain. Such an investigation is urgently needed, both for the clarification of the Negro's record and for the discovery of significant factors in the causation of homicide.

CHAPTER VII

THE PUNISHMENT OF HOMICIDE

THE ADMINISTRATION of criminal justice in the United States has for years been the subject of vigorous criticism. The point of attack has been directed against almost every feature of the present system, ranging from the corruption of the judiciary to the inefficiency of the detective bureaus. This disapproval has been especially keen in current discussions of legal technicalities, capital punishment, prison administration, and the incompetence and venality of the police.

In the majority of cases, it seems, this censure has been aroused by the treatment of charges of homicide. The public is usually little concerned with the handling of minor offenses under the criminal code and even less with the administration of civil law. A man may serve twenty years of a life sentence imposed for stealing a cheap watch or be sent to a prison camp upon vagrancy charges because he ventured to go to a distant city in search of a job, and no voice will be raised in protest; but if a murderer is more severely punished than the readers of the newspapers consider proper, thousands will demur. In other words, the people are indifferent to the punishment of lesser crimes but are quite partisan concerning the treatment of a murderer. Every celebrated homicide trial reveals a striking conflict in public opinion, vehement demands for stern treatment being met by equally vehement demands for clemency. A survey of the opinions of the people concerning such notable homicide cases as those of Harry K.

Thaw, Loeb and Leopold, Gray-Snyder, and Hall-Mills reveals a striking contrast. There is little moderation in belief; one group asserts that the accused are indubitably guilty and should receive condign punishment, another is convinced that the defendants are being "persecuted" and that their conviction would be "a national disgrace." This division of public opinion should be kept in mind when considering the outcome of jury trials dealing with murder cases. If the attorneys for the defense can secure a jury of those who usually sympathize with the slayer, the verdict will often be unaccountably favorable to the accused. If, however, the prosecution can get a jury composed of those who customarily are antagonistic to the defendants in such cases, the verdict is quite likely to be severe. The European observer's unfamiliarity with this situation frequently contributes to his astonishment or mystification concerning the outcome of jury trials in the United States.

This tendency towards sympathy with the slayer results in a lower conviction rate for homicide than for other offenses, if South Carolina is typical in this respect. In that state during the period, 1920-1925, the reports of the solicitors (prosecuting attorneys) showed that in the circuit courts (superior courts) 18,097 cases were tried for offenses other than homicide. Of these 13,993 or 77.3 per cent were convicted. But of the 1689 trials for murder or manslaughter during the same period only 889 or 52.6 per cent resulted in verdicts of guilty. If this is an adequate sampling, of every four persons charged with serious offenses other than homicide [in South Carolina misdemeanors and minor offenses do not reach the superior courts except upon appeal], three are found guilty, but of every four charged with murder or manslaughter only two are convicted. This, of course, does not mean that half of the persons who commit a homicide actually receive punishment. The cases of plainly justifiable homicide are rarely docketed in the superior courts, the slayers being freed after a favorable decision of the coroner's jury. Second, solicitors, who are anxious to present records favorable to themselves, report as a conviction any verdict of guilty, whether or not referring to the principal charge of the indictment. In at least a few cases the conviction was actually for carrying concealed weapons, or even for "disorderly conduct," rather than for the major offense of murder or manslaughter. Third, many of those convicted at the first trial secure a new hearing and are later acquitted or receive a mistrial decision. Fourth, others with the aid of petitions signed by the sympathetic group of the public obtain pardons or sentences of probation from judges, governors, or pardon and parole boards.

This leniency toward the slayer is not confined to South Carolina. In Cook County, Illinois, during the two years, 1926 and 1927, the police or the coroner's jury named 701 principals and accessories in *murder* cases. Of these, only 153, or 21.8 per cent, were actually convicted by the courts. In addition, 42 cases, 6 per cent of the total, were still pending at the end of the period under study. Of these 153, one person was placed on probation, 2 were sent to the house of correction, 4 to the hospital for the insane, 136 to prison, and 10 were sentenced to death. But of 349 persons named as principals or accessories in homicides other than premeditated murder, only 14, or 4 per cent, were punished, one being sent to the house of correction and 13 to prison.[1] Surveys of criminal justice in Cleveland, Ohio, and in Missouri reveal a similar tendency toward sympathy with the slayer.[2]

EXTENT OF PUNISHMENT FOR HOMICIDE IN THE UNITED STATES

The census bureau's study of the prisoners committed to state and federal prisons during the first six months of 1923 gives a basis for estimating the amount of imprisonment inflicted upon persons convicted of homicide.[3] For the first six months of the year 1923 there were committed to prison 1.8 persons per 100,000 estimated population of the United States. If it be assumed that the commitments for the second half of the year were at the same rate, this would mean that during 1923 a total of 3.6 persons were sent to prison for homicide for every 100,000 inhabitants of the country. For 1923, however, the actual homicide rate was 8.1 per 100,000 estimated population. Now if it be assumed further that the actual homicide rate for the territory not in the vital statistics registration area was approximately the same as for that within the registration area, then an imprisonment ratio for homicide can be secured by dividing 3.6 by 8.1. This result gives a ratio of 44.4.

Apparently, therefore, in the United States, between four and five persons are sent to prison for every ten homicides actually committed. Since the number of executions is quite small and since homicide is rarely punished

---

[1] *Illinois Crime Survey*, pp. 627 and 633.

[2] Alfred Bettman, "What the Criminal Justice Surveys Show," *Proceedings of the National Conference of Social Work 1927*, pp. 50-60.

[3] U. S. Bureau of the Census, *Prisoners 1923*, p. 41.

other than by imprisonment, the ratio of 44.4 prison sentences for each 100 actual slayings probably represents nearly all the legal punishment imposed upon such offenders. This ratio should, however, be accepted with caution since it is based upon a number of assumptions. In addition to those already mentioned above, it involves the assumption that two or more persons are slain by one as frequently as one slays two or more victims, that the commitments in 1923 for homicides that took place in 1922 or even earlier were equal to the number of 1923 slayers who were not sent to prison until 1924 or later, and that the data for prison commitments were practically complete. The last assumption is defensible, at least, since the report states that it covers all important institutions and all of the minor ones except "about 750 jails and workhouses not reporting, but which in nearly all cases had few sentenced prisoners or none at all."[4] The later reports for 1926 and 1927 were not used since they were less complete.

The imprisonment ratio described above does not vary materially from that revealed by an investigation of the punishment of homicide in the state of Rhode Island during the years, 1896-1927.[5] While there were actually 421 homicides committed during this time, only 330 individuals were charged in the courts with illegal killing. Concerning the remaining 91 cases there were no court records indicating prosecution. A total of 172 persons were punished, not including 12 who were declared insane. Of the 172 verdicts of guilty, 23 were for first degree

---

[4] *Ibid.*, p. 3.

[5] H. A. Phelps, "Rhode Island's Threat Against Murder," *Journal of the American Institute of Criminal Law and Criminology*, XV, 552-567.

murder, 43 for second degree murder, 104 for manslaughter, and 2 for assault with a deadly weapon.   If
the number of cases brought over from 1895 was equal to
those pending in the courts at the close of 1927, then
Rhode Island had for these years a punishment ratio of
only 40.9 per cent of the total number of homicides.

In South Carolina during the period, 1920-1926, there
were 1,646 homicides, according to the mortality records.
During the same period 1,902 persons were indicted for
murder or manslaughter in the circuit courts of the state,
according to the reports of the clerks of court.   Of these
persons, 978, or 51.5 per cent, were convicted of some offense, 27 of them suffering death by electrocution.   This
gives a punishment ratio of 59.4 as compared with 40.9
in Rhode Island.   Since Rhode Island abolished the death
penalty in 1852, there were no executions in this state.
Yet for the period, 1918-1926, the average homicide rate
of South Carolina was 12.9 per 100,000 persons, while
for Rhode Island it was only 2.6.   In other words, the
homicide rate in South Carolina is approximately five
times greater than it is in Rhode Island, even though
South Carolina punishes about six persons for every ten
homicides while Rhode Island punishes only four for
every ten.

These statistics compare rather favorably with those
of England, where the punishment of homicide is thought
to be unusually certain and severe.   According to a report
issued in 1922 by the British Home Office, there were during a four year period 390 murders known to the police.
In 83 cases the supposed murderer committed suicide,
19 cases were unsolved, and in the remaining 288 cases

313 persons were arrested. Of these 313 defendants, 76 were adjudged guilty but insane and were sent to hospitals, 74 were convicted of lesser offenses, 5 were "extradited or dealt with in other ways," and 94 were sentenced to death, of whom 55 were actually executed, 39 having their sentences commuted to life imprisonment. Only 64 of the accused were discharged.[6] From these data it seems that for every 100 murders only 44.4 persons, exclusive of those adjudged insane, were punished by the courts. If it be assumed that the large number of suicides was due to the fear of retribution and the 83 suicides be added to the number of convictions, even then for every 100 murders only 65.6 persons received punishment. It is, perhaps, worthy of note that 23.3 per cent of the accused were held to be insane and hence, from the legal point of view, "irresponsible" for their offense.

In Canada, also, the punishment of homicide is not extraordinarily severe. "In all Canada 54 charges of murder were preferred in 1925. Convictions were registered in 18 cases; four murderers were sent to asylums for the criminal insane; a few cases were not tried owing to lack of evidence, and trials in the balance resulted in acquittals."[7] Exclusive of those adjudged insane, only one third of the murderers were punished by the courts. Yet the same authority states that for the year 1925 in Canada "indictable offenses were charged against 21,685 persons and resulted in 17,219 convictions." This shows that while only 33.3 per cent of the murderers were sentenced, 79.4 per cent of the total number of offenders of

[6] Roy E. Calvert, "Murder and the Death Penalty," *Nation*, CXXIX, 405-07.
[7] William Banks, "Canada's Effective Criminal Law System," *Current History*, XXVIII, 405-07.

all classes were convicted in the courts. Canada, there-fore, seems to be more lenient with homicide than with other types of crime.

If the data for England and Canada as given above are representative of the situation in these countries, their low homicide rates do not seem to be due to their severity of punishment, unless, as has been suggested previously, the percentage of justifiable slayings increases as the total number of homicides decreases. It should be noted, how-ever, that the proportion of unsolved murders is quite small, both in England and in Canada.

In South Carolina for 1920-1926, the relationship be-tween homicide and punishment for murder and man-slaughter was studied by means of coefficients of correla-tion. For the 46 counties of this state during this seven year period the coefficient, calculated by the Pearsonian method, between the homicide rate per 100,000 popula-tion and the percentage of convictions in trials for murder and manslaughter was only —.16 with a probable error of ±.097. If certainty of conviction were an important deterrent of homicide, the relationship between the two factors should be expressed by a large negative coefficient. The calculated result, however, shows little or no relation-ship between frequency of punishment and a low homicide rate. This, of course, may be due to the whole state's be-ing so lax in law enforcement that county differences did not prove to be significant. This is not likely, however, since the percentage of convictions ranged from 28 to 90. Incidentally, the county having the highest percentage of convictions had the second highest homicide rate.

Yet since many cases of homicide never reach the

superior courts, the percentage of convictions may misrepresent the extent of punishment. Consequently, punishment ratios for each of these counties were calculated by securing the number of convictions in superior courts during the seven year period and by then dividing the convictions by the number of homicides reported. This punishment index or ratio was then correlated with the homicide rate for each county and the resultant coefficient was —.52 with a probable error of ±.07. This is a fairly high coefficient, but its significance is somewhat doubtful due to the possibility of convicting several persons for one murder, to changes of venue from one county to another, and to second trials after a successful appeal to the higher courts.

If these two coefficients of correlation be accepted at their face value, they show that certainty of conviction after arraignment in the criminal courts was apparently not a potent deterrent of homicide. High homicide rates seem to be found more frequently, however, in those counties where the slayer is not very liable to arrest and prosecution before the superior courts, even when the percentage of convictions is relatively high for those who are actually brought before these courts. This suggests the possibility that certainty of arrest and prosecution may be more of a deterrent from crime than a large percentage of convictions among the few who do not escape criminal proceedings. In Canada and England, as has already been pointed out, the punishment ratios are not very different from those in the United States, but the number of unsolved slayings and of "exonerations" by coroner's juries is quite small. This may, in part, explain the rarity of murder in these countries.

In conclusion, there is little unequivocal evidence that homicide is greatly reduced by severity of punishment of a relatively small proportion of the offenders. "Making an example" of a few of the more heinous slayers is probably less efficacious than certainty of arrest and prosecution, followed by a high percentage of moderate penalties. The whole problem of the relative value of punishment as a deterrent from crime is, however, in need of further clarification.

CAPITAL PUNISHMENT

The problem of the efficacy of punishment is emphasized by the controversy over the abolition of the death sentence. The number of lives that would be saved by substituting life imprisonment for capital punishment would, according to Sutherland, be quite small. "At most, less than one hundred executions occur each year in the United States. In view of the high death rate from industrial accidents and diseases, from street accidents, athletics, impure food, adulterated milk, and similar conditions and activities, this number of deaths need not attract attention. Its importance is due, rather, to the fact that it is the point of conflict between those who favor revenge or retaliation, though they generally attempt to conceal these attitudes by more civilized arguments, and those who look upon the criminal as a problem requiring scientific understanding and control based upon this understanding."[8] As this quotation explains, the question of capital punishment is quite unimportant in the

[8] *Criminology*, p. 376.

number of persons affected but it is of far-reaching significance as an attack upon the value of severe punishment
as a deterrent of crime.

Capital punishment is inflicted upon relatively few
of those who commit homicide. Sutherland estimates
that there is one execution for approximately 80 homicides.[9] In South Carolina during the period, 1920-1926,
there were officially reported 1646 homicides. In this
time there were 27 electrocutions for murder.[10] There
was, accordingly, only one execution for every 61 homicides. In Manhattan Borough of New York City there
were, from 1922 through 1928, a total of 1551 homicides.
For these offenses only 22 persons were convicted of first
degree murder, one for every 70.5 homicides.[11] (It is
probable that some of the 22 had their sentences commuted to life imprisonment.) In Chicago and Cook
County, Illinois, during the years 1926 and 1927 there
were 1045 homicides, exclusive of "auto manslaughters,
undetermined abortions, and undetermined violence."
For these slayings 10 persons were sentenced to death,
less than one for every hundred homicides.[12] The threat
of capital punishment is not, therefore, a very menacing
one.

The states that have abolished the death penalty have
much lower homicide rates than do those that have retained it. "The average homicide death rate in 1922 in
the North Central States that had retained the death penalty was 7.7, as contrasted with a rate of 4.4 in the North

[9] *Ibid.*, p. 371.
[10] Letter of J. B. Pearman, Superintendent of the South Carolina Penitentiary,
July 26, 1928.
[11] *World's Almanac 1930*, p. 567.   [12] *Illinois Crime Survey*, p. 627.

Central States that had abolished the death penalty. The median homicide rate in 1922 in cities of 100,000 population or more in states that retained the death penalty was 8.1, as contrasted with a rate of 6.5 in states that had abolished the death penalty."[13] The states of Kansas, Maine, Michigan, Minnesota, North Dakota, Rhode Island, and Wisconsin no longer execute persons found guilty of first degree murder, yet these states have homicide rates that are much lower than those in states that have not abolished the death penalty.[14] Perhaps the rarity of murder led to the abolition of the death penalty. It is probable, moreover, that in these states human life is held sacred and that this high valuation results in both the low homicide rate and the opposition to capital punishment.

According to its opponents, capital punishment has been tried as a panacea for crime and has signally failed. During the seventeenth and eighteenth centuries England punished even trivial crimes by the death penalty. In 1780 the penal code included 240 capital offenses; during the reign of Henry VIII, 72,000 executions took place.[15] In spite of this severity crime apparently increased. A chaplain reported that, of 167 men for whom he had prayed at the gallows, 161 had attended one or more public hangings. Many persons escaped punishment altogether because of the reluctance of juries and judges to impose the death penalty. In 1830 a petition signed by over 1000 bankers asked the English Parliament to remove forgery from the list of capital offenses on the

---

[13] Edwin H. Sutherland, "Murder and the Death Penalty," *Journal of the American Institute of Criminal Law and Criminology*, XV, 522-29.

[14] F. L. Hoffman, "The Homicide Record for 1929," *Spectator*, March 22, 1930.

[15] Fred E. Haynes, *Criminology*, pp. 184-5.

ground that the severity of the punishment prevented the conviction of the guilty.[16]

On the other hand, defenders of the death penalty insist that some "condign punishment" must be reserved for heinous offenders. They agree with the *San Francisco Chronicle* that "the killer who has been executed never kills again. A reasonable certainty of the extreme penalty will stay the arm of most slayers. . . . The surest way to stop murder is to exterminate the murderers."[17] This position is sharply attacked by the opponents of capital punishment, who believe with Warden Lewis E. Lawes of Sing Sing Prison that "the death penalty is a relic of savagery, perpetuated by custom and in ignorance, maintained by false assumptions and consumated in a killing that is legal in name only."[18] These strikingly diverse conclusions are almost typical of the controversy concerning the efficacy of capital punishment, a controversy in which, it seems, few speak or write with moderation. More investigation and study are needed before the criminologist can be sure of his position—"we are slowly learning that common sense is not an adequate basis for policies of social control."[19] Meanwhile, it appears that the weight of authority and evidence is with those who hold that capital punishment is not of great value in preventing murder.

THE "DEATH WATCH"

In many prisons persons accused of capital offenses or under sentence of death are very carefully guarded in

[16] *Ibid.*, p. 185.

[17] Editorial of August 27, 1927, quoted by Fred E. Haynes, *Criminology*, p. 19.

[18] Quoted by Fred E. Haynes, *Criminology*, p. 186.

[19] Edwin H. Sutherland, "Murder and the Death Penalty," *Journal of the American Institute of Criminal Law and Criminology*, XV, 522-9.

order to prevent their suicide.   In particular, a prisoner
about to be executed is usually watched night and day to
keep him from "cheating the gallows."   Whenever one
of the condemned, in spite of this death watch, succeeds
in taking his own life, a section of the public is quite harsh
in its criticism of the negligence of the authorities.   For
example, Hoffman, although a zealous advocate of the
abolition of capital punishment, protests against the care-
lessness of officials who had charge of a prisoner who, just
previous to his trial, killed himself with a safety razor,
"There has obviously been gross neglect on the part of
the responsible authorities to safeguard the interests of the
state.   Murderers and other offenders on the eve of trial
have frequently committed suicide, but the lessons of such
experience seem not to have been taken to heart.   While
it may relieve the State of the expense of a costly trial, the
ends of justice are not met.   Criminals under indictment
require to be carefully watched and no means should be
in their possession for ending their own existence. . . .
There should be a thorough inquiry into the facts of such
cases and the responsibility for their occurrence should
be placed where it belongs."[20]

If, as is generally assumed, the true purpose of punishment is to protect the public from the criminal, the
suicide of the accused or the condemned merely makes this
protection more certain.   If this is correct, suicide should
be encouraged rather than prevented.   This practice was
followed by the ancient Romans, who executed some
classes of offenders only when the condemned failed to
end their own lives.   Logically, then, it would seem proper

[20] *The Homicide Problem,* p. 106.

to supply those sentenced to death with suitable means for committing suicide, provided precautions are taken to prevent their injuring others instead. As a matter of fact, those who criticize officials for permitting the suicide of prisoners are usually far less interested in the protection of the public than in wreaking vengeance upon the offender. They are angered, therefore, that the victim has not "paid the penalty" to revenge and "justice" has thereby been "cheated."

The prisoner who wishes to commit suicide is not afraid of death, as his actions prove; he is more fearful of facing others, of being a public spectacle in his hour of agony. His dread of death is less than his fear of being thought a coward, of his being unable to play the man. If capital punishment is to continue as a practice in order to protect the public from its worst offenders, the "death watch" might with reason be abolished and suicide be encouraged rather than thwarted. This would, perhaps, reduce some of the psychological torture of the condemned and would lessen the sadistic pleasure of those who enjoy an execution and clamor for seats in the "death chamber" or for the newspapers describing the grim details.

DETECTION AND ARREST OF SLAYERS

The large number of unsolved homicides in the United States each year has caused grave concern. Few investigations of the extent of the failure to arrest slayers have been made, but their results show a much greater laxity in this country than in Europe. For example, during a four year period, there were in England 390 cases of supposed murder reported to the police. In 83 slayings the murderer committed suicide and in 288, arrests were made, leaving only 19 unsolved murders, 4.9 per cent of the total.[21]   In Chicago and Cook County, Illinois, there was, on the other hand, a total of 36 per cent unsolved cases out of 760 supposedly premeditated murders committed in the years, 1926 and 1927.   For the murder of white males the proportion of "mysteries" was even higher, reaching 50.8 per cent of the total.   This greater proportion of unsolved murders among the white males is probably due in part to the 130 slayings by gangsters, in which there were few arrests and no convictions during the two years covered by the survey.[22]   In Manhattan Borough of New York City there were, during the years 1922-1928, a total of 1551 homicides, according to the chief medical examiner.   Yet during the same time there were only 834 indictments and 303 convictions in homicide cases.[23]   The number of unsolved slayings is not recorded, but it must be large since the indictments total only 53.8 per cent of the number of homicides.

These unsolved murders, mentioned by the newspapers almost every day, are generally believed to be due to the inefficiency of the police and the detective bureaus. The United States has no body of law enforcement officers who have the prestige and public confidence of Canada's mounted police nor a detective agency equal to England's Scotland Yard.   As Parmelee says, "The excessive amount of homicide in this country is probably due in part to disregard for human life, which is in turn due at least in part to the new and somewhat unsettled conditions in

---

[21] Roy E. Calvert, "Murder and the Death Penalty," *Nation*, CXXIX, 405-7.
[22] *Illinois Crime Survey*, p. 620.   [23] *World's Almanac 1930*, p. 567.

this country. But it is certainly due to a considerable extent to the inefficiency of the police. This inefficiency has unfortunately been seconded often by the weakness of the courts in repressing crime on account of technicalities in the procedure."[24] This appears to be the consensus of opinion among criminologists.

Many explanations have been offered for the relative inefficiency of the police in the United States. In order to prevent abuse of authority laws have been passed that seriously hinder officials. If it were not that the police habitually disregard these laws, even more criminals would escape arrest. Geographical distinctions also aid offenders to escape. A murderer who flees from one state to another must be extradited with almost as much formality as if he had crossed the boundary of another nation. Officers of the law rarely have authority to pursue criminals beyond the boundaries of their city or county. Unless a heavy reward for capture is offered, local officers do not often diligently look for persons who have escaped from distant territory. Rapid communication has made crime a national, or even an international, problem. The police and detective system should, accordingly, be nation-wide in its scope. The experience of New York and Pennsylvania has already demonstrated the superiority of the state police over the employment of sheriffs, constables, and patrolmen. Not only are the police handicapped by antiquated laws and obsolete boundary lines, they are also handicapped by lack of professional training. The few police schools in the larger cities reach only a small proportion of the total number of officers. The

---

[24] *Criminology*, p. 351.

others are forced to learn from experience while the public suffers. The professional criminal is more than a match for the untrained constable. And by the time the officer has become fairly well trained through experience he is often discharged through a change in political power. The hazardous nature of the work, the uncertain tenure of office, the lack of prestige of the profession, and the very low salaries often prevent the employment of high class personnel. When these and many similar hindrances and handicaps are taken into account, it is small wonder that the police are inefficient, especially when dealing with the professional criminal. Until improvements are made, the public need not be surprised at the large number of "mystery murders."

THE COURTS AND HOMICIDE

Criticism of the police system is, however, almost insignificant in comparison with the volume of complaints against the courts and the administration of justice in the United States. From the jury to the supreme bench the entire judicial system is under attack, often because of the handling of cases of homicide. A few of these complaints are (1) the jury system is unsuited to modern conditions since its members are no longer personally acquainted with the defendant and the prosecutor; (2) the requirement that the jury vote unanimously for conviction results in the escape of many of the guilty; (3) juries are "miniature mobs" easily swayed by appeals to prejudice and passion; (4) the talents of lawyers are for sale to the highest bidder, either to convict the innocent or to acquit the guilty; (5) the courts are more concerned with what was done a century ago than with what ought to be done today; (6) judges and lawyers, like primitive savages, worship ritualism, the change of a word or a phrase operating to destroy the magic of the formula; (7) those too poor to pay for competent counsel rarely receive just treatment from the "lawyers' union" and its "walking delegate," the judge; and (8) technicalities provide a means of escape from punishment for the rich and the influential.

Needless to say, many of these complaints are exaggerated, but at the same time they show the trend of public opinion and portray a lack of confidence that seriously impedes the work of the courts. How this lack of respect for the judicial system may result in an increase of homicide is clearly shown in a letter to a newspaper in which the correspondent first cited cases to prove his contention that "most state courts have forfeited the respect of the people" and then concluded his arraignment with these words: "I am not an alarmist, and certainly no Bolshevist, but I am convinced that unless thinking men and women begin to disregard their personal financial interests and speak out against injustice in whatever form it appears, we might as well join the ranks of those who win uncertain justice with fists, brick-bats, and sawed-off shotguns."[25]

Not only do miscarriages of justice impel men to seek to redress their wrongs by deeds of violence, they also produce a sense of security from punishment that leads inevitably to crime. When Charles Birger, a gang leader of southern Illinois, was sentenced to death, one of his attorneys was quite overcome by the result of the trial. "This is," he said, "the first hanging verdict returned in 181 murder cases I have defended." Such a record of

[25] E. S. M. in the Columbia, S. C., *State*, June 21, 1929.

aiding and abetting murderers is not exceptional. Every state contains one or more attorneys who command extraordinary fees in murder cases because of their ability to take advantage of legal technicalities and to arouse the emotions of juries. Such lawyers, it seems fair to assume, increase the number of premeditated murders among those who have the funds necessary to employ them.

Two devices used by shrewd criminal lawyers have especially aroused public disapproval. The first of these is the appeal to legal technicalities, many of which were developed centuries ago as protection against the excessive infliction of the death penalty. When an indictment for murder is quashed because it stated that after the attack the victim "did then die" rather than "did then and there die," as required by the legal formula, the confidence of the public is seriously impaired. If a grand juror has failed to pay his poll tax or if a word in the indictment is misspelled once out of three times, delay in prosecution or conviction is almost certain, and every delay increases the chances of ultimate release without punishment. Appeals are frequently sustained because of minor errors which actually did no damage to the rights of the defendant.

Public confidence is also destroyed by the frequent plea of insanity or mental defect as a defense. In homicide cases if the defendant cannot claim "self-defense" or "the unwritten law," he usually resorts to a plea of lack of responsibility. This may be alleged to be due to mental defect, such as definite feeble-mindedness, or to mental aberration, such as permanent or "temporary" insanity. Logically, however, such claims should add to instead of reduce the chances of conviction, for criminals who are mentally disordered are exceptionally dangerous to the public. As a matter of fact, pleas of insanity are usually quite efficacious in securing acquittals, since both juries and judges generally believe that the "irresponsible" should not be punished. Since, as Parmelee has pointed out, in the scientific investigation of human behavior "the theological and metaphysical freedom of the will fades away into nothingness," the courts would be more in accord with present day psychology and psychiatry if they postponed the question of mental state until after the verdict of the jury. Then, if the accused is found guilty, his mental condition should be taken into account in deciding whether he should go to a prison or to an institution for the insane or the feeble-minded. If the sentence is for the infliction of death, mental state should be no bar to execution, for the anti-social defective and the criminal insane are among the most irreclaimable of offenders and should, perhaps, supply the victims if the use of the death penalty is adjudged to be necessary for the protection of society.

EFFECT OF UNCERTAINTY OF PUNISHMENT

The inefficiency of the judicial system, as described above, greatly reduces whatever good effects punishment might have. Whenever the chances of escaping the hand of the law are rather large, the criminally inclined will quite naturally arrive at the conclusion that he is sufficiently clever to act with impunity. And the chances are large enough to encourage the timid. Of 4,264 felonies committed in Cleveland, Ohio, only 495 even reached trial by jury. Although the juries convicted 367 of the cases brought before them, the number of convictions was exceedingly small in proportion to the number of offenses. The *Missouri Crime Survey* reported a similar situation. In that state only 12 per cent of the prosecutions for felonies actually reached a petit jury. Of the total cases only 5 per cent received release because of acquittal by jury, while 57 per cent were discharged because of the failure of the grand jury to find a true bill of indictment, the exercise of *nolle prosequi* by the prosecuting attorney, indefinite postponement of the case, etc.[26] When the chances for escaping arrest or arraignment for investigation are added to those for escaping conviction and punishment, it is little wonder that the typical prisoner under sentence feels that he has been unfairly "picked upon." As Blackstone once observed concerning capital punishment and the laxity of its application, "Among so many chances of escaping, the needy and hardened offender overlooks the multitude that suffer; he boldly engages in some desperate attempt to relieve his wants or supply his vices; and, if unexpectedly, the hand of justice overtakes him, he deems himself peculiarly unfortunate in falling at last a sacrifice to those laws, which long impunity has taught him to contemn."[27] This is certainly the attitude of the usual prisoner in the United States today, as those familiar with penal institutions will confirm. The chances of arrest and punishment for homicide are, perhaps, greater than for the other felonies, since there are less unsolved slayings than un-

---

[26] Alfred Bettman, "What the Criminal Justice Surveys Show," *Proceedings of the National Conference of Social Work 1927*, pp. 50-60.

[27] Quoted by Fred E. Haynes, *Criminology*, p. 19.

solved burglaries, robberies, etc., but even then only four
or five finally go to prison or to execution for every ten
persons done to death.

The importance of promptness and certainty in the
treatment of murderers has been well stated by the Man-
chester, England, *Guardian*, "In countries like Norway
and Sweden, Denmark, Holland, and several of the German states where the death penalty has been abolished or
has not been enforced for years past, but where the chances
of escaping punishment are very small, homicide is extremely rare. . . . Punishment, to be an effective deterrent, must follow the crime surely and swiftly. Its severity
is of secondary importance. If none were executed and
none escaped punishment, it is possible that crime would
diminish."[28] If this is a fair statement, and it doubtless
is, punishment has never been given a fair trial as a deterrent of crime in the United States.

THE PUNISHMENT OF ATTEMPTED MURDER

The legal penalties for attempted murder are in most
states far less than those for successful perpetration of the
deed. This anomalous and illogical distinction is due,
doubtless, to the concept of retribution, "an eye for an
eye." The administration of justice, being more concerned
with the deed than with the offender, assumes that since
little damage was done the criminal should be treated
leniently. As a matter of fact, however, this position is
equivalent to excusing the criminal because of his poor
marksmanship or because of the agility or resourceful-
ness of his intended victim. A man lay for hours in ambush to shoot a neighbor but in his excitement missed his

[28] Quoted by the *Literary Digest*, XCVIII, 17, July 21, 1928.

aim. His punishment was negligible, although the chief difference between him and an actual murderer was his inferiority in skill with firearms. In Scotland, France, and Japan this distinction is not made, at least in certain types of cases, and an attempt to murder may receive even the death penalty.[29]

PRISON SENTENCES FOR HOMICIDES

During the year 1926, according to the census of prisoners for that year, there were committed to state and federal prisons to serve sentences for homicide 2,552 persons —2,391 males and 161 females.[30] These data represent approximately 88 per cent of the commitments to prisons but do not include any commitments to work-houses and prison camps or chain gangs. They give, nevertheless, an adequate sampling of homicide sentences, with, perhaps, some tendency to minimize the shorter prison terms since short term prisoners are more likely to be sent to work-houses.

For these 2,552 prisoners the average sentence, exclusive of life imprisonment and indeterminate sentences, was 11.5 years. When a life sentence was arbitrarily assumed to be for 40 years, the average of the definite sentence group was found to be 23.23 years for the males and 17.16 years for the females. Those who had no previous prison record were punished as severely as the recidivists or "repeaters." For the males having definite sentences the first offenders averaged 27.37 years and recidivists 27.15 years, life sentences being estimated at

[29] L. D. Burling, "Stages of Evolution and Relation to Crime," *Scientific Monthly*, XXIV, 431-9.

[30] U. S. Bureau of the Census, *Prisoners 1926*, p. 1.

40 years. For those under indeterminate sentences the average for males was a minimum of 6.57 years and a maximum of 17.90 years and for females an average of 4.73 years for the minimum and 14.11 years for the maximum. Of the total of 2,552 prisoners committed for homicide, colored persons numbered 1,234. Negroes alone were represented by 1,153 prisoners, 45.2 per cent of the total, although they comprise less than ten per cent of the population of the United States.[31]

The most interesting part of this report, however, is its information concerning the 1,889 prisoners who were discharged during 1926 after serving sentence for homicide. The average time served by this group was 4.98 years for the males and 3.14 years for the females. Yet the average original sentence for this group was 18.10 years for the males and 13.68 years for the females. In other words, in this group of 1,889 persons discharged after serving sentence for committing homicide the males completed only 27.5 per cent of the maximum sentence they had originally received and the females completed only 22.9 per cent of their original maximum. Besides, 231 of these prisoners served less than one year and only 231 served more than 10 years. Pardons or paroles were responsible for the discharge of 967 of the total, over fifty per cent. This was not exceptional, for of the 40,-210 persons discharged from sentences of all kinds during this same year, 19,277, or nearly one half, were paroled or pardoned. These facts indicate quite clearly that lenient treatment of those who commit homicide does not end when they are sentenced to prison.

[31] *Ibid.*, pp. 22-32.

CONCLUSION

The evidence available shows clearly that in the United States punishment for homicide is far from being swift and certain. There is, moreover, little assurance that an increase in efficiency of the administration of criminal justice would be followed by any marked decline in the homicide rate. The task of bringing the courts and the police system from the slough of medieval enactments and procedures is an important one, but its success will not necessarily affect the problem of crime to any great extent. As Bettman has so clearly explained, "The crime producing factors are the products of years and decades and generations; the cures inevitably require long periods of time to be effective. At any rate no available data prove that severity of punishment in and of itself is seriously to be relied upon as the main preventive of crime. We know that the human organism inevitably produces protective devices against mere severity of punishment. For instance, we know that our whole system of criminal procedure, with its numerous technical defenses for the accused, was developed as a protective device against the system of excessive punishment that prevailed in sixteenth and seventeenth century England."[32]

If homicide and other crimes are to be reduced, relatively little reliance can be placed in the efficacy of punishment. One of the plainest lessons of sociological inquiry is that legal enactments and administrative devices are puny weapons against the strength of public opinion, social standards, and the *mores*. Until attitudes and val-

[32] "What the Criminal Justice Surveys Show," *Proceedings of the National Conference of Social Work 1927*, pp. 50-60.

ues, especially those emphasizing the worth of human life, are appreciably changed, reforms in the machinery of criminal justice will likely be of little avail in the reduction of homicide.

CHAPTER VIII

HOMICIDE AND OTHER SOCIAL PHENOMENA

A NY STUDY of the relationship between two types of social phenomena is to be undertaken with caution since errors of interpretation are so easily and frequently made. Except for the fallacy of oversimplifying the cause of complex sociological problems, the fallacy of "false cause" seems most often to deceive the unwary social scientist. Two phenomena may be closely related, as measured statistically, yet neither may be the "efficient cause" of the other—both may arise from a common cause, or their apparent kinship may be a mere matter of chance. For example, a writer recently presented a graph showing the increase in homicide in 31 large cities of the United States compared with the decrease in lynching in the country as a whole.[1] Since the homicide rates showed a rather steady increase and the number of lynchings, a similar decrease, the author drew the conclusion that homicide was being substituted for lynching, a few members of a potential mob slaying the offender at sight rather than waiting for the gathering of a crowd. This may be a proper inference, but it does not necessarily follow from an examination of the data presented. In the first place, the homicide rates shown were those for large cities, where lynchings do not usually occur. As a matter of fact, however, the rural rates show the same tendency. Besides, the mere presentation of similar rate-curves upon a chart does

[1] H. B. Davis, "A Substitute for Lynching," *Nation*, CXXX, 12-14.

not explain any connection between the two.   The illiteracy rates have also steadily decreased.   Does this
mean that homicide is being substituted for illiteracy?
In the examination of the evidence presented below the
reader should, therefore, be careful to avoid the fallacy of
post hoc, ergo propter hoc, the error of believing that one
phenomenon is caused by any preceding one, as when the
little boy assumed that the crowing of the cock made the
sun rise.

ILLITERACY

In spite of the fact that in the United States illiteracy
rates are steadily falling and homicide rates are rising,
it is a general assumption that lack of an education is a
cause of murder.   Logically, this assumption is defensible
enough, for an untrained person is quite likely to be unable to handle social conflict except by physical violence.
Additional support is found in studying the educational
background of convicted persons.   For example, in North
Carolina out of 200 persons sentenced to be executed for
capital crimes during the period from 1909 to 1928 only
29 per cent were able to read and write.[2]   Of 19,080
commitments to state and federal prisons during the first
six months of 1923, illiterates composed 10.7 per cent of
the total, although in that year the estimated illiteracy of
the general population of the United States was only 7.1.
For every 100,000 adult illiterates, according to the census of 1920, there were 42.7 prison commitments, while
for every 100,000 adults able to read and write there were
only 27.3 commitments during the first six months of
the year 1923.[3]   These statements apply, of course, to

[2] Fred E. Haynes, *Criminology*, p. 82.
[3] U. S. Bureau of the Census, *The Prisoner's Antecedents*, p. 19.

persons who were caught, convicted, and sent to prison.
It is quite possible that the better educated were less liable
to arrest and imprisonment because of their superior skill
in eluding the officers of the law. A compensating factor,
however, was the presence of a very large group of persons
from 15 through 34 years of age, among whom illiteracy
was much less frequent than in the general population.

Besides, illiteracy seems to be more characteristic of
slayers than of many other groups of criminals. In the
study described above, the percentage of illiteracy was
10.8 for all males committed, but for those sentenced for
homicide the percentage was 19.7, higher than for any
group of offenders except those committed for violent assault, who were 24 per cent illiterate. The median school
grade of prisoners sentenced for homicide was the fifth,
for those sentenced for violent assault it was the fourth,
for all other offenses it was higher.[4] Dr. Stearns found
that of 100 murderers "only 12 could be described as
highly educated, whereas 62 were distinctly characterized
by illiteracy."[5]

On the contrary, a study of the illiteracy and homicide rates of the 46 counties in South Carolina revealed
little relationship between the two. The coefficient of
correlation between illiteracy according to the census of
1920 and the homicide rate for the mean of the seven
years, 1920-1926, was only +.113 with a probable error
of ±.098. This coefficient means that the relationship
between the two factors is apparently negligible. In order to see whether or not the relationship was being ob-

---

[4] *Ibid.*, pp. 20-21.
[5] Quoted in the Columbia, S. C., *State*, August 24, 1925.

scured by the close association of illiteracy and sparseness of population, a partial correlation was calculated. In this procedure when the density of population was held mathematically constant, the coefficient of correlation between homicide and illiteracy was increased to $+.290$, still too small to indicate a very significant relationship.

For the 43 states for which homicide rates are available, the coefficient of correlation between the mean rate of homicide, as given in Table I, and the percentage of illiteracy on January 1, 1920, was $+.658$ with a probable error of $\pm.06$. This coefficient apparently indicates a close relationship between the two factors. Further evidence, however, shows that this is probably due to the fact that the southern states are high in both illiteracy and homicide, partly at least because of the presence of the Negro. But when 90 southern cities were studied by the same method the coefficient between illiteracy in 1920 and the homicide rate for 1920 and 1925 combined was only $+.154$ with a probable error of $\pm.07$. For 94 cities chosen at random from each of the northern and western states, the relationship between illiteracy and rate of homicide was also practically negligible. These three calculations seem to indicate that within the South illiteracy and homicide are not closely associated and that within the states outside the South the two factors are also only slightly related.

Unless the coefficients of the correlations described above have been materially reduced by the interference of other factors, it seems that *within* either the South or the North and West the percentage of illiteracy offers little aid in estimating the rate of homicide. Still illiteracy and homicide rates for the 43 states in the registration area were positively correlated. This is very probably due to the South's unfavorable showing with regard to both traits being studied. The high rate of illiteracy among prisoners committed for deeds of violence may also be due in part to the inclusion of a large number of Negroes among such offenders. (In 1920 Negroes were 22.9 per cent illiterate.) Besides, if illiteracy seriously affects the rate of crime, it should, perhaps, increase the number of crimes against property rather than against the person, since it is so often associated with economic inadequacy.

Although further investigation is necessary, the results already presented tend to cast doubt upon the popular assumption that illiteracy and homicide are causally connected. The apparent association of the two factors may arise from similar background causes rather than from any direct influence of illiteracy upon the rate of homicide.

POPULATION CHANGES

Since 1798, when T. R. Malthus published his *Essay on the Principle of Population*, the sociological significance of changes in the number of inhabitants in any specific area has received much attention. The general belief is that an increase in population pressure aggravates such social problems as crime and poverty. Parmelee says, "If the population increases more rapidly than the production of wealth, the standard of living falls, and poverty and its attendant evils increase. In other words, the economic welfare of the community diminishes. Inasmuch as the reproductive power of mankind is very great, it is the tendency for population to be pressing constantly upon the means of subsistence, and thus to increase economic misery. Consequently, rapid growth of population is likely to accentuate the economic factors for crime."[6]

Within the city of Chicago, however, Clifford R. Shaw and his associates found that high rates of delinquency were associated with decreasing population.[7] When the city was laid out in radials, somewhat resembling the spokes of a wheel, Shaw found that for radial II the coefficient of correlation, by the rank method, between male juvenile delinquency and increase of population was —.89. For radial V the coefficient was —.56.[8] These results indicate that population increase and male juvenile delinquency are negatively related, delinquency being greater where the population was decreasing. This may be due to special conditions prevailing *within* the city, as when business encroaches upon a residence area and causes a deterioration in the quality of its inhabitants. Shaw's findings do not, therefore, indicate that, other things being equal, cities with stationary or decreasing populations would be liable to be more criminalistic than those with increasing numbers.

An indication that rapidly growing cities may expect an increase in homicide is shown by the data for Florida cities for the years 1920 and 1925. By the latter date the "Florida boom" in land values and population was well under way. In the six cities of the state there were 57 homicides in 1920 and 208 in 1925. An analysis of

---

[6] *Criminology*, pp. 64-5.   [7] *Delinquency Areas*, p. 214.

[8] C. R. Shaw, "Correlation of Rate of Juvenile Delinquency with Certain Indices of Community Organization and Disorganization," *Proceedings of the American Sociological Society*, XXII, 174-9.

the individual cities shows even more clearly the effect of increasing numbers. Jacksonville during this period increased from 92,700 to 135,800 population, while the homicides increased from 31 to 69, giving for the two years combined a rate of 43.74 per 100,000 persons. Key West showed a decrease in population; its corresponding homicide rate was only 6.16. Miami increased in numbers from 30,800 to 69,700 and in homicides from 10 in 1920 to 86 in 1925, giving for the two years combined a rate of 95.46 per 100,000. Pensacola had a decrease in population and the homicides dropped from 4 to 2. St. Petersburg increased from 14,700 to 26,800 in population and from 1 to 8 in homicides. Tampa changed from 51,200 to 94,900, and its homicides went up from 10 to 42. These cities may not be typical and their number is too small for reliability, but it seems significant that in each of the six there was a clear indication of the unfavorable effect of population increase upon the amount of homicide.

In preparing the homicide rates included in this volume it was observed that there was an apparent freedom from homicide in those counties and cities which did not increase in population from 1910 to 1920 and for which, consequently, no population data were estimated for the year 1925. Of 133 cities which did not increase in numbers between 1910 and 1920, there were 13 that had no homicides in 1920 and 1925—9.78 per cent of the total. But of 580 cities increasing in population between 1910 and 1920, only 37, or 6.38 per cent, had no homicides in 1920 and 1925. Approximately 6 per cent of the growing cities had no homicides in the two years studied, while nearly 10 per cent of the cities with stationary or decreasing population were free from slayings.

The data for counties, exclusive of cities of 10,000 or more, indicate the same tendency for growth of population to increase homicide. Of 1390 counties having homicides reported for the year 1920 or 1925, there were 428 that failed to increase in population between 1910 and 1920—30.79 per cent of the total. But of 717 counties free from homicide during these years, 350 or 48.81 per cent failed to increase in numbers in the previous decade. In this tabulation the states of Idaho, Iowa, and North Dakota were not included since the data for them could not be easily secured. For Alabama and West Virginia the homicide records were based upon 1925 only. These differences should not, however, affect the validity of the results. Nearly half of the counties with stationary or decreasing population were free from homicide during the period studied, while less than one third of the growing counties had no slayings.

The three studies reported above, although somewhat limited in scope, indicate the probability that cities and counties with increasing population may expect an increase in homicide as one of the prices to be paid for higher real estate values, "progress," and the fetich of numbers. This is probably due not so much to population "pressure" upon the actual means of subsistence as to inadequate housing facilities, an increase of migrants, and the social disorganization accompanying an influx of strangers.

URBAN AND RURAL HOMICIDE

Urban homicide rates are consistently higher than those for rural communities. This is in accord with the

general observation that in proportion crime is more frequent in the city than in the country.   For example, it has
been shown that in Italy in 1881, the urban population
of 32 per cent contributed 43 per cent of the total crimes;
In France in 1880 the 30 per cent living in cities had about
50 per cent of the crime; and in 1913 Aschaffenburg estimated that in German cities of more than 20,000 inhabitants there were 134.2 criminals per 100,000 adults, while
in the rural districts there were only 96.6.[9]   This preponderance of urban criminality is illustrated by the homicide rates per 100,000 population for the urban and rural
parts of the states in the United States Registration Area
for the period 1918-1927.

TABLE IV. URBAN AND RURAL HOMICIDE, 1918-1927

YEAR	Urban	Rural	YEAR	Urban	Rural
1918	8.2	4.8	1923	9.6	6.4
1919	8.8	5.7	1924	10.1	6.5
1920	8.2	5.4	1925	10.5	6.4
1921	9.1	7.2	1926	10.3	6.8
1922	9.1	7.0	1927	10.3	6.8

This shows that homicide rates are about fifty per cent
higher for city than for country.   If, however, it were
not for the infrequency of homicide in the New England
and North Atlantic states, where there is a heavy concentration of urban population, the record of the cities
would be even more unfavorable.   This is demonstrated
by an examination of Table V, based upon the combined
estimated population for urban and for rural parts of the
registration states for the years 1920 and 1925 and the
corresponding homicide data.[10]

[9] M. Parmelee, *Criminology*, p. 55.
[10] Original data from the files of the U. S. Division of Vital Statistics.

TABLE V. URBAN AND RURAL HOMICIDES PER 100,000 POPULATION, 1920
AND 1925 COMBINED
(Data in italics are based upon less than 5 deaths)

STATES	Urban	Rural	STATES	Urban	Rural
Alabama*	41.11	12.13	Montana	16.27	5.79
California	7.98	8.18	Nebraska	10.82	2.08
Colorado	9.56	8.02	New Hampshire	1.50	1.61
Connecticut	4.20	2.12	New Jersey	5.19	3.81
Delaware	3.86	3.93	New York	5.64	2.18
Florida	43.66	23.65	North Carolina	22.90	7.37
Idaho*	2.42	4.07	North Dakota*	5.73	1.70
Illinois	12.02	5.01	Ohio	10.84	2.90
Indiana	10.16	2.42	Oregon	4.27	3.92
Iowa*	5.70	1.64	Pennsylvania	7.53	4.06
Kansas	11.91	2.67	Rhode Island	2.16	0.00
Kentucky	19.06	10.81	South Carolina	35.53	11.02
Louisiana	32.79	13.29	Tennessee	40.28	9.44
Maine	2.23	1.62	Utah	6.43	4.71
Maryland	7.68	4.27	Vermont	0.00	1.65
Massachusetts	2.61	1.53	Virginia	18.42	7.94
Michigan	10.50	2.00	Washington	6.43	4.33
Minnesota	5.97	1.99	West Virginia*	17.03	10.98
Mississippi	44.43	18.71	Wisconsin	3.23	1.19
Missouri	18.74	4.13	Wyoming*	20.47	8.73

Only five of the forty states—California, Delaware, Idaho, New Hampshire, and Vermont—have higher rural than urban rates. In four of these the number of killings is small enough to cast some doubt upon the results. In California, however, there is a small reliable excess of rural homicides. This may be due to the number of tourist camps located outside the cities, the outdoor life encouraged by the mild climate, or the presence of many transient laborers engaged in fruit packing and similar occupations.

In comparing relative urban and rural homicide rates, it should be borne in mind that the homicide records of the bureaus of vital statistics are based upon the *place of*

* Based upon data for 1925 only.

death. Consequently, if a person who is mortally wounded in an affray outside the city limits dies in a hospital within the city, he is reported as an urban rather than a rural homicidal death. This practice increases the urban rates and decreases the rural rates from what they would be if there were a differentiation based upon the place of injury. The number of deaths thus transferred from rural to urban records is difficult to estimate, but it is probably not large, since mortally wounded persons cannot usually be carried to a distant hospital.

Urban rates are also increased by homicides among non-residents who have come to the city for business or pleasure. This increase affects the homicide rates of all cities, it is presumed, but it seems to affect some more than others. Hoffman found that for the period, 1924-1928, non-residents contributed 32.0 per cent of the homicides in Memphis, 19.4 per cent of those in New Orleans, 19.0 per cent for Birmingham, and 19.5 per cent for Boston.[11] This tendency for urban homicide rates to be increased by the presence of strangers, many of whom are residents of rural areas, should be taken into account in contrasting city and country records. Nevertheless, the city cannot be held entirely blameless for these slayings of non-residents, for often it is the city's unwholesome amusements, vice, and commercialized lawlessness, which attract the visitor.

This preponderance of urban homicide is only one feature of a general tendency in the distribution of crime. According to *The Prisoner's Antecedents*, giving a study of 19,080 persons committed to federal and state re-

---

[11] "The Homicide Record for 1929," *Spectator*, March 22, 1930.

formatories and prisons during the first six months of 1923, urban communities were the scenes of 77.8 per cent of the prisoners' crimes, although only 70.4 per cent of those committed were residents of cities. Besides, the 48.6 per cent of the total population living in rural areas contributed only 22.2 per cent of the crimes, even though 29.6 per cent of the criminals resided in the country.[12] This shows clearly that the cities had about three times as many commitments as did the country and that there is a tendency for delinquents to migrate cityward, since more offenders dwell in the country than are sent to prison for acts committed in the country. This migration may be due to the opportunity for greater booty or more ready concealment in the city, or it may be partly an error in reporting the place of the crime, offenses in the suburbs beyond city limits being incorrectly reported as urban.

Country dwellers seem, however, to have a tendency to commit more than a proportionate share of the crimes of violence. In the United States in 1910 the farmers, who constituted 18.6 per cent of the male population ten years of age or over, furnished only 3.3 per cent of the males committed to penal and reformatory institutions, yet they contributed 18.6 per cent of those sent to prison for grave homicide and 19.8 per cent of those committed for lesser homicide.[13] This may be due in part to the large number of Negro farmers in the South, whose rate of commitment for homicide is exceptionally high. Nevertheless, it has been observed that "in gen-

[12] U. S. Bureau of the Census, *The Prisoner's Antecedents*, p. 13.
[13] Edwin H. Sutherland, *Criminology*, p. 95.

eral the more serious the offense the greater is the proportion of farmers and farm laborers among the total number of males committed for it."[14]   This preponderance
of deeds of violence among rural delinquents has often
been noted. Lombroso says, "The urban and the rural
districts have each their own specific type of criminality.
The crimes in the country are more barbarous, having
their origin in revenge, avarice, and brutal sensuality.
In the city the criminal is characterized by laziness, a
more refined sensuality, and by forgery."[15]   Sutherland's
conclusion is that "crime increases with the density of
population, but the major crimes increase less than the
minor crimes." This may be due to such conditions as
the custom of overlooking minor evil-doing in rural communities, the greater number of laws regulating urban
areas, the inability of the country dweller to call upon the
police for aid in settling disputes, the farmer's greater
familiarity with firearms and other dangerous weapons,
etc.

Yet in spite of the rural dweller's propensity for crimes
of violence and the cityward migration of the lawless,
homicide rates are clearly higher among urban communities. Many further explanations of this have been suggested. Density of population increases the chances of
personal conflict. If the number of people grows faster
than the production of wealth, the resultant fall in the
standard of living incites the submerged classes to deeds
of violence. The complexity and strain of modern city
life with its noisy bustle destroys the mental equilibrium

[14] *Ibid.*
[15] C. Lombroso, *Crime: Its Causes and Its Remedies*, p. 74.

of many who in a rural setting might avoid abnormal behavior. The accumulated wealth of cities tempts the highwayman and the burglar. In the country and in villages all the residents are somewhat acquainted with each other; this prevents a man from visiting resorts of ill repute, if he expects to retain the respect of his neighbors. In the city it is otherwise; an easily secured anonymity permits and encourages the commercialization of vice. In the areas where vice becomes institutionalized, crime flourishes.[16] In Seattle, Washington, for the years 1914 to 1924, almost 25 per cent of the homicides were committed in a very small district about four blocks wide and about ten blocks long, which "the conventionally proper never visit save under exceptional circumstances." In this territory there were many cheap rooming houses, the former "red light district," several lotteries and gambling resorts, "joss" houses, and other accompaniments of a "delinquency area."[17] If Seattle is typical in this respect, the development of organized vice in urban communities must have an important effect upon the amount of homicide.

If the explanations advanced above are substantially correct, the proportionate extent of crime should increase with the size of the city. This, however, is not true; the larger cities have lower delinquency rates than would be expected if comparison were made with smaller cities. A study of 19,080 persons committed to prisons and reformatories in 1923 shows that the commitments per 100,000 population were: for rural communities 7.6, for

[16] M. Parmelee, *Criminology*, pp. 62-64.
[17] C. F. Schmidt, "A Study of Homicides in Seattle, 1914 to 1924," *Social Forces*, IV, 745-56.

cities of more than 100,000 inhabitants 22.5, for cities of
10,000 to 25,000 persons 25.8, for towns of 2500 to
10,000 population 28.4, and for cities of 25,000 to 100,-
000 the highest ratio, 28.6.[18]   An examination of Table
X indicates that this tendency is also followed by the homicide rates, large cities often having more creditable records than smaller ones.   It is possible that this apparent
contradiction between explanations and statistical investigations may be due to the activity of the police.   The
law enforcement officers may be more efficient in the
larger cities.   The percentage—not the actual number
—of non-resident criminals and victims may be less.   No
indubitable conclusion may be drawn, except that homicide is more frequent in urban than in rural areas.

OTHER RELATIONSHIPS

For the 46 counties of South Carolina the average
homicide rate for the years 1920-1926 has been correlated
with data for several other sociological phenomena, the
mathematical relationships being calculated by means of
the Pearsonian formula.   The number of counties is too
small to give very conclusive results, but since few investigations of this type have been published, these coefficients are presented as indicating some interesting
tentative generalizations.

In the predominantly agricultural sections of this state
it is often believed that the presence of the textile industry increases the homicide rate.   On the contrary, the
coefficient of correlation between homicide and the value
of manufactured goods per capita during 1925 was —.168,
with a probable error of ±.097, indicating no relationship

---

[18] Fred E. Haynes, *Criminology*, p. 15.

between the amount of slaying and the county's relative industrialization.

The ownership of property is generally assumed to be a preventive of crime, yet in South Carolina the coefficient of correlation between homicide and the percentage of farm tenancy for the year 1925 was —.15 with a probable error of ±.097. This result lends no support to the belief that tenant farmers are unusually likely to commit crimes of violence.

Since homicide rates are higher for urban than for rural areas, it was supposed that there would be a close relationship between density of population and the number of slayings per 100,000 persons. The coefficient of correlation was, however, only +.195 with a probable error of ±.096, indicating an insignificant relationship. This result may be due in part to the fact that the entire state of South Carolina is not very densely settled, the lack of great variation in the number of persons per square mile partially obscuring the relationship. Besides, the coefficient may be lowered by the small sample. The evidence is too scanty to cast much doubt upon the criminologists' conclusion that, other things being equal, crimes of violence increase with density of population.

The coefficient of correlation between homicide and the percentage of church members in the United States registration states is, according to Miner, —.340 with a probable error of ±.098. This means that states with large proportions of church members are more likely to have low homicide rates than are those with smaller percentages. Miner also reports that states having a large proportion of Roman Catholics have on the average lower homicide rates than those with smaller proportions and that states with large percentages of Methodists and Baptists are more likely to have high homicide rates than those with smaller percentages.[19] This may, of course, be due to the predominance of Methodists and Baptists in the South, where homicide rates are high, and to the large numbers of Roman Catholics in the Northeast, where murder is relatively infrequent.

In England and Wales there is "little connection" between business conditions and the amount of homicide, according to Dorothy S. Thomas. The coefficient of correlation between the business cycle and crimes against the person was only + .06.[20] If this result holds true in the United States, murder is not increased by financial depressions, as many have assumed.

From the evidence presented in this chapter homicide is, it seems, associated with rapidly increasing population and the growth of cities. There are, however, only slight relationships between homicide and such social phenomena as illiteracy, industrialization, farm tenancy, density of rural population, church membership, and business conditions. Yet the data for several of these studies are insufficient to warrant more than tentative conclusions. Besides, actual relationships may be obscured by the interference of other factors.

[19] *Social Science Abstracts*, II, 947.
[20] D. S. Thomas, *Social Aspects of the Business Cycle*, pp. 143-4.

CHAPTER IX

SEASONAL VARIATION IN HOMICIDE

FROM THE TIME of Hippocrates, about 460 to 370 B. C., men have speculated concerning the effect of meteorological conditions upon human behavior. After Hippocrates many Greek, Roman, and medieval writers discussed the evidence for and against this relationship. Of these, doubtless, the most important was the Arabian philosopher, Ibn Khaldun. In the preface to his *Universal History*, composed between 1374 and 1378, he delineated the influence of climate upon civilizations and races, tracing, for example, to this origin the skin color of the Negroes and their characteristic traits and culture.[1] Jean Bodin, 1530-1596, is generally considered to be the founder of the modern school of geographical sociology. Among his successors have been Montesquieu, Ritter, Buckle, Ratzel, Semple, and Huntington.[2]

Among the earliest to apply the theories of the geographical school to the problems of criminology was Guerry, who found that for the period, 1826-1830, crimes against the person were twice as numerous in southern as in central or northern France. His results were as follows:[3]

	Crimes Against the Person	Crimes Against Property
Northern France	2.7	4.9
Central France	2.8	2.34
Southern France	4.96	2.32

[1] A. H. Koller, *The Theory of Environment*, pp. 12-14.
[2] P. Sorokin, *Contemporary Sociological Theories*, pp. 99-193.
[3] M. Parmelee, *Criminology*, p. 45.

[161]

Lombroso reported that for every 100,000 persons there were 7.22 homicides in northern Italy, 15.24 in central Italy, and 31.00 in southern Italy.[4] The homicide data already presented show that in the United States the highest rates are found in southern territory and the lowest in the northern states. In fact, the worst quarter with respect to homicide consists of the South and the state of Wyoming—and Wyoming is included by only a narrow margin. On the other hand, all of the best quarter of states, except Iowa and Nebraska, lie on or near the northern border.

Such facts as those given above led Quetelet (1796-1874) to formulate his famous *thermic law of delinquency*, according to which crimes against the person are more prevalent in southern regions and those against property in northern areas. His belief in this law and his observation that the number of crimes in a geographical unit could be predicted with fair accuracy influenced Quetelet to conclude that crime is almost a matter of destiny, that the individual criminal is in the grip of forces which imperceptibly but inevitably draw him into conflict with the rules and regulations of the state. In his *Social Physics*, published in 1869, he went so far as to state, "Society prepares the crime; the criminal becomes its executive."[5]

If, then, the climate is largely responsible for the type and amount of delinquency, the criminal is to that extent free from blame—he is merely a puppet in the hands of nature. This fatalistic attitude toward crime is almost

---

[4] *Ibid.*
[5] Bernaldo de Quiros, *Modern Theories of Criminality*, p. 10.

characteristic of the geographical school of sociology. For example, Lacassagne says that criminality is like a microbe in that it is of no significance until it finds a favorable social environment. Furthermore, he observes, "Communities possess the criminals whom they deserve."[6]

THE EFFECT OF TEMPERATURE

If, however, this thermic law of delinquency is to be accepted, some explanation of its method of operation is necessary. This, according to its advocates, is because of the effect of higher temperatures in increasing the rate of crimes against the person. (Besides, in warm countries there is usually a more abundant food supply and less need for clothing and shelter. These conditions decrease the crimes against property.) There is a considerable body of evidence in support of this contention. For example, Lombroso reports that 54 per cent of the murderous attacks in England and Wales occur in the spring and summer and only 46 per cent in the autumn and winter.[7] He believed that his studies, especially those based upon Italian data, indicated that "the preponderant influence of temperature is plainly evident, even if it is not exclusive."[8] Enrico Ferri summarizes as follows his analysis of the crimes committed in France from 1827 to 1869: "I have been able to prove that the greatest variations in crimes against the person in France may be either at times of political revolution or in years when the summers have been hottest and when there has been the greatest consumption of meat, cereals and wine."[9] (Here Ferri intends

---

[6] *Ibid.*, p. 58.

[7] Franklin Thomas, *The Environmental Basis of Society*, p. 101.

[8] *Crime: Its Causes and Its Remedies*, pp. 12-15.

[9] *Criminal Sociology*, p. 210.

to convey the idea that such heating foods as cereals, meat, and wine intensify the effect of the high temperatures.)

In Germany from 1882 to 1893, Aschaffenburg found that all crimes against the person, with the exception of infanticide, increased during the summer months. Infanticide is more prevalent during February and March, he explains, because of the excess of illegitimate births in those months. This, in turn, is a result of heightened sexual interest during the late spring and early summer of the preceding year. In support of this hypothesis he quotes data gathered by Ferri showing that for the years, 1863-1871, the number of conceptions among French women was lowest in January, 7.84 per cent, and highest in May, 9.21 per cent. Besides, in the same country during the years 1827 to 1869 the number of sexual crimes committed against adults reached its minimum in November, 6.24 per cent, and its maximum in June, 12.67 per cent. Sexual crimes against children varied from 4.95 per cent in November to 13.03 per cent in June.[10] Since sexual motives often result in deeds of violence, any increase of such interests during the warmer months of the year would naturally augment the number of homicides.

LEFFINGWELL'S STUDIES

One of the most important studies concerning the effect of meteorological conditions upon human behavior is Albert Leffingwell's *Illegitimacy and the Influence of the Seasons upon Conduct*—Two Studies in Demography— published in 1892. The second of these essays, summarized here because of its relative inacessibility, contains a wealth of material in support of the author's hypothesis

[10] *Crime and Its Repression,* pp. 16-17.

that "either by the gradual increase of solar light or of solar heat, or else in some other manner quite mysterious at present, the breaking up of winter and the advent of spring and summer seasons produces upon all animated nature a peculiar state of excitement or exaltation of the nervous system."[11]

Suicide and attempted suicide are apparently far more frequent in spring and summer than in autumn and winter. In the Japanese empire from 1882 through 1885 the total suicides were distributed as follows: spring 27.4 per cent, summer 30 per cent, autumn 22.6 per cent, and winter 20 per cent. Of suicides due to insanity there occurred, during the spring and summer, 64.4 per cent of the cases in Italy, 58.9 per cent of those in France, and 56.3 per cent of those in Belgium. Of suicides due to causes other than insanity the proportions for spring and summer were in Italy 59.0 per cent, in France 56.7 per cent, and in Belgium 57.1 per cent.[12] Since suicide is often associated with homicide, Leffingwell's data are significant, especially since they have been confirmed by other studies.[13]

Mental disorder also seems to increase in spring and summer. From a study of 38,678 admissions to "insane asylums" in Scotland during the years 1865-1874 and 1880-1887 Leffingwell concludes, "Whether for men or for women, for one period or another or for single years, about 53 per cent of all persons attacked with insanity in Scotland are admitted to asylums and retreats during the

---

[11] P. 32.

[12] The dates for these percentages were not given by Leffingwell. He was probably quoting Morselli.

[13] Irving Sands and Phyllis Blanchard, *Abnormal Behavior*, p. 342.

six months following the first of March."[14] Since mental disorder leads to an increase of crimes against the person, seasonal variation in the extent of homicide might naturally be expected to follow the increase of insanity during the spring and summer.

Data for other social phenomena show the effect of a heightened emotionality during the spring and summer. In Italy duels have been found to be far more frequent in spring and summer, especially in spring. Popular insurrections usually take place in the spring or early summer. Sex interests apparently increase during the spring.

More germane to the subject of this volume, however, are Leffingwell's data concerning the seasonal distribution of crime. His principal summary table is given below, showing percentages for spring and summer and for autumn and winter:

Homicide and Murderous Assault	*Spring and Summer*	*Autumn and Winter*
England and Wales 1878-1882......	54.1	45.9
England and Wales 1883-1887......	54.9	45.1
Crimes against Chastity		
England and Wales 1878-1887......	60.1	39.9
France 1860-1869	62.9	37.1
All Crimes against the Person		
England and Wales 1878-1882......	54.0	46.0
England and Wales 1883-1887......	54.9	45.1
Ireland 1878-1887	53.4	46.6
France 1830-1869	55.0	45.0

[14] Ellsworth Huntington, *Civilization and Climate*, p. 157, gives June as the month of maximum admissions to hospitals for mental diseases in New York state, 1919-1920.

The quarterly distribution of the 3,950 homicides and murderous assaults summarized in the preceding table was as follows:

	PER CENT EACH QUARTER	
Period	*1878-1882*	*1883-1887*
January, February, March.............. 21		23
April, May, June..................... 25		25
July, August, September.............. 29		28
October, November, December......... 25		24

If these results are typical, crimes against the person are more prevalent in the warm months.

The precise mechanism through which changes in the seasons affect human behavior was not clear to Leffingwell. Besides the theory of the effect of greater heat and light, he proposed other explanations, one based upon circulatory changes and another upon the effect of sun spots. He says, "Upon evidence not yet sufficient for demonstration, I am disposed to believe that one effect [of springtime] both in higher animals and in man is an actual increase in the quantity of blood sent through the system; or that the heart in reality beats at a quicker rate, with stronger impulse in April and May than in November and December."[15] The theory of Jevons that the number and size of the spots upon the sun result in changes in the business cycle is suggested by Leffingwell's comment, "One summer's day the opportunity was mine to look through a telescope at a large spot on the sun. Into that dark chasm our planet might drop, without even touching the edge of flame on either side. That may yet be its fate. But even now, it is not impossible that what we call 'a mere sunspot'

[15] P. 132.

in midsummer may have some influence, in our little world, upon the ebb and flow of passion, the excitement of emotion, and all that make up the profound mystery of human life."[16]   This observation is supported, at least in part, by recent investigations showing the effect of sun spots upon the weather and upon the rate of reproduction of such animals as rabbits, mice, and lemmings.[17]

One evidence of Leffingwell's good judgment is his unwillingness to overstate his case.   He is confident that the seasons affect human behavior, but he is far from being dogmatic as to the extent of this influence or its explanation.   His warning is "It cannot therefore be too clearly stated that cosmic influence upon human conduct *is always very slight when we take into account the totality of action in any direction.*   What appears to me clear is its existence as a true factor of causation—no matter to how small an extent."[18]

DEXTER'S INVESTIGATIONS

A most interesting and important series of investigations of the effect of meteorological conditions upon conduct is reported in *Weather Influences,* published in 1904 by Edwin G. Dexter, professor of education at the University of Illinois.   The principal studies showing the effect of the weather upon crime are summarized here, since this volume, like that of Leffingwell, is not generally available.   Among Dexter's chief sources of information were the meteorological records of New York City and Denver, Colorado, and the police reports of arrests, the

[16] P. 138.
[17] Julian Huxley, "Mice and Men," *Harper's,* CLVI, 42-50.
[18] P. 136.

punishment records in the New York City Penitentiary, the seasonal distribution of 184 homicides in Denver, etc.

The monthly distribution of 36,627 arrests of males for assault and battery in New York City during the years, 1891-1897, shows a dome-shaped curve, rising from a low in January to a high in July and then falling to another low in December. Dexter, unfortunately, fails to give his raw data, but he presents a chart showing variation from "expectancy." This expectancy is really the average or arithmetic mean. According to this chart, the months of January, February, March, April, October, November, and December are below expectation, while those of May, June, July, August, and September are above expectation. The range is from approximately 22 per cent below expectation in January to about 24 per cent above in July. Dexter believes that since this graph "is very nearly identical with the curve of monthly means for temperature, one must conclude that temperature, more than any other condition, affects the emotional states which are conducive to fighting."

The graph representing the relationship between fighting and temperature shows that up to temperatures between 65 and 70 degrees Fahrenheit the arrests for assault and battery were at or below the expectancy. From that point they increased rapidly until a temperature of 85 to 90 degrees was reached, when there was a sharp decline. This decrease in fighting during the hottest days is explained by Dexter as being due to "the devitalizing effect of the intense heat." According to him, "For fighting purposes one must have not only the inclination, but also the energy to support his position *vi et armis*. Heat of considerable intensity seems productive of emotional states, furnishing the former (i. e. inclination) but at a certain point the latter is depleted by extra demands made upon it by the processes of life under such conditions."

The graph giving the monthly distribution of 3,134 arrests of women for assault and battery in New York City during 1891-1897 shows, with one exception, the same tendency as that for men. The highest point for women is in August, about 63 per cent above expectancy, and the lows are also even more pronounced than for males. This, according to Dexter, is "a suggestion of what most of the curves show where a comparison of the two sexes is made —namely, a greater susceptibility of women to weather influence." The unusual excess of fighting among women during the month of August which is really cooler than July, "would seem to imply that there is a point in the endurance of heat at which 'forbearance ceases to be a virtue,' and after the months of June and July had been borne with some equanimity, the heat of August proved too much and its effects were noted in the police courts." If this hypothesis is correct, a similar difference should appear in the arrests for assault and battery among men, yet their percentages above expectancy are for June approximately 23 per cent, for July 24 per cent, and for August only about 21 per cent. Yet it may be true, as Dexter suggests, that, if women are more susceptible than men to the ill effects of hot weather, they would give greater indications of the emotional stress due to long continued heat.

Other graphs show that a hot day in the spring or autumn is more likely to increase the arrests for assault

and battery than is an equally warm day in midsummer.
For example, a temperature of 65 to 70 degrees Fahrenheit during October was accompanied by a marked increase
in fighting, but the same degree of heat resulted in slightly
less than the expected number of arrests for July and
August. Dexter believes this to be due to the failure to
dress in accordance with the demands of comfort. It
seems more probable, however, that such a difference
arises from the fact that *relative* temperature is more significant than absolute temperature. For example, 65 degrees Fahrenheit seems warmer in winter than the same
temperature appears to be during midsummer.

Low barometric pressure apparently indicates an increase in fighting as well as the approach of storms. As
Dexter says, "If the emotional effects of such conditions
be what seem to be indicated by our curves, we would do
well at such a signal of storm not only to keep our shipping
in port, but keep away from our enemies, especially if they
are better fighters than ourselves."

Other meteorological conditions affect the number of
arrests for assault and battery. High humidity decreases
fighting—"on such days we perhaps feel like fighting but
such a thing is altogether too much exertion and the police
records are none the wiser." Cloudy and rainy days seem
freest from personal violence. Calms are accompanied by
a decrease in fights. This, Dexter suggests, may be due
to the presence of too much carbon dioxide in the air of
cities during calm weather.

The results described above, based upon arrests for
assault and battery in New York City, are generally in
accord with those secured by Dexter in his analysis of 184

homicides occurring in Denver, Colorado, during the years 1884-1896. He believes that homicides and fighting have about the same relationship to temperature. "At temperatures below 70° a deficiency is shown, beginning with 60 per cent for 15°—the lowest group studied—the curve gradually rising till an excess of 80 per cent is reached at a mean temperature of 90°." One striking difference between New York and Denver was observed in the effect of low humidity. In New York a low humidity resulted in a slight excess of brawls, about 20 per cent; but in Denver a similar mean humidity of from 10 to 15 sent the homicide rate up to an excess of 400 per cent. Under such conditions, "for the thirteen years covered by the study, murders were four times as prevalent as under ordinary conditions." This situation, Dexter thought, was brought about by the "crackling, dry Colorado day" that causes an "increased potential of atmospheric electricity" so that "in some way, which in the present stage of investigation cannot be explained, the result is disastrous to seemly behavior." A parallel study of the extent of flogging in the Denver schools supports this finding, low humidity being accompanied by an excess in floggings of 400 per cent above expectancy.

At Denver, high winds also increased homicide. For winds moving at the rate of about 400 miles a day there was an excess of more than 400 per cent in the number of murders. This is also due, according to Dexter, to "the super-induced electrical potential of the atmosphere which increases with the wind."

The chief objection to be found with Dexter's study of homicides is that his data are insufficient to give confidence in his results. Only 184 slayings scattered over a period of thirteen years is an inadequate sample, since chance factors might seriously affect his findings. Nevertheless, his homicide study is only one of several investigations, the general results of which corroborate one another.

In addition to the studies already described, Dexter made other investigations of the effect of weather upon conduct. Some of his results in terms of highest and lowest points above or below expectancy can be summarized as follows:

PHENOMENA	HIGHS	LOWS
Suicides, New York City	Spring and summer	Winter
Arrests for insanity in New York City...	High and low temperatures	Moderate temperatures
Arrests for insanity in New York City...	Low barometer	High barometer
Arrests for insanity in New York City...	Low humidity	High humidity
Punishments in the N. Y. City Penitentiary 1891-1897........	High temperatures	Low temperatures
Punishments in the N. Y. City Penitentiary 1891-1897.........	Low humidity	High humidity
Punishments in the N. Y. City Penitentiary 1891-1897.........	Low barometer	High barometer
Drunkenness New York City.....	Cold weather	Hot weather
Drunkenness New York City.....	High barometer	Low barometer
Drunkenness New York City	High humidity	Low humidity
Homicides in India.....	Summer	Winter[19]

Dexter admits that some of the seasonal variations that he observed may be due to the *indirect* effects of the

[19] The data for homicides in India were quoted by Dexter from S. A. Hill, "Effects of the Weather upon Death Rate and Crime in India," *Nature*, XXIX, 338.

weather. For example, in discussing the increase of fighting in New York City during hot weather, he comments, "It is possible that the greater publicity of life practiced in the summer time, when most of the people of the poorer classes are in the streets to escape the torture of the stifling rooms, would tend to bring to the notice of the police, altercations which, under the conditions of life in the winter time, would have escaped them. . . . It seems very probable, too, that opportunities for fistic encounter would be increased by summer customs, and this, too, would prove a factor." Nevertheless, he believes "we cannot suppose that any considerable part of the summer's excess and the winter's deficiency [is] due to these accidental causes but for the most part to the weather conditions themselves." Whether or not this contention is ultimately sustained by the preponderance of evidence, Dexter's painstaking investigations and his scepticism of extreme or hasty conclusions have made a definite contribution toward the understanding of the relationship between the weather and human behavior.[20]

SUMMARY AND CRITICISM

The apparent close correlation of crime with meteorological conditions has led to several ambitious attempts to derive a formula that will permit mathematical prediction of the extent of delinquency. For example, De Quiros quotes from Kropotkin's *Prisons*, published in 1890, "By the statistics of previous years one could foretell with astonishing exactness the number of crimes to be committed during the following year in every country of Europe. Through a very simple mathematical operation

[20] *Weather Influences*, pp. 141-165.

we can find the formula that enables us to foretell the number of crimes merely by consulting the thermometer and the hygrometer. Take the average temperature of the month and multiply it by 7, then add the average humidity, multiply again by 2 and you will obtain the number of homicides that are to be committed during the month."[21] This somewhat ambiguous declaration, if correctly quoted by De Quiros, is, at best, a gross oversimplification of the problem. In addition, Kropotkin apparently neglected to state whether the resultant number of homicides would be the rate per 100,000 population or merely the total for the European countries.

Nevertheless, the investigations described above, together with others showing that crimes against property usually reach a maximum in winter and a minimum in summer, apparently justify Gillin in stating, "Studies in every country indicate that crimes against the person are more numerous in summer than in winter, while crimes against property are more numerous in winter than in summer."[22] This position is generally held by criminologists.

Several studies, however, tend to throw some doubt upon the universal applicability of the principle, as stated by Gillin. Upon the island of Guadaloupe, lying well within the tropics, Corre found that crimes of all kinds decreased when the temperature rose above 85 degrees Fahrenheit. He found the total number of crimes against property to be about the same for the hot and the cool seasons but crimes against the person were twice as fre-

[21] Bernaldo de Quiros, *Modern Theories of Criminality*, p. 34.
[22] *Criminology and Penology*, p. 83.

quent in the cool season.[23]   Parmelee offers two credible
explanations of Corre's findings.   First, within the tropics
crimes against property should not show such marked seasonal changes since there is not as much variation in human
needs between the hot and the cool seasons as there is in
the temperate zones.   Besides, the correlation between
high homicide rates and high temperatures seems to hold
only up to a certain point; when the heat is excessive, it
tends to depress activity of all kinds, even acts of passion
and violence.[24]

In Schmidt's analysis of 252 homicides in and near
Seattle during the period 1914-1923 he found that December was the month of greatest frequency, closely followed by January and April.   In the winter months there
were 84 homicides, while only 47 were reported for the
summer months.   The explanation of this excess of homicide during the winter, according to Schmidt, is the dis-
tress and disorder among the large number of migratory
workers who make the city their headquarters during cold
weather.[25]

The homicide reports for 77 large cities in the United
States for the year 1924 have been analyzed by Hoffman
in order to discover the extent of seasonal variation.   A
total of 2,798 cases was distributed as follows: January
192, February 197, March 226, April 213, May 227, June
239, July 251, August 246, September 209, October 227,
November 237, and December 258.[26]   The greatest number in any one month was for December, closely followed

[23] C. Lombroso, *Crime: Its Causes and Its Remedies*, p. 12.
[24] *Criminology*, pp. 47-48.
[25] "A Study of Homicides in Seattle, 1914 to 1924," *Social Forces*, IV, 751.
[26] *The Homicide Problem*, pp. 101-03.

by July. This study shows, however, that the three summer months with a total of 736 materially exceed the winter months with a total of 647. Consequently, even though the month of December had the highest record for homicides, the study as a whole indicates a possible correlation between high temperature and homicide.

SEASONAL VARIATION IN HOMICIDE IN SOUTH CAROLINA

An analysis of the seasonal distribution of 1601 homicides that occurred in South Carolina during the period, 1920-1926, raises further doubt concerning the effect of temperature upon crimes against the person. Table VI gives the result of this analysis.

TABLE VI. MONTHLY DISTRIBUTION OF HOMICIDES IN SOUTH CAROLINA, 1920-1926

MONTH	Lowest	Highest	Range	Total	Corrected for 31 Days
January	13	24	11	133	133.0
February	9	21	12	100	109.5
March	10	26	16	128	128.0
April	13	24	11	127	131.2
May	8	23	15	112	112.0
June	12	28	16	132	136.4
July	12	33	21	153	153.0
August	12	26	14	145	145.0
September	10	33	23	131	135.4
October	10	24	14	119	119.0
November	13	30	17	150	155.0
December	15	32	17	171	171.0
Mean	11.4	27.0	15.6	133.4	135.7

Even a casual examination of this table will indicate the lack of a consistent pattern in the data. For example, July varies from 12 to 33 and September from 10 to 33. It is also worthy of note that in ten of the twelve months the range from lowest to highest number in any one year is greater than the minimum. December is appreciably higher than either July or August, the two warmest months. When corrected so that each month's total would represent the equivalent of 31 days each, the lowest months were found to be February, May, and October, and the highest were December, November, and July.

The distribution of cases by seasons also failed to show any close relationship between the temperature and the amount of homicide. The results of this analysis were:

Season	Gross Number	Number Corrected for 31 Days
Winter	404	413.5
Spring	367	371.2
Summer	430	434.4
Autumn	400	409.4

These statistics should be compared with such findings as that of Lombroso, who reported that 54 per cent of the homicides in England and Wales occur in the spring and summer. In South Carolina, however, the total for the autumn and winter was 804, while for the spring and summer it was 797, slightly less.

In addition to the tabulations described above, the relationship between temperature and homicide was also studied by means of the Pearsonian coefficient of correlation. Unfortunately, the mean temperature for each of the months of 1920 could not be secured. Consequently, this part of the investigation was based upon the data for the 72 months from January 1, 1921, through December 31, 1926, the uncorrected number of homicides in each month being correlated with the mean monthly temperature according to the United States Weather Bureau's

Climatological Data.[27] When this coefficient was calculated, it proved to be only $+ .128$ with a probable error of $\pm .078$. This result shows that, unless it is obscured by the presence of other conditions, the relationship between the two factors is negligible. This corroborates the conclusions obtained by inspection of the enumerations.

But since the number of homicides was greater for both summer and winter, it appeared possible that the factor of deviation from the mean temperature might be of importance, changes causing increased discomfort, and, perhaps, greater emotionality. Accordingly, the mean temperature for each of the 72 months in the years being studied was compared with the normal annual temperature, 63 degrees Fahrenheit. The deviations in either direction from the normal average temperature were then correlated with the number of homicides in each month, the Pearson formula being used. The coefficient was only $+ .135$ with a probable error of $\pm .072$. The relationship, therefore, between the number of deaths by homicide and the changes from the average temperature appears to be one of mere chance, as far as this method of measurement is to be relied upon. The secular trends appeared to be negligible in their effect upon both of the coefficients reported above.

HOLIDAYS AND HOMICIDE

In studying the seasonal distribution of homicide in South Carolina, it was observed that a large number of slayings took place during the Christmas holidays. By a special tabulation of the daily distribution of the 171 homicides reported for December during the years, 1920-1926,

[27] Number 13 of volumes XXIV-XXIX.

it was found that 23 slayings took place on Christmas Day, while 66 took place in the week from December 23 to December 29, inclusive.   In other words, while the average day of the year during this period had only 4.38 homicides, December 25 had a total of 23, over five times greater than the average.   The average week in the year had only 30.79 slayings, but the week December 23-29 had 66, more than twice the average.   (It is interesting to note that there were no homicidal deaths reported for December 25, 1921, when Christmas fell upon Sunday, although the total for that December was 25, which was about the monthly average for the seven years under survey.   This fact, if not due to chance or other factors, apparently indicates that the people of this state respect the sanctity of the Sabbath Day more than they respect the sanctity of human life.)

Although little information is available concerning any tendency for holidays to result in an increase of crimes against the person, it is probable that the facts reported above are not exceptional, even though in South Carolina the number of homicides on Thanksgiving Day and on July the Fourth was not much above the average.   In Russia, for example, the Moscow Institute of Criminology reported that for March, 1928, there were 1,044 persons injured in personal encounters, while for April of the same year the number increased to 1,603.   "The increase in the latter was due to Easter holidays' vodka."[28]   Excessive drinking of alcoholic liquors also doubtless increased the number of Christmas slayings in South Carolina, for in that state and other parts of the South it is the custom to

[28] Associated Press report, May 12, 1929.

celebrate Christmas in a somewhat boisterous manner as the Fourth of July is commemorated in other sections of the country.

In Dexter's study of 39,761 arrests for personal assault in New York City during the years, 1891-1897, a similar condition was found. Dexter describes "the increase of arrests for assaults upon holidays and occasions of unusual celebration in the city. Even political campaigns can be plainly determined from a study of the data alone, and the Christmas season deflects materially the occurrence curve."[29]   If these reports are typical of the situation generally, it is little wonder that Ferri advocated a reduction in holidays since "they are always the occasion of numerous crimes and misdemeanors by bringing the people together for enjoyment."[30]

SEASONAL DISTRIBUTION OF HOMICIDE IN THE UNITED STATES

Few extensive investigations have been made concerning the seasonal variation in the number of homicides committed in the United States. For 1930, however, the *Uniform Crime Reports* of the Department of Justice give definite information upon this subject for about 80 per cent of the cities of 25,000 or more population. When defective and incomplete returns had been excluded, murder and non-negligent manslaughter made up the following percentages of the total number of important offenses reported: for January 0.5 per cent, for February 0.4, for March 0.5, for April 0.5, for May 0.5, for June 0.5, for July 0.6, for August 0.6, for September 0.6, for October 0.4, for November 0.4, and for December 0.4 per cent.

[29] *Weather Influences*, p. 142.   [30] *Criminal Sociology*, p. 273.

This indicates that homicide comprises a *relatively* larger proportion of the offenses of importance during the late summer and early autumn than at any other period. For 58 cities of 100,000 or more inhabitants, however, the gross number of slayings reached its maximum in August and September, the minima being in February and November. Since the chart presenting this part of the data shows that homicide was more frequent in March than in April, May, or June, and more prevalent in December than in October or November, it lends little support to the theory that slayings rise and fall with the temperature.[31]

This same chart, showing the monthly distribution of principal offenses in 58 large cities during the year 1930, offers other evidence concerning the relationship between weather and crime. For aggravated assault the high point was in May rather than in midsummer, as Dexter reported, although the lows were in January and December, two cold months. Rape was least in February and most prevalent in June, the marked increase supporting Aschaffenburg's belief in a periodic variation in the sex interests of man reaching its height in late spring or early summer.[32] The number of robberies, moreover, showed a marked decline in the early summer and an almost 100 per cent increase by December. Larcenies were also slightly more frequent during the winter months. Since, however, the year 1930 was unusual both for its extremely hot summer and the severity of its economic depression, the evidence presented above may not be typical and should not, therefore, be accepted without confirmation.

[31] Vol. I, no. 5, pp. 1-6, December, 1930.
[32] *Cf.* p. 164.

In order to secure more representative data, the monthly distribution of homicides in the United States registration area for the years, 1923-1928, was obtained.[33] During these six years 51,798 homicides were reported for the registration states. The table below shows the results obtained from an analysis of these cases.

Season	Total	Total Corrected for 31 Days
Winter	12,511	12,870.11
Spring	12,666	12,806.04
Summer	13,626	13,764.91
Autumn	12,995	13,283.88
Total	51,798	52,724.94

From this table it is seen that when the number of homicides are corrected mathematically in order to compensate for the shortness of some months, winter has more homicides than spring does, while summer has more than any other season. These results partly confirm and partly refute the thermic law of crime against the person.

A further analysis was then attempted, showing the number of homicides for each month of the six years being studied. In Table VII are given the results of this investigation. An examination of this table shows that there is little uniformity of results. For example, in three years the January homicides exceed those for February; in the other three February exceeds January. In three years December leads in total homicides; in the other three August leads. Once more the results seem somewhat equivocal.

[33] Original data from the files of the U. S. Division of Vital Statistics.

TABLE VII. HOMICIDES BY MONTHS, U. S. REGISTRATION STATES,
1923-1928

YEAR	Jan.	Feb.	Mar.	April	May	June	July	Aug.	Sept.	Oct.	Nov.	Dec.	Total
1923.......	597	505	600	594	588	589	711	694	660	641	610	768	7,557
1924.......	554	580	678	645	631	641	724	850	653	697	681	680	8,014
1925.......	606	661	733	686	681	665	770	811	773	630	674	750	8,440
1926.......	690	638	654	726	762	734	794	804	727	747	680	784	8,740
1927.......	720	689	734	717	804	720	794	758	751	772	731	807	8,997
1928.......	734	747	778	827	828	809	922	836	866	854	848	1,001	10,050
Totals.....	3,901	3,820	4,177	4,195	4,294	4,158	4,715	4,753	4,430	4,341	4,224	4,790	51,798

In Table VIII are presented the results secured when
the short months are corrected in order to make them comparable on the basis of 31 days.   December has the highest
average number of homicides but is closely followed by
August and July.   As a group, the summer months have
an excess of homicides, but the winter months, due chiefly
to the high record for December, are not as low as they
should be in order to accord with the relative temperature.

TABLE VIII. HOMICIDES BY MONTHS, CORRECTED FOR 31 DAYS EACH,
U. S. REGISTRATION STATES, 1923-1928

YEAR	Jan.	Feb.	Mar.	April	May	June	July	Aug.	Sept.	Oct.	Nov.	Dec.	Total
1923..	597.00	559.24	600.00	613.80	588.00	608.53	711.00	694.00	682.00	641.00	630.23	768.00	7,692.80
1924..	554.00	620.00	678.00	666.50	631.00	662.47	724.00	850.00	674.87	697.00	703.70	680.00	8,141.54
1925..	606.00	731.91	733.00	708.97	681.00	687.27	770.00	811.00	798.87	630.00	696.57	750.00	8,604.59
1926..	690.00	706.49	654.00	750.20	762.00	758.57	794.00	804.00	751.13	747.00	702.77	784.00	8,904.16
1927..	720.00	762.91	734.00	740.90	804.00	744.00	794.00	758.00	775.93	772.00	755.47	807.00	9,168.21
1928..	734.00	798.56	778.00	854.67	828.00	836.07	922.00	836.00	894.97	854.00	876.37	1,001.00	10,213.64
Mean.	650.17	696.52	696.17	722.51	715.67	716.15	785.83	792.17	762.96	723.50	727.52	798.33	8,787.49

Figure 4 has been prepared in order to portray the
extreme variation in the monthly distributions of homicides
for the six years examined.   It is based upon the data
given in Table VIII, which is the most significant, per-

haps, of the tables showing the relationship between homicide and the seasons. The heavy line representing the average for six years, corrected to equalize the length of the months, should be carefully observed. Except for the months of November and December, this graph supports the conclusions reached by Dexter, as have already been

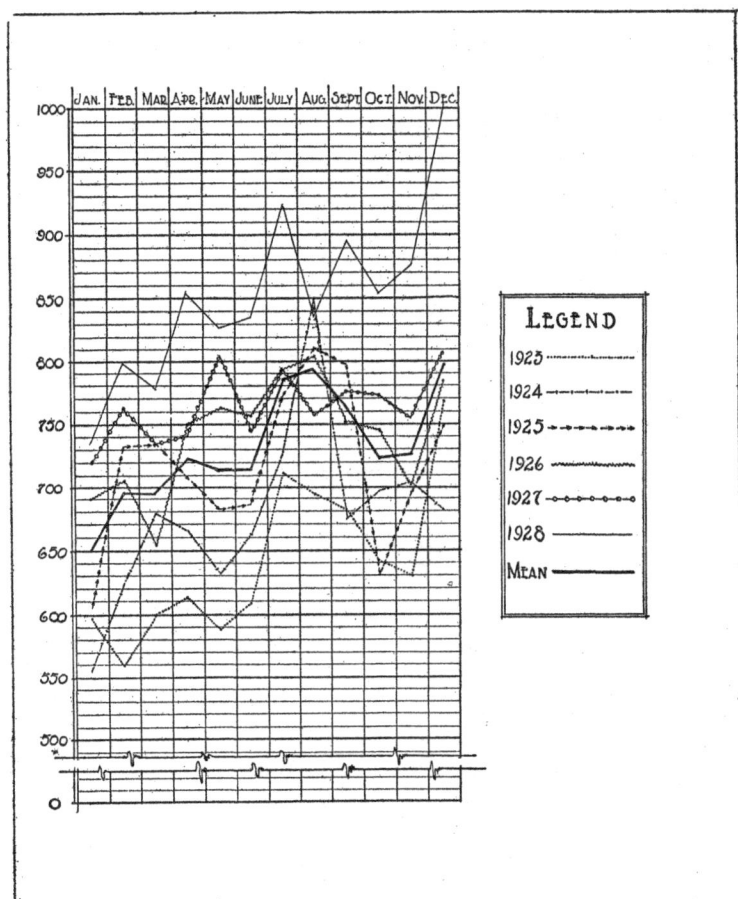

FIGURE 4. HOMICIDES BY MONTHS, UNITED STATES, 1923-1928.

described. May and June have less slayings than April, but Dexter pointed out the effect of the warm days in spring when the heat was less bearable because heavy winter clothing had not yet been discarded. He explained also that August should be higher than July because a short period of heat could be borne with more equanimity than a longer one. Consequently, after the hot days of June and July the warm weather of August may prove too uncomfortable to be endured with patience. Other equally credible explanations are possible, however, as, for example, the preoccupation of the rural communities with planting and harvesting during the spring and autumn and the lack of travel and social intercourse during the months of January and February.

On the other hand, an examination of the graphs representing the individual years shows clearly that there is little uniformity in the results secured. For example, although May is on the average a month having only a moderate number of homicides, in 1927 it exceeded all of the months except December. In the same year August, although usually a high month, was below February, May, July, September, October, and December. If climate and season exert any potent influence, it should, it seems, appear in every year, since the annual totals of over seven thousand cases are apparently large enough to cancel out any chance interference.

Besides, the data for November and December are distinctly at variance with the mean temperatures for these months. This fact, together with the lack of uniformity for the yearly seasonal trends, seems sufficient to prove the absence of any close relationship between homicide and mean temperature. There is the possibility, however, that the records for November and December, especially for the latter, are materially affected by the Thanksgiving and the Christmas holiday seasons. As has already been described, in the state of South Carolina the homicide record for December was greatly increased by the excess of slayings taking place during Christmas week. For example, during the period, 1920-1926, December had a total of 171 homicides, but when this number was mathematically corrected to compensate for the large number of homicides committed within the week of December 23-29, the new total was only 135.6. The latter figure was only slightly above the average for the twelve months when these were corrected to be equivalent to 31 days in length. In South Carolina, however, there was no noticeable excess of homicides at the Thanksgiving season. This may be due to the fact that Thanksgiving is not in that state generally celebrated in as boisterous a manner as Christmas is. If in the United States the customary way of observing Thanksgiving tends to increase the chances of homicide and if the same condition is true in an exaggerated form of the celebration of Christmas, then the relative number of slayings in November and December might more closely approach the comparative temperatures, if the excess of homicidal deaths occurring during the holiday seasons could be eliminated. Unfortunately, the data necessary to calculate this mathematical correction were not available, except for the state of South Carolina, for which the exact day of the month on which the death took place was secured by copying the original certificates filed by the undertakers.

It is to be regretted that this crucial point could not be more thoroughly investigated.

To discover whether the presence of colored persons affects materially the monthly distribution of homicides an analysis of colored homicidal deaths was made for the years 1923-1927. In this study 11,382 cases were surveyed. They came from the District of Columbia, Alabama, Arkansas, Florida, Georgia, Kentucky, Louisiana, Maryland, Mississippi, North Carolina, South Carolina, Tennessee, and Virginia. In Table IX are shown the results of this tabulation.

TABLE IX. MONTHLY DISTRIBUTION OF COLORED HOMICIDAL
DEATHS 1923-1927

January	839
February	869
March	958
April	955
May	936
June	876
July	1,029
August	1,055
September	924
October	915
November	928
December	1,098
Mean	948.5

An examination of this table reveals little evidence that the seasonal distribution of colored homicidal deaths differs appreciably from that of the whites. If the results were corrected to compensate for the shortness of several months, they would practically coincide with the results already presented in Table VIII. Clearly, therefore, the presence of colored persons has little or no effect upon seasonal variation in homicide.

For the period, 1923-1927, the monthly distribution of homicides for each state was tabulated. The results are presented in Table XIII of Chapter X. Even a casual examination of this table will reveal the lack of uniformity in the seasonal trends. For example, in the New England states the highest month was October and the lowest was November. The periods when homicide is at the maximum generally fall in the mid-summer or in December, but there are many exceptions. In the tier of states extending downward from Virginia to Florida the month of greatest homicide incidence is December, but in the group immediately west of this one—Alabama, Tennessee, and Kentucky—December is not a high month. As a rule, there seems to be little difference between the monthly distribution of homicides in the northern and the southern states. It has already been pointed out, however, that the prevailing rates of homicide are lower in the North than in the South, this result lending support to the thermic law of crime. But when homicides do occur in the North, they are likely to be distributed through the year in almost the same way as in the South. If any variation is noticeable, it is the slightly greater tendency for an excess of homicides during the summer. This, of course, may be due to the difficulty of social intercourse during the winter rather than to any direct effect of temperature.

The series of extended investigations reported above does not, unfortunately, enable one unequivocally to reject or support the thermic law of crime. If this law describes the seasonal distribution of crimes against the person in the European countries, that fact is of significance. But that it applies to the United States with equal accuracy is not yet certain. Since the data are somewhat contradictory, they have been presented here in detail in order that further investigations may carry forward the study of the problem. Meanwhile, the criminologist is forced to suspend judgment. Temperature trends may affect the seasonal distribution of homicide in the United States, and, again, they may not. The relationship may actually exist, obscured by interfering factors, but the evidence already presented does not lend much support to this conclusion.

EXPLANATIONS OF POSSIBLE SEASONAL VARIATION
IN HOMICIDE

Even if further studies prove the significance of seasonal changes in the amount of homicide committed in the United States—and at present there is ample ground for scepticism—there still would remain the important problem of explaining how and why the variations take place. Until the precise manner in which the weather causes an increase in deeds of violence is determined, the relationship between these two factors will necessarily be open to question.

In general, the weather appears to play a rôle of diminishing importance in the affairs of men. The invention of mechanical refrigeration and of improved methods of ventilation and heating has greatly lessened the discomfort arising from extremes of temperature. Meanwhile, the tendency to explain human behavior by reference to climate and seasons has also greatly decreased. As the etymology of the words themselves indicates, lunacy was once thought to be due to the influence of the moon, while malaria was the result of "bad air" and miasma arising from swampy regions. Even in 1748 Montesquieu in his *Spirit of Laws* by means of climatic differences explained the variations in such phenomena as racial traits, the extent of slavery, the type of government, the form of marriage, and the amount of sobriety.[34] Such explanations of regional differences would receive little credence today.

In addition to the theories already presented, one of the most interesting of the attempts to show the relationship between the weather and conduct is Dexter's "reserve energy" hypothesis.[35] According to this theory, "varying meteorological conditions affect directly, though in different ways, the metabolism of life." The general effect of high temperature, strong winds, fair days, and low humidities is to increase bodily vigor and health and to build up a reserve of energy. "As a corollary, misconduct is the result of an excess of reserve energy, not directed to some useful purpose." Although the weather also affects the emotional states, Dexter thinks that this influence is less important than its effect upon "that portion of the reserve energy which is available for action."

If this hypothesis is correct, the time for expecting the maximum number of homicides would be in the spring and autumn rather than in the summer and the winter, for in a temperate climate the former seasons more nearly approach conditions of optimum efficiency. According to Huntington, "the optimum or most favorable condition for human health is an average outside temperature of about 64° F. for day and night, a relative humidity of about 80 per cent, and a fairly high degree of storminess

[34] J. P. Lichtenberger, *The Development of Social Theory*, pp. 214-32.
[35] *Weather Influences*, pp. 266-70.

or at least of variability from day to day."[36] Such weather is characteristic of spring and autumn over most of the United States, yet homicide is generally less during these seasons of increased health and energy, when, if Dexter's theory is correct, they should be at the maximum. Furthermore, Dexter found that both fighting and homicides were at or below expectancy up to temperatures between 65 and 75 degrees and reached a maximum between 85 and 90 degrees. But Drever reports, "It has been shown that the physical efficiency at a temperature of 68 degrees is 37 per cent greater than it is at 86 degrees."[37] Drever's findings, supported by experimental evidence, clearly conflict with the reserve energy hypothesis. Moreover, even in the southern states homicide is generally more frequent in August than in June and July, yet in August the vitality of the body is often impaired by the debilitating effects of long continued heat. Consequently, Dexter's theory cannot be accepted as a satisfactory explanation of the increase of homicide during the summer months. If an excess of energy actually tends to result in more crimes of violence, the maxima of homicide would occur in the spring and autumn, unless, of course, the effect of this factor is obscured by others more powerful or more numerous.

According to Mary Borden, the climate of the United States is too variable. "No extremes of cold or tropical heat are good for us." The excellence of the English climate is that "it does not tolerate exaggerations; it exerts a soothing influence even upon mob psychology." On the other hand, "there is only one great danger looming over America, the climate. It is bad for white men. It has

---

[36] *Civilization and Climate*, pp. 161-2.
[37] *The Psychology of Industry*, p. 97.

produced more skyscrapers, more machinery, more labor-saving devices, more religious maniacs, more psycho-analysts, more nervous wrecks, more drunkards, more dyspeptics, more patent foods, more gamblers and gunmen and yellow journalists than any other country in the world. Its keynote is extravagance."[38]

A similar hypothesis is upheld by Huntington, who represents geographical determinism in its extreme form. According to him, climate almost decides the fate of nations. In the United States regional differences are due largely to differences in the weather, and the nation's tendency toward anti-social behavior apparently proceeds from the same source. His point of view is illustrated by the following quotation:

In the South we find less energy, less vitality, less education, and fewer men who rise to eminence than in the North, not because southerners are in any way innately inferior to northerners, but apparently because of the adverse climate. In the far West people seem to be stimulated to such a degree that nervous exhaustion threatens them. In the North we see still another handicap. In spite of a wonderfully stimulating climate most of the year, the people suffer sudden checks because of the extremes of temperature. These conditions favor nervousness and worst of all they frequently stimulate harmful activities. That, perhaps, is why American children are so rude and boisterous or why so staid a city as Boston has six times as many murders as London in proportion to the population. Our country takes immigrants of every mental caliber, and stimulates some to noble deeds and others to commit murder, break down respect for law, and give us city governments that shame us in the eyes of the world. All these things would apparently not happen to such an extent were our

[38] "A Defense of the English Climate," *Harper's*, CLXI, 28-31.

climate less bracing and did not its extremes often weaken the power of self-control.[39]

Extremes of temperature may, of course, result in a tendency toward erratic behavior, as Huntington believes. Evidence to this effect is given by Agar's experiments with invertebrate water-mites. These Hydrachnids were placed in tubes of wates kept at constant temperatures and their locomotor activity was recorded. At optimum temperatures the mites typically travelled up and down the whole length of the tube. But at both higher and lower temperatures their behavior was more erratic, there being frequent unforced reversals of direction. "At optimal temperatures, then, this organism is active but in a routine straightaway manner; whereas at abnormally low and abnormally high temperatures its behavior shows *variability* in high degree. The variability in the behavior increases in direct proportion to the degree of lack of balance between internal and external temperature conditions."[40] This experiment deals, of course, with a relatively simple organism and its results may not be applicable to human beings.

But so far as Borden's and Huntington's observations apply to the homicide problem, they can be easily answered from an examination of the map and tables previously presented. Homicide is not excessive on the mid-western plains where extremely hot summers and exceedingly cold winters are generally experienced. On the other hand, the Pacific coast states and the South have

[39] *Civilization and the Climate*, p. 404.
[40] J. F. Dashiell, *Fundamentals of Objective Psychology*, pp. 240-2.

less variation in climate but more than their share of the homicides.

An interesting theory concerning the effect of high temperature upon the mental state of the murderer was presented by J. Marro at the Sixth International Congress of Criminal Anthropology in 1906. This paper has been summarized as follows: "The determining cerebral condition of the murderer is essentially a psychic hyperæsthesia, now morbid, now physiologic, which renders some subjects so sensitive to the impressions touching their personality that it is impossible for them to tolerate them without a sudden and violent reaction against the person from whom they proceed. The unfolding of puberty, the effect of heat and alcoholic intoxication mainly favor so dangerous an hyperæsthesia."[41] Unfortunately, little evidence for or against this hypothesis appears to be available. As has been shown already, alcoholic intoxication does predispose toward violence, but that high temperatures have the same effect is open to doubt.

DIRECT AND INDIRECT WEATHER INFLUENCES

Meteorological conditions, such as temperature and humidity, apparently affect human beings *directly* by influencing the exchange of energy through the skin tissue. Under ordinary conditions the body produces more heat than is necessary for the maintenance of normal temperature. The amount of this heat varies to some extent in proportion to the degree of muscular, glandular, and nervous activity. Obviously, a rise in the temperature of the surrounding air decreases the efficiency of the radiation

[41] Bernaldo de Quiros, *Modern Theories of Criminality*, p. 93.

from the body, and if the air becomes hot enough the exchange of energy will proceed in the opposite direction. The body may defend itself against this loss of efficient radiation by an increase in the amount of perspiration through the pores of the skin. But if the humidity of the surrounding air is very high, evaporation from the surface of the body will be correspondingly retarded. When, therefore, the temperature and the humidity of the surrounding air rise beyond a certain optimum, the individual organism is placed under stress in its endeavor to maintain normal temperature. This stress, in turn, results in a feeling of discomfort or, perhaps, irritability. Then the *physical* efficiency is seriously impaired, as has already been pointed out, but experiments indicate that "apparently no immediate impairment of mental efficiency may take place even when the conditions are extremely adverse as far as physical efficiency is concerned."[42] Unfortunately, no important studies have been made, it seems, of the *emotional* effects arising from high temperature and humidity. Such an investigation would assist greatly in solving the problem of the relationship of crime and the weather. All that can be said at the present stage of inquiry is that hot, humid weather reduces physical or motor efficiency but has, apparently, little or no effect upon *mental* efficiency. Other than the commonly observed feeling of discomfort, the effect upon emotional health is not known. If it were, it might be possible to state more unequivocally the effect of summer weather upon the homicide rate.

On the other hand, when the surrounding air becomes

[42] James Drever, *The Psychology of Industry*, pp. 96-97.

so cold and dry that energy exchanges from the skin are facilitated, the organism becomes chilled and suffers from the attempt to keep its body temperature up to normal. Under such conditions some animals hibernate for protection; others are stimulated to greater activity, thus producing internal heat to counteract the external cold.

Two influences, however, tend to counteract the effect of the weather. One is acclimatization, the process by which the organism's metabolic activities are adjusted to suit the prevailing weather. In some ways, *relative* meteorological conditions are more significant than absolute thermometer, barometer, and hygrometer readings. The newspaper article reproduced below illustrates this:

Along with a really serious water shortage, England is experiencing a change from her customarily cool summer weather and is suffering what people here are pleased to call a terrific heat wave.

Today newspapers printed streaming headlines announcing the news that the temperature reached a maximum of 81 degrees Fahrenheit in the shade at noon.

People are fleeing to the seaside for the weekend, and roads are blocked with motor traffic.

American tourists, finding it comfortably warm in England, smiled broadly.[43]

Not only is the influence of the weather lessened, accordingly, at least in part by the organism's adapting itself to its meteorological environment; it is also materially affected by the mechanical equipment and the social customs of the human group. The civilized man may be more comfortable at the equator or within the Arctic circle than were his ancestors who dwelt within the

[43] Associated Press report, July 20, 1929.

temperate zones. As Cleveland Abbe has observed, "When speaking of climatic influences we must not forget that clothing, food, national customs, or other features of our environment, may very largely counteract the climatic influences proper."[44]

If the extent or type of crime is seriously affected by meteorological conditions, it seems likely that the *indirect* effect is greater than the influence of the weather itself. For example, in winter the scarcity of food may produce a greater incentive toward thievery while the long nights give a better opportunity for such an undertaking. Similarly, in summer the increase of outdoor life and social gatherings may result in more personal conflicts leading to fighting and homicide. As Parmelee has pointed out, the activities of pickpockets depend upon the presence of large crowds. If the weather is bitterly cold or a heavy rain is falling, people will remain indoors, and the pickpockets will be restricted in their operations. In many other ways the weather may have an indirect influence upon crime, as by attracting migratory workers during the rush of harvest, by causing seasonal unemployment, by increasing the need for food and clothing during winter, etc.

In South Carolina, predominantly an agricultural state, homicide was low during the months of February, May, and October for the period, 1920-1926. In May and October farm activities are usually at their height, and laborers are busily engaged in planting or harvesting. In February the country roads are likely to be in poor condition after the winter rains, the money left from the sale of the previous crop has been exhausted, and credit for the

---

[44] R. G. Dexter, *Weather Influences*, p. xxii.

new crop cannot usually be secured so early in the season. Consequently, during February a large part of the rural population remains indoors except when preparing land for the spring planting. On the other hand, farm work is in greatly diminished volume during midsummer and during December and January.[45] During these two seasons there is also a great increase of social life and festivity, especially in July and in December. Correspondingly, the number of homicides reach their maxima during July and December. Apparently, periods of leisure are likely to result in more homicides, while seasons of heavy labor are accompanied by fewer slayings. This seems to be an illustration of the indirect effect of the weather—the interrelationship of meteorological and cultural factors.

CONCLUSION

The exhaustive inquiry reported in this chapter leads, therefore, to the conclusion that in the United States the positive relationship between temperature changes and variation in the number of homicides is not established. There is some evidence that might indicate such an interpretation, but there is also much evidence in the opposite direction. There appears to be, moreover, even less chance that any correlation between these two factors is due to weather influences directly. If the seasons do affect the distribution of homicide, they probably do so indirectly through their effect upon the social behavior of the people.

[45] O. E. Baker, "Agricultural Regions of North America, Part II," *Economic Geography*, III, 77; and U. S. Department of Agriculture, *Seedtime and Harvest*, Circular 183, 1922, pp. 36-9.

CHAPTER X

PREPARATION AND TABULATION OF DATA

ATTEMPTS TO STUDY the extent of anti-social conduct usually meet with almost insuperable difficulties. As one criminologist has concluded, "Crime statistics are the most difficult of all statistics." The reason for his despondency will be apparent when the more obvious inaccuracies in the data are enumerated. The United States Bureau of the Census at intervals makes a special census of the prisoners serving sentence in penal and reformatory institutions. In addition to securing the number of those present upon the date specified, this census collects statistics of commitments and discharges for a six months period. As an index of actual crime this census is not reliable, for such reports include a disproportionate number of the poor and friendless who are unable to employ skilled lawyers for their defense or to secure petitions for clemency after conviction. Furthermore, the number of prisoners serving sentence varies with the strictness or laxity of law enforcement in states, counties, and municipalities, and with the extent of the use of substitutes for imprisonment, such as probation, parole, and fines. In addition, several of these enumerations use different systems of classification of offenses, thus making comparisons difficult or valueless.

A second source of crime statistics is the reports of arrests by police officers and of commitments after arrest to the county and city jails. Once more comparisons are difficult, for in some places offenders are first committed to jail and then released upon bond, in others those who can give bail are rarely committed to jail except when charged with serious offenses. Moreover, arrests vary with the relative skill of the police and of the offenders. Their validity is also often vitiated by indiscriminate arrests in the "drag net" after a notorious crime. Besides, every city and every state seems to have a different method of classifying and reporting criminal offenses.[1] A frequent error in the use of these reports is due to an investigator's inability to discover whether few arrests and commitments are to be interpreted as an indication of the absence of delinquency or of laxity in law enforcement. If they are taken at their numerical value, they may misrepresent the law-abiding regions, where offenders are promptly apprehended, or may reflect undue credit upon places where arrests are infrequent because the laws are being violated with impunity. For example, an inexperienced investigator once reported that a certain region was exceptionally free from crime, since very few persons had been arrested and committed to jail, when in reality many forms of delinquency were being tolerated by both the public and the officers of the law. Crime was rampant, yet arrests were rare.

A third source of information concerning crime is the reports of complaints made to police headquarters. Only a few cities keep such records, however, and they are of doubtful validity since many articles are alleged to be stolen when they have been merely lost and since serious crimes are often concealed for fear of vengeance upon

---

[1] This condition may improve because of the publication of the census bureau's *Instructions for Compiling Criminal Statistics* with a standard classification of crimes, and of a guide for the preparation of police reports, sponsored by the Committee on Uniform Crime Records.

complainants. Court records provide another source of crime statistics, but they are no more valid than the enumeration of arrests or jail commitments, and for about the same reasons. Other sources of lesser importance are newspaper files, reports of such coöperative organizations as the American Bankers' Association, records of insurance and surety companies, and special investigations, such as the Illinois Crime Survey.

Until there are more uniform methods and greater precision in securing records of crime, Robinson's conclusion should be accepted, "The statistics are, from the point of view of the student of criminology, almost without exception bad."[2]   Sutherland's evaluation is approximately the same, "In view of the difficulties and inaccuracies in criminal statistics, little dependence can be placed upon them for scientific purposes."[3]   For investigations of the relative frequency of anti-social conduct there is, it seems, only one fairly reliable and valid source of information, the homicide reports of the state and Federal bureaus of vital statistics, based upon the certificates of death required by law to be filed with the local registrars in the United States death registration area, which in 1927 comprised 91.3 per cent of the population of the country.[4] Violent deaths are rarely concealed from these registrars and are practically always reported to the central bureaus, although the exact nature of the death may, for numerous reasons, be disguised.   These reports, therefore, probably minimize the extent of homicide, but if it be assumed that the proportion of discrepancies is somewhat uniform because they arise from causes that operate throughout the

[2] *Criminal Statistics*, p. 94.   [3] *Criminology*, p. 54.
[4] *Mortality Statistics 1927*, Part II, pp. 7-9.

nation, they provide a trustworthy means of comparing
the relative frequency of homicide in communities and
regions.

DEFINITION OF HOMICIDE

The homicide rates presented in this volume are based
upon the records of the United States Division of Vital
Statistics, which defines homicide as follows: "Homicide,
as here used, includes murder, manslaughter, justifiable
homicide, and incendiarism, but not legal execution."[5]
This definition is also followed, perforce, by the state and
local registrars of the death registration area.   As a description of homicide it is open to serious criticism.   In the
first place, it is couched in legal phraseology rather than
in terms describing the situation as it exists at the time the
death certificate is prepared, which is usually within a few
hours after the victim's life has ceased.   Technically, manslaughter or murder cannot be determined for weeks or
months by judicial procedure.   Furthermore, accidents due
to criminal behavior or gross negligence, as in driving an
automobile or handling firearms, are often classed by the
courts as manslaughter or in exceptional cases as murder.
Yet, however criminalistic, automobile accident deaths are
not reported as homicides.[6]   Homicide, therefore, is primarily the purposive killing of one person "by the act,
procurement, or omission of another," as the New York
penal code states.   It is an inclusive term, almost a syn-
onym of the word *slaying,* and covers all classes of violent
deaths due to the intentional acts of others, whether or not

[5] *Ibid.,* p. 138.
[6] H. A. Phelps, "Rhode Island's Threat Against Murder," *Journal of the
American Institute of Criminal Law and Criminology,* XV, 552-7.

"with malice aforethought," and whether or not blame-worthy.[7]

But, regardless of difficulty of definition, homicide is in reality a very specific term, with easily distinguished confines. Table II of the annual *Mortality Statistics* divides deaths from "external causes" into three classes: "suicide," "homicide," and "accidental, other, or undefined external causes." This is further clarified by the use of the International Classification of Causes of Death, in which the subdivisions are: "by firearms" (number 197); "by cutting or piercing instruments" (number 198); and "by other means" (number 199) such as by poison, bludgeon, or strangulation. During 1927, for example, there were 6,310 homicides by firearms, 1,495 by cutting or piercing instruments, and 1,665 by other means.[8] Gunshot and knife wounds, accordingly, cause about eighty per cent or more of the annual homicide toll. Since 1921, infanticide, the slaying of a child less than one year of age, has been enumerated separately as number 200 of the International Classification but has been included in the homicide totals. For practical purposes, then, it is proper to describe a homicide as a violent death which is neither a suicide nor an accident. This is essentially the meaning of the official definition quoted above.

RELIABILITY OF RATES

In the principal tables presented in this volume the homicide rates of cities and counties are based upon the

---

[7] This sociological use of the term *homicide* should be sharply distinguished from its use in law and sometimes in common speech to denote all cases of the killing of human beings, including accidents and suicides as well as purposive slayings.

[8] *Mortality Statistics 1927*, Part I, Table II.

records for the two years, 1920 and 1925, combined. This is, unfortunately, necessary, since mortality statistics for smaller cities and minor civil divisions can now be secured only at five year intervals. The number of homicides committed in 1930 will not be available for several years afterwards, unless the United States Division of Vital Statistics is able to tabulate and publish them more promptly than usual. When the homicide statistics for 1930 may be obtained, it is hoped to revise the rates published in this study, basing them upon three years—1920, 1925, and 1930—rather than upon only two.

Meanwhile, it is quite important to know how reliable are the rates based upon the number of homicides for two years. What would be the result if the rates were based upon a much longer period? A tentative answer can be derived from an analysis of the statistics for the counties in South Carolina. From a previous investigation homicide rates for each of the counties of this state were available for a seven year period, 1920-1926. These rates were compared with those based upon the official records for the years, 1920 and 1925. Six counties having cities of 10,000 or more inhabitants were excluded since slayings in urban areas were treated differently in the two investigations. This procedure left 40 counties having two comparable homicide rates—one based upon the records for 1920-1926 and the other upon the data for the years 1920 and 1925. A coefficient of correlation by the rank-difference method was then calculated. It was found to be + .77, with a probable error of ± .04, indicating a very close relationship between the rates based upon two years and those based upon seven years. This conclusion was further supported by an examination of the relative rank of each of the 40 counties in the two tables, 19 differing less than five positions in rank when the seven year rates were compared with the two year rates. For example, the county having the highest homicide rate for 1920 and 1925 was also the highest for the years 1920-1926. In the same way the county having the lowest rate for 1920 and 1925 was also the lowest for the years 1920-1926. Provided these results are typical of the situation prevailing in the registration area, homicide rates based upon the years, 1920 and 1925, are fairly reliable for, even if the sample were increased by the addition of five years' records, about half of the rates would not be materially changed and the general results would be very closely related.

Yet even if the rates presented are statistically reliable, they should not be accepted without caution. In the first place, they are "crude" rather than "refined" rates. If a city with an excess of females has the same crude homicide rate as another where the sexes are approximately equal in numbers, its refined rate is really higher, since women slay and are slain less frequently than men. Besides, the urban rates are often increased by deaths of those wounded elsewhere and brought to hospitals for treatment. Furthermore, the percentage of justifiable homicides included in the total number of slayings may vary greatly from city to city or county to county. Nevertheless, even with the defects mentioned above homicide rates represent the best information now available concerning the extent of any one crime in the cities and counties of the United States registration area.

PREPARATION OF TABLES

In the preparation of the tables presented in this volume many precautions have been taken to prevent errors and inaccuracies. The original data were copied upon the calculation sheets and were then checked by comparison with the primary source. Whenever possible, this work was done by persons other than those who did the copying, and even when the workers were the same, the tasks were different. Unfortunately, primary sources must be accepted at face value, even though typographical errors and minor inaccuracies are almost unavoidable. For example, official United States government publications were found to contain inconsistent population statistics. Especial care was taken to insure accuracy in the tables showing homicide rates. The calculations were first made upon a computing machine and were then checked by another person using a slide rule. Conflicting results were investigated further until the source of error was discovered. By these precautions it is hoped that clerical errors have been practically eliminated and that mistakes of all types have been reduced to a minimum.

TABLE X

In Table X are presented the homicide rates per 100,-000 population for the years, 1920 and 1925, combined, for the registration area cities having 10,000 or more inhabitants on January 1, 1920. Unless otherwise noted, these rates are based upon the sum of the number of homicides in the years 1920 and 1925 divided by the sum of the estimated populations for July 1, 1920, and for July 1, 1925. This quotient, when the decimal point is properly placed, gives the annual rate per 100,000 persons. An improvised illustration may make this procedure somewhat clearer:

CITY	HOMICIDES			ESTIMATED POPULATION			HOMICIDE RATE PER 100,000
	1920	*1925*	*Total*	*July, 1920*	*July, 1925*	*Total*	
XYZ	4	6	10	23,000	27,000	50,000	20.00

This method gives a result that is more trustworthy than the rate for either of the two years, if they were calculated individually. If the rates for the two years were calculated separately and an average of the two were then taken, this result would be less reliable than the rate secured by the method illustrated above. Besides, the "weighted" averages, as given in Table X, have the further advantage of permitting the inclusion of additional data with a minimum of effort.

The number of homicides for the years, 1920 and 1925, was copied from unpublished records of the United States Division of Vital Statistics. The estimated population for each city for July 1, 1920, and for July 1, 1925, was secured from Table I B of *Mortality Statistics* for 1920 and 1925. For fifteen cities the Census Bureau did not estimate the population as of July 1, 1925, because of such difficulties as change in rate of growth. For these cities the estimated population as of July 1, 1920, was added to the enumerated population on April 1, 1930. The sum was then divided by two in order to get the average (mean) and the quotient was adopted as a fair representative of the probable population in 1925.

In interpreting this table it should be recalled that all urban homicide rates are probably increased a little by deaths occurring at hospitals in the city, although the victim was actually injured in the rural territory nearby. The transportation of mortally wounded persons to hospitals, therefore, slightly increases the urban rate of homicide and correspondingly decreases the rural rate.

TABLE X. HOMICIDES PER 100,000 POPULATION, CITIES OF 10,000 OR MORE, U. S. REGISTRATION AREA, 1920 AND 1925 COMBINED
(Data in italics are based upon less than 5 deaths.)

ALABAMA CITIES

Anniston[1]	29.27	Dothan[1]	68.97	Mobile	24.37
Bessemer[1]	36.36	Florence[1]	23.62	Montgomery	34.35
Birmingham	51.65	Gadsden[1]	0.00	Selma[1]	29.41
				Tuscaloosa[1]	30.53

ARKANSAS CITIES

Fort Smith[1]	15.82	Little Rock[1]	44.47	North Little	
Hot Springs[1]	42.75			Rock[1]	6.37

CALIFORNIA CITIES

Alameda	3.28	Oakland	3.38	San Francisco	7.01
Bakersfield	11.78	Pasadena	2.92	San Jose	5.98
Berkeley	4.88	Pomona	10.32	Santa Ana	5.66
Eureka	0.00	Richmond	5.02	Santa Barbara	0.00
Fresno	4.62	Riverside[8]	4.48	Santa Cruz	18.32
Glendale	2.83	Sacramento	17.29	Santa Monica	8.56
Long Beach	2.69	San Bernardino	28.69	Stockton	9.08
Los Angeles[8]	9.47	San Diego	8.22	Vallejo	14.52
				Venice	7.92

COLORADO CITIES

Boulder	0.00	Denver	9.26	Trinidad	13.69
Colorado		Greeley	8.47		
Springs	0.00	Pueblo	19.56		

CONNECTICUT CITIES

Ansonia	0.00	Fairfield	3.81	Naugatuck	0.00
Bridgeport[8]	5.82	Greenwich	6.29	New Britain	4.68
Bristol	4.38	Hartford	3.33	New Haven	3.21
Danbury	4.48	Manchester	2.52	New London	7.26
Derby	8.34	Meriden	1.40	Norwalk	8.68
East Hartford	0.00	Middletown	4.43	Norwich	6.64
Enfield	4.05	Milford	0.00	Orange	5.48

[1] Based upon 1925 data only.

[8] Population for 1925 not estimated. In place of it there was used the average of the estimated population for July 1, 1920, and the enumerated population upon April 1, 1930.

Stamford *4.60*	Torrington ... *4.14*	Willimantic .. 0.00
Stonington ... *9.48*	Waterbury[3] ... 5.28	Windham 0.00
Stratford *3.47*	Wallingford .. 0.00	

DELAWARE CITIES

Wilmington ... 3.86

DISTRICT OF COLUMBIA

Washington ... 11.18

FLORIDA CITIES

Jacksonville ... 43.74	Miami 95.46	St. Petersburg . 21.63
Key West *6.16*	Pensacola 10.57	Tampa 35.38

GEORGIA CITIES

Albany[1] *7.41*	Augusta 29.63	La Grange[1] ... *8.51*
Athens[1] 31.92	Brunswick 15.91	Macon[1] 32.65
Atlanta[3] 40.22	Columbus[1] 27.15	Savannah 16.36
		Waycross[1] *14.93*

IDAHO CITIES

Boise 0.00	Pocatello[1] *5.46*

ILLINOIS CITIES

Alton 11.61	East St. Louis . 34.63	Maywood 0.00
Aurora *5.20*	Elgin 8.26	Moline *4.62*
Belleville *3.85*	Evanston *4.89*	Murphysboro .. *17.12*
Berwyn *2.99*	Forest Park ... 0.00	Oak Park 9.75
Bloomington .. 0.00	Freeport *4.94*	Ottawa 49.15
Blue Island ... 20.18	Galesburg 12.31	Pekin *7.84*
Cairo 32.43	Granite City .. *12.06*	Peoria 5.69
Canton *4.56*	Herrin 57.15	Quincy *5.34*
Centralia *7.48*	Jacksonville ... 25.29	Rockford 4.89
Champaign ... *2.87*	Joliet 10.10	Rock Island .. 11.89
Chicago 12.67	Kankakee *11.25*	Springfield 8.10
Chicago Heights 26.21	Kewanee *5.58*	Streator *6.69*
Cicero *3.68*	La Salle *3.70*	Urbana *4.62*
Danville 11.27	Lincoln *8.22*	Waukegan 12.08
Decatur 9.16	Mattoon 0.00	

INDIANA CITIES

Anderson *4.69*	Crawfordsville . 0.00	Elwood. *4.61*
Bloomington .. *8.24*	East Chicago .. 27.90	Evansville 10.58
Clinton 28.22	Elkhart *5.81*	Fort Wayne .. 3.78

[1] Based upon 1925 data only.

[3] Population for 1925 not estimated. In place of it there was used the average of the estimated population for July 1, 1920, and the enumerated population upon April 1, 1930.

Frankfort	....	4.03	La Porte	.....	0.00	New Castle	...	6.31
Gary	....	42.46	Lafayette	.....	8.62	Peru	....	0.00
Hammond	....	18.35	Logansport	...	0.00	Richmond	....	5.22
Huntington	...	3.33	Marion	......	3.98	South Bend	...	9.88
Indianapolis	..	9.01	Michigan City	.	5.03	Terre Haute	..	13.81
Jeffersonville	..	4.95	Mishawaka	...	0.00	Vincennes	....	2.81
Kokomo	.....	4.41	Muncie	......	3.77	Whiting	......	0.00
			New Albany	..	2.18			

IOWA CITIES

Boone[1]	....	0.00	Des Moines[1]	..	5.66	Keokuk[1]	......	0.00
Burlington[1]	...	3.79	Dubuque[1]	....	2.44	Marshalltown[1]	.	0.00
Cedar Rapids[1]	.	1.98	Fort Dodge[1]	..	23.04	Mason City[1]	..	8.82
Clinton[1]	......	0.00	Fort Madison[1]	.	0.00	Muscatine[1]	....	0.00
Council Bluffs[1].		2.51	Iowa City[1]	...	0.00	Ottumwa[1]	....	3.79
Davenport[1]	...	5.72				Sioux City[1]	...	13.09
						Waterloo[1]	....	10.88

KANSAS CITIES

Arkansas City	.	0.00	Fort Scott	....	8.90	Parsons	......	0.00
Atchison	.....	10.85	Hutchinson	..	12.09	Pittsburg	.....	8.02
Chanute	......	4.96	Independence	..	13.11	Salina	....	9.68
Coffeyville	....	6.73	Kansas City	..	17.88	Topeka	......	8.51
El Dorado	...	9.57	Lawrence	.....	8.06	Wichita	......	14.85
Emporia	.....	12.70	Leavenworth	..	10.58			

KENTUCKY CITIES

Ashland	.....	30.51	Lexington	....	39.44	Owensboro	...	10.13
Covington	....	12.12	Louisville	....	18.43	Paducah	......	13.80
Henderson	...	12.09	Newport	.....	13.64			

LOUISIANA CITIES

Alexandria	....	36.37	Lake Charles	..	22.08	New Orleans	..	28.00
Baton Rouge	..	14.02	Monroe	......	70.11	Shreveport	....	71.16

MAINE CITIES

Auburn	......	0.00	Bath	....	0.00	Portland	.....	1.38
Augusta	......	3.48	Biddeford	....	2.74	Sanford	......	0.00
Bangor	......	5.70	Lewiston	.....	2.99	Waterville	....	3.59

MARYLAND CITIES

Annapolis	....	12.43	Cumberland	..	12.52	Hagerstown	...	6.70
Baltimore	.....	7.56	Frederick	.....	0.00			

MASSACHUSETTS CITIES

Adams	....	0.00	Attleboro	.....	4.93	Boston	....	3.85
Amesbury	....	4.70	Belmont	.....	3.81	Braintree	.....	8.37
Arlington	....	2.27	Beverly	......	2.20	Brockton	.....	1.51

[1] Based upon 1925 data only.

Brookline	3.71	Lowell	3.13	Quincy	0.92
Cambridge	3.05	Lynn	0.49	Revere	0.00
Chelsea	2.20	Malden	0.99	Salem	2.34
Chicopee	0.00	Marlborough	0.00	Saugus	0.00
Clinton	0.00	Medford	0.00	Somerville	0.52
Danvers	0.00	Melrose	0.00	Southbridge	0.00
Dedham	0.00	Methuen	2.78	Springfield	4.75
Easthampton	0.00	Milford	0.00	Taunton	1.31
Everett	3.64	Natick	4.20	Wakefield	0.00
Fall River	2.00	New Bedford	0.83	Waltham	4.56
Fitchburg	1.18	Newburyport	3.19	Watertown	0.00
Framingham	2.61	Newton	1.01	Webster	0.00
Gardner	0.00	North Adams	0.00	Westfield	2.63
Gloucester	2.16	Northampton	6.49	West Springfield	3.45
Greenfield	0.00	Northbridge	0.00	Weymouth	9.25
Haverhill	3.86	Norwood	0.00	Winchester	4.52
Holyoke	0.83	Peabody	2.52	Winthrop	3.14
Lawrence	5.31	Pittsfield	1.12	Woburn	2.86
Leominster	2.38	Plymouth	0.00	Worcester	3.49

MICHIGAN CITIES

Adrian	0.00	Hamtramck	3.75	Muskegon	3.74
Alpena	0.00	Highland Park	1.65	Owosso	0.00
Ann Arbor	4.77	Holland	0.00	Pontiac	8.46
Battle Creek	1.27	Ironwood	12.02	Port Huron	1.78
Bay City	0.00	Ishpeming	4.76	Saginaw	2.20
Benton Harbor	3.79	Jackson	5.60	Sault Ste. Marie	0.00
Detroit	16.82	Kalamazoo	2.93	Traverse City	4.58
Escanaba	7.63	Lansing	3.09	Wyandotte	20.71
Flint	4.36	Marquette	3.82		
Grand Rapids	1.37	Monroe	3.84		

MINNESOTA CITIES

Austin	4.51	Mankato	7.61	St. Paul	5.40
Duluth	5.69	Minneapolis	6.79	Virginia	0.00
Faribault	0.00	Rochester	0.00	Winona	5.17
Hibbing	15.02	St. Cloud	2.86		

MISSISSIPPI CITIES

Biloxi	4.22	Hattiesburg	25.51	Meridian	37.67
Columbus	22.75	Jackson	57.94	Natchez	15.53
Greenville	78.18	Laurel	27.62	Vicksburg	96.84

MISSOURI CITIES

Cape Girardeau	4.06	Independence	12.25	Moberly	7.46
Carthage	4.88	Jefferson City	19.73	St. Joseph	11.52
Columbia	9.52	Joplin	11.71	St. Louis	16.32
Hannibal	2.55	Kansas City	31.64	Sedalia	6.82
				Springfield	4.88

MONTANA CITIES

| Anaconda | 12.37 | Butte | 28.36 | Helena | 4.15 |
| Billings | 17.99 | Great Falls | 9.17 | Missoula | 3.95 |

NEBRASKA CITIES

| Grand Island | 3.37 | Lincoln | 2.58 | Omaha | 13.81 |
| Hastings | 0.00 | North Platte | 20.44 | | |

NEW HAMPSHIRE CITIES

Berlin	2.86	Keene	0.00	Nashua	1.72
Concord	0.00	Laconia	0.00	Portsmouth	3.50
Dover	3.84	Manchester	1.24		

NEW JERSEY CITIES

Asbury Park	11.44	Garfield	0.00	New Brunswick	11.23
Atlantic City	13.43	Gloucester	3.85	Orange	4.36
Bayonne	3.00	Hackensack	23.97	Passaic	11.25
Belleville	0.00	Harrison	0.00	Paterson	3.23
Bloomfield	4.13	Hoboken	5.14	Perth Amboy	1.12
Bridgeton	6.96	Irvington	8.42	Phillipsburg	0.00
Camden	8.52	Jersey City	2.60	Plainfield	5.02
Carteret		Kearney	1.71	Rahway	4.32
(Roosevelt)	0.00	Long Branch	22.11	Summit	4.54
Clifton	4.85	Millville	3.25	Trenton	6.72
East Orange	0.00	Montclair	1.61	Union City	1.62
Elizabeth[3]	7.40	Morristown	19.88	West New York	0.00
Englewood	8.23	Newark	5.28	West Orange	5.88

NEW MEXICO CITIES

Albuquerque[1] .. 14.29

NEW YORK CITIES

Albany	1.30	Fulton	0.00	Lackawana	2.61
Amsterdam	4.35	Geneva	3.26	Little Falls	7.84
Auburn	4.17	Glen Falls	2.89	Lockport	4.64
Batavia	10.26	Gloversville	2.26	Middletown	5.13
Beacon	13.26	Herkimer	0.00	Mount Vernon	3.20
Binghampton	2.15	Hornell	9.71	Newburgh	6.57
Buffalo	5.82	Hudson	12.76	New Rochelle	3.71
Cohoes	0.00	Ilion	0.00	New York	6.46
Corning	0.00	Ithaca	0.00	Niagara Falls	4.59
Cortland	3.67	Jamestown	4.84	North Tona-	
Dunkirk	5.08	Johnstown	0.00	wanda	0.00
Elmira	1.06	Kingston	1.82	Ogdensburg	3.16

[1] Based upon 1925 data only.

[3] Population for 1925 not estimated. In place of it there was used the average of the estimated population for July 1, 1920, and the enumerated population upon April 1, 1930.

Olean	7.12	Port Jervis	9.66	Syracuse	4.78
Oneida	4.69	Poughkeepsie	2.82	Tonawanda	0.00
Oneonta	0.00	Rensselaer	0.00	Troy	4.85
Ossining	4.26	Rochester	3.09	Utica	1.53
Oswego	0.00	Rome	3.51	Watertown	0.00
Peekskill	5.90	Saratoga		Watervliet	3.10
Plattsburg	4.45	Springs	3.70	White Plains	6.17
Port Chester	5.55	Schenectady	3.84	Yonkers	1.40

NORTH CAROLINA CITIES

Asheville	29.86	Greensboro	16.38	Salisbury	9.40
Charlotte	16.95	High Point	20.97	Wilmington	18.36
Durham	20.35	New Bern	57.38	Wilson	21.18
Gastonia	9.95	Raleigh	32.68	Winston-Salem	21.98
Goldsboro	42.70	Rocky Mount	37.41		

NORTH DAKOTA CITIES

Fargo	2.12
Grand Forks[1]	13.19
Minot[1]	0.00

OHIO CITIES

Akron[8]	13.78	East Liverpool	18.41	Middletown	5.40
Alliance	12.79	East Youngs-		New Phila-	
Ashtabula	8.44	town	7.26	delphia	4.38
Barberton	4.70	Elyria	8.98	Newark	0.00
Bellaire	15.89	Findlay	5.66	Niles	3.26
Bucyrus	4.50	Fremont	0.00	Norwood	0.00
Cambridge	0.00	Hamilton	26.73	Piqua	12.85
Canton	11.30	Ironton	17.51	Portsmouth	17.95
Chillicothe	0.00	Kenmore	0.00	Salem	4.66
Cincinnati	14.30	Lakewood	2.00	Sandusky	6.31
Cleveland	13.42	Lancaster	0.00	Springfield	5.37
Cleveland		Lima	2.26	Steubenville	14.80
Heights	0.00	Lorain	12.50	Tiffin	0.00
Columbus	6.93	Mansfield	6.67	Toledo	11.24
Coshocton	4.44	Marietta	3.28	Warren	17.62
Cuyahoga Falls	4.13	Marion	1.64	Youngstown	14.93
Dayton	5.19	Martins Ferry	33.01	Zanesville	8.33
East Cleveland	0.00	Massillon	18.97		

OKLAHOMA CITIES

Oklahoma City[8] 12.95

OREGON CITIES

Astoria	9.76	Eugene	0.00	Portland[8]	3.69
				Salem	10.65

[1] Based upon 1925 data only.

[8] Population for 1925 not estimated. In place of it there was used the average of the estimated population for July 1, 1920, and the enumerated population upon April 1, 1930.

PENNSYLVANIA CITIES

Allentown	2.90	Easton	1.41	Phoenixville	0.00
Altoona	3.94	Erie	6.00	Pittsburg	10.47
Ambridge	9.96	Farrell	26.05	Pittston	15.62
Beaver Falls	15.42	Greensburg	9.61	Plymouth	6.06
Berwick	0.00	Harrisburg	5.00	Pottstown	0.00
Bethlehem	3.40	Hazleton	7.28	Pottsville	8.94
Braddock	28.13	Homestead	16.69	Punxsutawney	4.68
Bradford	19.14	Jeannette	8.92	Reading	4.07
Bristol	4.32	Johnstown	5.03	Scranton	4.64
Butler	2.04	Lancaster	1.82	Shamokin	0.00
Canonsburg	4.09	Lebanon	0.00	Sharon	14.88
Carbondale	5.23	McKeesport	24.98	Shenandoah	4.04
Carlisle	4.48	McKees Rocks	11.46	Steelton	3.72
Carnegie	4.17	Mahanoy City	0.00	Sunbury	0.00
Carrick	4.21	Meadville	16.52	Swissvale	4.17
Chambersburg	0.00	Monessen	0.00	Tamaqua	0.00
Charleroi	8.26	Mt. Carmel	5.72	Uniontown	31.53
Chester	12.55	Nanticoke	4.21	Warren	0.00
Coatesville	0.00	New Castle	5.25	Washington	11.21
Columbia	0.00	New Kensington	26.31	West Chester	0.00
Connellsville	17.76	Norristown	4.45	Wilkes-Barre	2.64
Dickson City	0.00	North Braddock	0.00	Wilkinsburg	5.76
Donora	19.11	Oil City	4.47	Williamsport	1.26
Du Bois	0.00	Old Forge	7.97	Woodlawn	6.26
Dunmore	2.38	Olyphant	0.00	York	6.20
Duquesne	7.49	Philadelphia	7.91		

RHODE ISLAND CITIES

Bristol	4.13	East Providence	2.08	Warwick	0.00
Central Falls	0.00	Newport	6.88	West Warwick	0.00
Cranston	1.56	Pawtucket	1.49	Woonsocket	0.00
Cumberland	0.00	Providence	2.77		

SOUTH CAROLINA CITIES

Anderson	78.28	Columbia	34.16	Greenville	35.43
Charleston	23.32	Florence	82.07	Spartanburg	30.99

TENNESSEE CITIES

Chattanooga	57.68	Johnson City	14.81	Memphis	59.68
Jackson	36.03	Knoxville	22.35	Nashville	21.59

TEXAS CITIES

Beaumont	17.43	Fort Worth[1]	15.48	Houston[3]	20.55
Dallas	24.78	Galveston	19.35	San Antonio	15.99
El Paso	26.05				

[1] Based upon 1925 data only.

[3] Population for 1925 not estimated. In place of it there was used the average of the estimated population for July 1, 1920, and the enumerated population upon April 1, 1930.

UTAH CITIES

Ogden 8.56	Provo *4.64*	Salt Lake City. 5.99

VERMONT CITIES

Barre 0.00	Burlington ... 0.00	Rutland 0.00

VIRGINIA CITIES

Alexandria ... 24.59	Newport News . 23.84	Richmond 12.54
Charlottesville . *4.56*	Norfolk 21.28	Roanoke 26.45
Danville 17.91	Petersburg ... 23.86	Staunton *18.85*
Lynchburg ... 24.79	Portsmouth ... 12.30	

WASHINGTON CITIES

Aberdeen 44.29	Hoquiam *9.41*	Tacoma 7.94
Bellingham ... *3.86*	Seattle[3] 4.38	Vancouver *3.66*
Everett 8.76	Spokane 6.09	Walla Walla .. *6.45*
		Yakima *7.23*

WEST VIRGINIA CITIES

Bluefield[1] 26.18	Huntington[1] .. 18.90	Moundsville[1] .. 0.00
Charleston[1] ... 28.57	Martinsburg[1] .. *14.82*	Parkersburg[1] .. *4.70*
Clarksburg[1] ... *13.16*	Morgantown[1].. *21.74*	Wheeling 8.01
Fairmont[1] *19.05*		

WISCONSIN CITIES

Appleton 0.00	Kenosha 5.43	Racine 4.72
Ashland 0.00	La Crosse *3.29*	Sheboygan ... *1.55*
Beloit 8.62	Madison 5.86	Stevens Point . *4.10*
Eau Claire *6.91*	Manitowoc ... 0.00	Superior *2.52*
Fond du Lac .. *2.01*	Marinette *3.67*	Waukesha 0.00
Green Bay 0.00	Milwaukee ... 3.40	Wausau *2.57*
Janesville *2.54*	Oshkosh 0.00	West Allis 0.00

WYOMING CITIES

Casper[1] 35.64	Cheyenne[1] *12.90*

TABLE XI

In Table XI are given the homicide rates for the whites and for the colored persons in those cities for which such data could be secured. Unfortunately, the southern cities are chiefly represented. This is because no separation of slayings by races is given by the vital statistics records when the number of colored persons is not large. For the year 1925, however, important additions were made to the list of northern and western cities reporting homicides ac-

[1] Based upon 1925 data only.

[3] Population for 1925 not estimated. In place of it there was used the average of the estimated population for July 1, 1920, and the enumerated population upon April 1, 1930.

cording to the race of the victim. These cities are included in the rates given in the table whenever the number of colored persons in the population could be secured. In general, the method of preparing the rates and making the necessary calculations was the same as has been described above.

TABLE XI. WHITE AND COLORED HOMICIDES PER 100,000 POPULATION, U. S. REGISTRATION AREA CITIES, 1920 AND 1925 COMBINED
(Data in italics are based upon less than 5 deaths.)

ALABAMA CITIES

	White	Colored		White	Colored
Anniston[1]	0.00	92.31	Mobile	11.43	45.39
Bessemer[1]	31.25	40.32	Montgomery	13.92	60.06
Birmingham	17.44	104.46	Selma[1]	11.91	46.51
Dothan[1]	69.77	67.80	Tuscaloosa[1]	0.00	88.89
Florence[1]	9.90	76.92			

ARKANSAS CITIES

	White	Colored		White	Colored
Fort Smith[1]	14.04	32.26	Little Rock[1]	19.78	118.28
Hot Springs[1]	33.77	71.12	North Little Rock[1]	0.00	19.23

CALIFORNIA CITIES

	White	Colored
San Francisco[1] ..	6.10	17.65

DELAWARE CITIES

	White	Colored
Wilmington	2.85	13.29

DISTRICT OF COLUMBIA

	White	Colored
Washington	4.57	31.49

FLORIDA CITIES

	White	Colored		White	Colored
Jacksonville	13.21	88.77	Pensacola	0.00	32.01
Key West	3.85	15.41	St. Petersburg ...	0.00	83.33
Miami	43.59	207.92	Tampa	18.00	102.36

GEORGIA CITIES

	White	Colored		White	Colored
Albany[1]	0.00	14.49	Columbus[1]	15.53	58.33
Athens[1]	25.86	41.67	LaGrange[1]	0.00	33.33
Atlanta[2]	9.32	107.30	Macon[1]	15.11	55.78
Augusta	11.25	54.60	Savannah	11.53	64.80
Brunswick	18.49	13.15	Waycross[1]	35.71	0.00

[1] Based upon data for 1925 only.
[2] Based upon data for 1920 only.

	White	*Colored*		*White*	*Colored*
ILLINOIS CITIES					
Cairo[1]	46.30	*20.83*	East St. Louis[1]	17.43	228.92
Chicago[1]	10.79	102.80	Murphysboro[1]	*8.93*	0.00
INDIANA CITIES					
Indianapolis[1]	6.00	56.74	Jeffersonville[1]	0.00	*70.67*
KANSAS CITIES					
Kansas City[1]	11.38	87.64	Leavenworth[1]	*16.94*	*31.42*
KENTUCKY CITIES					
Henderson	0.00	*50.29*	Owensboro	*5.90*	*35.58*
Lexington	32.04	*56.98*	Paducah	*5.03*	45.61
Louisville	7.32	76.59			
LOUISIANA CITIES					
Alexandria	41.40	29.84	Monroe	44.18	106.61
Baton Rouge	*12.68*	*16.31*	New Orleans	11.44	75.01
Lake Charles	*5.50*	*55.72*	Shreveport	28.44	139.98
MARYLAND CITIES					
Annapolis[1]	0.00	*71.43*	Baltimore[1]	3.39	39.28
MASSACHUSETTS CITIES					
Boston[1]	2.76	*21.39*			
MICHIGAN CITIES					
Detroit[1]	12.64	113.66			
MISSISSIPPI CITIES					
Biloxi	*4.91*	0.00	Laurel	*5.71*	61.20
Columbus	*9.96*	*33.51*	Meridian	22.33	66.92
Greenville	*36.85*	106.22	Natchez	*16.61*	*14.59*
Hattiesburg	*11.64*	48.70	Vicksburg	28.03	163.90
Jackson	18.46	112.79			
NEW JERSEY CITIES					
Newark[1]	4.87	36.20			
NORTH CAROLINA CITIES					
Asheville	24.21	47.19	New Bern	*9.04*	97.47
Charlotte	*5.78*	41.81	Raleigh	*8.27*	79.76
Durham	*9.39*	42.26	Rocky Mount	0.00	89.16
Gastonia	*4.02*	*37.85*	Salisbury	0.00	*38.30*
Goldsboro	*20.61*	71.38	Wilmington	*9.24*	32.71
Greensboro	*6.10*	**44.47**	Wilson	*16.97*	*25.36*
High Point	*12.82*	*57.61*	Winston-Salem	*4.49*	44.69

[1] Based upon 1925 data only.

White	Colored		White	Colored

OHIO CITIES

	White	Colored		White	Colored
Cincinnati[1]	6.95	189.66	Columbus[1]	5.16	24.82
Cleveland[1]	8.91	101.21	Springfield[1]	4.96	36.59

PENNSYLVANIA CITIES

	White	Colored		White	Colored
Philadelphia[1]	4.63	61.16	Pittsburg[1]	7.16	54.82

SOUTH CAROLINA CITIES

	White	Colored		White	Colored
Anderson	50.62	152.21	Florence	21.14	167.04
Charleston	9.21	39.67	Greenville	33.01	40.04
Columbia	22.14	54.53	Spartanburg	18.90	54.01

TENNESSEE CITIES

	White	Colored		White	Colored
Chattanooga	16.98	156.25	Knoxville	12.58	85.32
Jackson	7.68	93.76	Memphis	19.18	129.13
Johnson City	16.87	0.00	Nashville	11.65	45.64

TEXAS CITIES

	White	Colored		White	Colored
Beaumont	12.93	26.75	Galveston	9.72	52.30
Dallas	12.47	99.39	Houston[2]	4.72	46.61
Fort Worth[1]	11.03	47.37	San Antonio	13.28	44.48

VIRGINIA CITIES

	White	Colored		White	Colored
Alexandria	10.45	76.00	Petersburg	13.08	38.13
Charlottesville	6.13	0.00	Portsmouth	4.73	21.86
Danville	8.92	45.24	Richmond	5.60	28.47
Lynchburg	8.98	68.88	Roanoke	13.30	87.57
Newport News	9.99	44.34	Staunton	16.50	32.85
Norfolk	12.13	37.07			

TABLE XII

The homicide rates given in Table XII show the records of each of the counties in the vital statistics registration area, if the necessary information could be secured. In many states the practice of changing county lines at frequent intervals prevents the census bureau from being able to estimate populations for intercensus years. Since, in general, the population of rural areas is fairly stationary, the records of the census of 1920 have been occasionally

[1] Based upon data for 1925 only.
[2] Based upon data for 1920 only.

used when later estimates could not be secured. When this has been done, proper notation has been made.

In presenting the data for cities the rates are given in italics whenever the calculation was based upon less than five homicidal deaths. For counties, however, this practice was not followed, since nearly all rates were calculated from a small number of homicides. The rates for counties should, therefore, be accepted with caution. Similarly, because of the small number of homicides represented rates were not calculated for whites and colored separately, even when the requisite data were available.

Unless otherwise noted, the omission of the name of any county means that for the years under survey there were no homicides reported from that territory. The rates for counties, moreover, do not include data for cities having 10,000 or more inhabitants according to the census of 1920.

TABLE XII. HOMICIDES PER 100,000 POPULATION FOR COUNTIES EX-
CLUSIVE OF CITIES OF 10,000 OR MORE INHABITANTS, U. S.
REGISTRATION AREA, 1920 AND 1925 COMBINED
(Counties omitted had no homicides reported.)

ALABAMA COUNTIES

County	Rate	County	Rate	County	Rate
Autauga[1]	10.6	Coosa[1]	6.7	Jefferson[1]	33.9
Baldwin[1]	13.5	Covington[1]	9.6	Lauderdale[1]	6.3
Barbour[1]	18.7	Crenshaw[1]	26.1	Lawrence[1]	39.1
Bibb[1]	17.2	Cullman[1]	5.6	Lee[1]	9.1
Bullock[1]	7.9	Dale[1]	8.6	Limestone[1]	3.0
Butler[1]	30.2	Dallas[1]	7.8	Lowndes[1]	19.7
Chambero[1]	2.3	DeKalb[1]	5.3	Macon[1]	25.5
Chilton[1]	4.4	Elmore[1]	24.9	Madison[1]	9.3
Choctaw[1]	31.8	Escambia[1]	16.3	Marengo[1]	13.9
Clarke[1]	15.2	Franklin[1]	4.3	Marion[1]	8.1
Cleburne[1]	7.5	Greene[1]	16.5	Mobile[1]	4.4
Coffee[1]	6.2	Hale[1]	4.1	Monroe[1]	13.4
Colbert[1]	11.1	Henry[1]	18.3	Montgomery[1]	20.4
Conecuh[1]	22.7	Houston[1]	11.7	Morgan[1]	20.6

[1] Based upon data for 1925 only.

Perry[1]	7.9	Shelby[1]	22.1	Walker[1]	12.0
Pickens[1]	3.9	Sumter[1]	15.6	Washington[1]	35.0
Pike[1]	24.9	Talladega[1]	11.7	Wilcox[1]	6.4
Russell[1]	14.1	Tallapoosa[1]	6.7	Winston[1]	6.6
		Tuscaloosa[1]	9.1		

CALIFORNIA COUNTIES

Alameda	3.3	Los Angeles[4]	7.1	San Luis Obispo	4.4
Amador	6.4	Madera	14.9	San Mateo	8.8
Butte	9.7	Marin	14.3	Santa Barbara	8.6
Calaveras	8.1	Mendocino	8.3	Santa Clara	4.7
Colusa	5.1	Monterey	15.4	Santa Cruz	16.3
Contra Costa	9.8	Napa	2.4	Shasta	18.7
Del Norte	17.3	Nevada	9.2	Siskiyou	10.8
Eldorado	7.8	Orange	6.7	Solano	2.4
Fresno	6.6	Placer	13.4	Sonamo	12.2
Humboldt	5.9	Plumas	17.2	Stanislaus	4.0
Imperial	19.0	Riverside	8.7	Tehama	15.0
Inyo	7.1	Sacramento	17.4	Tulare	5.3
Kern	3.9	San Benito	5.4	Tuolumne	12.9
Kings	10.5	San Bernardino	17.4	Ventura	7.8
Lake	18.5	San Diego	6.8	Yolo	2.8
Lassen	36.3	San Joaquin	10.0	Yuba	9.5

COLORADO COUNTIES

Adams	6.2	Huerfano	5.6	Otero[4]	13.3
Arapahoe	13.5	Jefferson	10.4	Ouray	19.1
Archuleta	13.5	Kiowa	25.0	Phillips	8.1
Bent	4.5	Larimer	8.7	Prowers	6.6
Boulder	2.4	Las Animas	21.9	Pueblo	22.1
Chaffee	12.9	Logan	11.8	Rio Blanco	29.5
Costilla[4]	9.9	Mesa	4.5	Rio Grande	6.1
Douglas	13.8	Mineral	64.2	Routt[4]	22.4
El Paso	7.1	Moffat[4]	29.3	San Juan	29.4
Fremont	8.4	Montezuma	7.5	San Miguel	9.2
Garfield	10.8	Montrose	2'0.3	Teller	14.9
Grand	17.2	Morgan	5.5	Weld	4.3
				Yuma	6.4

CONNECTICUT COUNTIES

Fairfield[4]	1.2	Middlesex	3.9	New London	1.2
Hartford	2.5	New Haven	3.3	Windham	6.2

DELAWARE COUNTIES

Kent	4.8	New Castle	2.5	Sussex	4.6

[1] Based upon data for 1925 only.

[4] Population for 1925 not estimated. In place of it the estimated population for July 1, 1920, was used.

FLORIDA COUNTIES

Alachua	35.8	Hardee[1]	39.3	Osceola	5.6
Baker	71.3	Hernando	32.4	Palm Beach	44.8
Bay	21.5	Highlands[1]	42.4	Pasco	34.2
Bradford	25.6	Hillsborough	12.0	Pinellas	7.7
Brevard	37.1	Holmes	11.8	Polk	23.2
Broward	56.8	Jackson	10.9	Putnam	9.5
Calhoun	14.9	Jefferson	24.7	St. Johns	40.7
Citrus	28.3	Lafayette	18.3	St. Lucie	40.7
Clay	28.6	Lake	25.2	Santa Rosa	3.5
Columbia	26.8	Lee	9.2	Sarasota[1]	59.7
Dade	36.5	Leon	18.4	Seminole	23.3
De Soto	41.1	Levy	43.8	Sumter	12.6
Dixie[1]	23.6	Liberty	40.5	Suwannee	11.1
Duval	46.4	Madison	12.5	Taylor	44.8
Escambia	5.5	Manatee	28.6	Volusia	25.2
Flagler	21.5	Marion	23.5	Wakulla	9.1
Franklin	18.9	Okaloosa	5.2	Walton	3.9
Gadsden	14.4	Okeechobee	47.7	Washington	18.0
Hamilton	5.1	Orange	15.5		

IDAHO COUNTIES

Bannock[6]	8.0	Boundary[6]	22.4	Lemhi[1]	37.0
Benewah[6]	14.3	Canyon[6]	7.4	Power[6]	19.6
Bingham[6]	5.5	Caribou[6]	45.6	Shoshone[1]	20.8
Blaine[6]	22.4	Cassia[6]	6.4	Washington[6]	21.2
Bonner[6]	7.7	Clearwater[6]	20.0		

ILLINOIS COUNTIES

Adams	14.2	Franklin	11.2	McDonough	1.8
Alexander	16.8	Fulton	5.4	McLean	1.2
Bureau	4.7	Gallatin	23.3	Macoupin	1.7
Carroll	5.1	Greene	2.2	Madison	14.3
Cass	2.8	Hancock	7.0	Marion	8.0
Champaign	1.7	Hardin	26.0	Marshall	10.2
Christian	10.1	Jackson	11.5	Mason	3.0
Clark	2.4	Jefferson	5.3	Massac	3.7
Clay	2.8	Kane	7.5	Mercer	2.7
Clinton	2.2	Kankakee	3.5	Monroe	3.9
Cook	11.5	Knox	2.2	Montgomery	8.1
Cumberland	3.9	Lake	5.9	Morgan	2.8
De Witt	5.2	La Salle	1.9	Ogle	1.9
Du Page	5.6	Lawrence	2.3	Peoria	4.2
Effingham	5.1	Lee	1.8	Perry	21.6
Fayette	1.9	Livingston	2.6	Piatt	3.2

[1] Based upon data for 1925 only.

[6] Homicide data for 1925, only. Estimated population for 1925 not available. In place of it the population for 1920 was used.

Pike 3.7	Sangamon 2.4	Wayne 2.2
Pulaski 20.5	Tazewell 9.2	White 2.5
Randolph 5.2	Union 2.5	Whiteside 1.4
Rock Island ... 3.5	Vermilion 3.8	Will 9.8
St. Clair 6.5	Wabash 3.6	Williamson 14.0
Saline 11.0	Warren 4.7	Winnebago 3.6
	Washington 2.8	

INDIANA COUNTIES

Adams 2.4	Jackson 2.1	Pike 2.7
Allen 16.0	Jay 2.1	Porter 4.9
Blackford 3.6	Jefferson 14.5	Putnam 2.5
Carroll 3.1	Jennings 7.5	Ripley 2.7
Clark 2.6	Johnson 2.4	Rush 5.2
Clay 1.7	Knox 1.6	Shelby 3.9
Crawford 8.9	Kosciusko 1.8	Spencer 2.7
Dearborn 2.5	Lagrange 3.6	Starke 4.9
Decatur 5.6	Lake 9.7	Vanderburg 14.2
Delaware 2.8	Lawrence 1.8	Vermilion 5.6
Dubois 2.5	Madison 1.8	Vigo 7.1
Fayette 2.8	Marion 2.8	Wabash 1.8
Floyd 6.4	Monroe 3.9	Warrick 2.5
Fountain 5.3	Morgan 5.0	Washington 3.0
Grant 1.9	Ohio 12.4	Wayne 2.4
Hamilton 4.1	Orange 5.9	Wells 2.4
Henry 2.5	Perry 3.0	White 2.9
Huntington 2.9		

IOWA COUNTIES

Appanoose[1] 3.5	Harrison[1] 4.2	Monona[1] 17.9
Benton[1] 4.3	Howard[1] 15.0	Monroe[1] 4.9
Butler[1] 5.6	Jefferson[1] 6.1	Montgomery[1] .. 6.0
Cedar[1] 5.9	Johnson[1] 6.9	Page[1] 4.3
Cherokee[1] 12.0	Jones[1] 11.2	Plymouth[1] 4.2
Clay[1] 6.5	Lucas[1] 6.4	Polk[1] 7.2
Crawford[1] 4.9	Madison[1] 6.8	Sioux[1] 7.5
Dubuque[1] 5.3		

KANSAS COUNTIES

Allen 2.1	Cowley ...,.... 5.8	Ford 6.7
Anderson 3.8	Crawford 8.2	Franklin 7.1
Atchison 4.7	Dickinson 5.9	Feary 7.5
Barton 2.6	Doniphan 3.7	Graham 6.4
Brown 4.7	Douglas 4.4	Harvey 2.4
Butler 1.7	Edwards 7.1	Johnson 2.5
Cherokee 3.0	Ellis 16.9	Kearney 18.4
Coffey 3.4	Ellsworth 4.9	Kiowa 16.4

[1] Based upon data for 1925 only.

Labette	2.9	Montgomery	4.2	Sheridan	8.7
Leavenworth	2.4	Morris	4.3	Sumner	5.2
Linn	3.6	Osage	2.5	Thomas	8.1
McPherson	4.7	Pratt	11.6	Trego	8.2
Marion	2.2	Rawlins	7.1	Wilson	4.9
Miami	2.6	Rice	3.5	Wyandotte	2.7
		Shawnee	5.0		

KENTUCKY COUNTIES

Adair	5.7	Grant	14.4	McCracken	8.0
Allen	2.9	Graves	7.7	McCreary[4]	30.0
Anderson	10.0	Grayson	2.5	Madison	20.9
Barren	3.9	Greenup	7.3	Magoffin	10.8
Bath	8.3	Hancock	7.2	Marion	6.4
Bell	16.8	Hardin	4.0	Martin	6.4
Boone	5.2	Harlan	77.6	Mason	2.8
Bourbon	16.0	Harrison	9.5	Mercer	6.7
Boyd	21.9	Henderson	6.6	Montgomery	12.3
Boyle	16.6	Henry	7.5	Morgan	6.0
Breathitt	27.8	Hickman	4.9	Muhlenberg	11.5
Calloway	4.7	Hopkins	20.5	Nelson	9.3
Campbell	7.5	Jackson	4.2	Ohio	9.4
Carter	2.2	Jefferson	5.4	Owen	8.0
Casey	5.6	Jessamine	4.1	Perry	40.9
Christian	15.3	Johnson	12.3	Pike	25.5
Clark	8.4	Kenton	6.0	Pulaski[4]	8.8
Clay	19.6	Knott	16.8	Rockcastle	3.2
Clinton	23.0	Knox	12.1	Rowan	21.1
Cumberland	4.6	Lawrence	14.2	Russell	4.1
Edmonson	4.5	Lee	7.9	Shelby	5.4
Elliott	11.3	Leslie	24.0	Trigg	3.5
Estill	15.1	Letcher	29.6	Union	16.6
Fleming	9.6	Lewis	9.5	Warren	3.2
Floyd	21.6	Lincoln	9.1	Wayne[4]	9.3
Franklin	5.2	Livingston	10.3	Webster	19.3
Fulton	19.3	Logan	4.2	Whitley[4]	12.6
Garrard	7.9	Lyon	11.4	Wolfe	11.4

LOUISIANA COUNTIES

Acadia	5.6	Caddo	23.9	East Baton Rouge	26.6
Allen[4]	19.0	Calcasieu[4]	7.6	East Carroll	31.2
Ascension	4.5	Cameron	25.3	East Feliciana	14.3
Avoyelles	8.4	Catahoula	8.9	Evangeline[4]	8.5
Beauregard[4]	26.5	Claiborne	19.1	Franklin	16.2
Bienville	11.9	Concordia	28.1	Grant	13.9
Bossier	15.6	De Soto	20.1	Iberia	3.7

[4] Population for 1925 not estimated. In place of it the estimated population for July 1, 1920, was used.

Iberville	7.5	Pointe Coupee	6.1	St. Mary	1.6
Jackson	3.4	Rapides	7.8	St. Tammany	7.1
Jefferson	11.1	Red River	12.1	Tangipahoa	15.6
La Salle	5.0	Richland	37.9	Tensas	41.4
Lafayette	7.9	Sabine	14.3	Terrebonne	1.9
Lafourche	3.3	St. Bernard	30.2	Union	12.7
Lincoln	8.8	St. Charles	17.5	Vernon	48.9
Livingston	4.2	St. Helena	5.9	Washington	23.2
Madison	9.2	St. James	2.4	Webster	13.3
Morehouse	51.4	St. John the		West Baton	
Natchitoches	28.0	Baptist	4.2	Rouge	4.5
Ouachita	24.8	St. Landry[4]	13.5	West Feliciana	4.1
Plaquemines	4.9	St. Martin	2.3	Winn	9.3

MAINE COUNTIES

Androscoggin	3.0	Knox	1.9	Piscataquis	7.2
Aroostook	2.4	Oxford	1.3	Somerset	4.0
Kennebec	1.4	Penobscot	.8	York	2.4

MARYLAND COUNTIES

Allegany	6.2	Harford	5.1	Somerset	6.1
Baltimore	4.5	Howard	6.3	Talbot	8.2
Calvert	5.1	Kent	6.7	Washington	6.1
Carroll	4.4	Montgomery	5.6	Wicomico	12.3
Cecil	2.1	Prince Georges	5.5	Worcester	4.5
Frederick	3.7	St. Marys	3.1		

MASSACHUSETTS COUNTIES

Berkshire	4.1	Middlesex	1.8	Worcester	2.1
Bristol	0.7	Norfolk	1.6		
Hampden	1.1	Plymouth	3.1		

MICHIGAN COUNTIES

Arenac	10.6	Gratiot	1.4	Muskegon	8.6
Bay	6.9	Ingham	3.9	Oakland	2.5
Berrien	1.0	Ionia	3.0	Ontonagon	3.7
Calhoun	1.3	Iron	6.2	Oscoda	28.0
Cass	4.9	Kent	1.1	St. Clair	3.2
Charlevoix	3.2	Lapeer	1.9	Schoolcraft	4.8
Cheboygan	3.6	Lenawee	2.8	Van Buren	3.3
Clinton	4.3	Macomb	5.0	Washtenaw	5.0
Dickinson	7.7	Marquette	11.3	Wayne	6.1
Eaton	1.7	Mecosta	2.8	Wexford	5.5
Emmet	6.4	Midland	2.7		

[4] Population for 1925 not estimated. In place of it the estimated population for July 1, 1920, was used.

MINNESOTA COUNTIES

Aitkin	6.1	Houston	3.6	Olmsted	3.5
Becker	2.1	Hubbard	4.9	Pine	4.4
Beltrami[4]	3.6	Itasca	5.8	Ramsey	4.9
Brown	6.5	Jackson	3.1	Red Lake	6.7
Carlton	2.5	Koochiching	3.2	Renville	2.1
Carver	3.0	Lake	12.0	Rice	2.9
Cass	2.9	Lyon	2.5	St. Louis	10.3
Clay	2.2	McLeod	2.4	Stearns	1.2
Crow Wing	3.7	Mahnomen	7.0	Swift	3.2
Dakota	5.0	Meeker	2.7	Wadena	4.4
Freeborn	2.0	Nicollet	3.3	Waseca	3.5
Goodhue	1.6	Norman	3.3	Watonwan	3.9
Hennepin	2.8				

MISSISSIPPI COUNTIES

Adams	48.3	Itawamba	6.3	Perry	5.3
Alcorn	15.7	Jackson	9.8	Pike[4]	15.7
Amite	5.3	Jasper	13.5	Pontotoc	10.0
Attala	8.1	Jefferson	6.3	Prentiss	16.8
Benton	5.1	Jefferson Davis	11.8	Quitman	40.2
Bolivar	29.0	Jones	5.2	Rankin	12.3
Calhoun	20.8	Kemper	22.9	Scott	6.1
Carroll	12.3	Lafayette	18.2	Sharkey[4]	35.2
Chickasaw	33.8	Lamar	11.4	Simpson	13.6
Choctaw	8.0	Lauderdale	6.8	Smith	6.2
Claiborne	23.0	Lawrence	19.7	Stone[4]	15.3
Clarke	2.8	Leake	20.6	Sunflower[4]	34.5
Clay	14.3	Lee	10.1	Tallahatchie	28.9
Coahoma	34.3	Leflore	28.0	Tate	15.3
Copiah	7.0	Lincoln	16.2	Tishomingo	6.4
Covington	13.5	Lowndes	3.0	Tunica	38.2
De Soto	40.4	Madison	8.5	Union	9.8
Forrest	6.5	Marion[4]	23.3	Walthal[4]	29.7
Franklin	7.1	Marshall	15.3	Warren	16.4
George	18.0	Monroe	12.3	Washington[4]	19.0
Grenada	22.1	Montgomery	29.0	Wayne	12.7
Hancock	19.3	Neshoba	7.6	Webster	7.9
Harrison[4]	27.4	Newton	16.9	Wilkinson	16.3
Hinds	10.4	Noxubee	16.9	Winston	32.5
Holmes[4]	20.3	Oktibbeha	8.9	Yalobusha	16.0
Humphreys[4]	33.9	Panola	14.4	Yazoo[4]	37.7
Isaqueena	32.8	Pearl River	26.5		

MISSOURI COUNTIES

Adair	4.7	Barton	5.9	Boone	5.2
Barry	2.1	Bates	2.1	Butler	11.9

[4] Population for 1925 not estimated. In place of it the estimated population for July 1, 1920, was used.

Callaway	2.2	Jackson	7.4	Pulaski	4.8
Carroll	2.4	Jefferson	3.8	Putnam	3.8
Cass	4.6	Knox	23.2	Ralls	9.6
Christian	6.6	Lafayette	1.7	Randolph	13.6
Clay	17.1	Lawrence	2.1	Ray	7.3
Clinton	3.5	Lincoln	9.4	St. Charles	2.2
Cooper	2.6	Linn	2.0	St. Clair	6.5
Crawford	8.1	Macon	3.6	St. Francois	3.2
Dallas	8.3	Madison	4.7	St. Louis	11.8
Daviess	3.0	Mississippi	19.4	Ste. Genevieve	5.1
DeKalb	4.3	Morgan	4.2	Saline	6.9
Dunklin	14.9	New Madrid	9.3	Scott	4.2
Franklin	5.3	Oregon	3.9	Stoddard	6.6
Gentry	3.2	Ozark	13.5	Stone	8.3
Henry	2.0	Pemiscot	19.1	Texas	2.4
Holt	3.6	Pettis	10.5	Vernon	5.8
Howard	3.6	Pike	2.5	Webster	6.0
Howell	4.7	Platte	7.1	Wright	2.8

MONTANA COUNTIES

Beaverhead	6.5	Hill[4]	7.2	Rosebud[4]	25.0
Blaine[4]	6.5	Judith Basin[5]	19.1	Sanders	37.9
Chouteau[4]	13.6	Lewis and Clark	15.1	Silver Bow	10.5
Custer[4]	8.2	Musselshell[4]	24.9	Stillwater[4]	13.1
Daniels[5]	18.0	Park	4.3	Teton[4]	8.5
Fergus[4]	8.8	Pondera[4]	8.7	Toole[4]	13.4
Flathead[4]	2.3	Powell	13.8	Valley[4]	21.7
Gallatin	3.0	Roosevelt[4]	9.7	Wheatland[4]	8.9
Garfield[4]	9.3				

NEBRASKA COUNTIES

Boone	6.9	Holt	5.7	Rock	13.5
Box Butte	11.0	Jefferson	3.1	Sarpy	10.7
Boyd	6.1	Kimball	9.5	Saunders	2.4
Cherry	8.2	Knox	5.3	Scotts Bluff	4.1
Dodge	2.1	Lancaster	3.2	Seward	3.2
Fillmore	3.7	Morrill	19.0	Sheridan	9.7
Garden[4]	10.9	Nemaha	4.0	Stanton	6.4
Hall	5.1	Pierce	4.6	Wayne	20.6
				York	11.7

NEW HAMPSHIRE COUNTIES

Carroll	3.3	Grafton	2.5	Merrimack	3.4
Coos	2.5	Hillsborough	3.5		

[4] Population for 1925 not estimated. In place of it the estimated population for July 1, 1920, was used.

[5] New county formed since 1920 census. Homicide rate based upon homicides committed during 1925 and the enumerated population for April 1, 1930.

New Jersey Counties

Atlantic	5.6	Essex	3.0	Morris	4.8
Bergen	3.6	Gloucester	2.9	Passaic	5.6
Burlington	3.5	Hudson	8.9	Salem	2.5
Camden	2.2	Mercer	2.3	Somerset	6.9
Cape May	5.1	Middlesex	3.6	Union[4]	4.4
Cumberland	4.5	Monmouth	5.5	Warren	5.4

New York Counties

Albany	2.7	Genesee	3.8	Saratoga	4.1
Allegany	1.4	Herkimer	1.6	Schenectady	8.9
Broome	2.7	Livingston	2.6	Schoharie	4.7
Cattaraugus	2.9	Monroe	1.5	Seneca	2.0
Chautauqua	3.3	Montgomery	4.0	Steuben	2.0
Chemung	2.2	Nassau	2.7	Suffolk	3.9
Clinton	1.5	Oneida	1.6	Sullivan	1.4
Columbia	1.7	Onondaga	2.6	Tompkins	2.6
Cortland	3.0	Ontario	1.3	Ulster	2.9
Delaware	5.8	Orange	4.8	Warren	3.2
Dutchess	3.1	Otsego	1.4	Wayne	1.0
Erie	2.2	Rensselaer	3.1	Westchester	1.7
Essex	1.6	Rockland	2.0	Wyoming	3.3
Franklin	3.4	St. Lawrence	0.7		

North Carolina Counties

Alamance	4.4	Craven	8.4	Johnston	2.9
Alexander	4.0	Cumberland[4]	22.8	Jones	4.9
Alleghany	13.5	Davidson	1.4	Lee	7.1
Anson	17.1	Duplin	6.3	Lenoir	9.5
Ashe	2.3	Durham[4]	4.8	Lincoln	8.3
Avery[4]	4.8	Edgecombe	12.2	McDowell	2.8
Beaufort	12.9	Forsyth	3.7	Madison	5.0
Bertie	6.2	Franklin	5.5	Martin	11.5
Bladen	2.5	Gaston	3.7	Mecklenburg	5.8
Brunswick	10.0	Gates	4.7	Mitchell[4]	17.7
Buncombe	2.6	Granville	7.3	Montgomery	10.3
Burke	8.4	Greene	8.7	Moore	6.6
Cabarrus	12.5	Guilford	3.1	Nash	4.1
Caldwell[4]	7.5	Halifax	12.1	New Hanover	12.7
Carteret	9.4	Harnett	5.0	Northampton	8.5
Caswell	6.2	Haywood	10.3	Onslow	10.1
Catawba	7.0	Henderson	13.2	Orange	2.7
Chatham	6.2	Hertford	3.0	Pamlico	5.5
Cherokee	3.2	Hoke	8.5	Pasquotank	13.9
Chowan	14.1	Iredell	6.4	Pender	6.8
Columbus	8.1	Jackson	3.7	Perquimans	4.5

[4] Population for 1925 not estimated. In place of it the estimated population for July 1, 1920, was used.

Person	5.1	Sampson	2.6	Wake	9.8
Pitt	14.5	Scotland	22.4	Warren	9.1
Polk	5.4	Stanly	8.4	Washington	8.7
Randolph	6.4	Stokes	12.1	Watauga	7.4
Richmond	7.3	Surry	4.5	Wayne	9.0
Robeson[4]	10.1	Swain	3.6	Wilkes	6.0
Rockingham	9.7	Transylvania	10.0	Wilson	21.7
Rowan[4]	3.3	Union	12.2	Yadkin	3.0
Rutherford	3.1	Vance	4.2	Yancey	6.2

NORTH DAKOTA COUNTIES

Bowman[1]	22.1	Mountrail[1]	7.9	Stark[1]	7.1
Cass[1]	5.2	Ramsey[1]	12.7	Ward[1]	11.7
McIntosh[1]	10.8	Sargent[1]	10.8		

OHIO COUNTIES

Adams	8.9	Guernsey	1.5	Muskingum	1.8
Ashtabula	4.6	Hamilton	4.3	Ottawa	2.3
Athens	5.9	Hardin	1.7	Perry	2.8
Belmont	7.3	Highland	3.6	Portage	6.6
Brown	2.2	Hocking	2.2	Richland	1.8
Butler	6.4	Huron	4.6	Ross	1.9
Carroll	6.3	Jackson	1.8	Sandusky	2.0
Clark	2.5	Jefferson	9.8	Scioto	6.4
Clermont	1.8	Lake	3.3	Seneca	5.3
Columbiana	2.9	Lawrence	9.9	Stark	6.4
Coshocton	5.5	Licking	1.8	Summit[4]	5.4
Cuyahoga	4.7	Logan	1.7	Trumbull	4.3
Defiance	2.0	Lorain	1.5	Tuscarawas	7.4
Erie	3.0	Lucas	1.5	Van Wert	5.3
Franklin	4.6	Mahoning	6.4	Washington	1.8
Fulton	2.1	Marion	3.6	Wayne	1.2
Gallia	6.4	Medina	1.9	Wood	2.2
Geauga	6.6	Montgomery	2.5	Wyandot	2.6
Greene	4.7	Morrow	3.2		

OREGON COUNTIES

Baker	5.6	Harney	12.5	Malheur	4.3
Benton	3.4	Jackson	7.4	Multnomah[4]	8.3
Clackamas	3.7	Klamath	24.4	Polk	6.9
Coos	2.1	Lake	12.5	Tillamook	5.2
Deschutes[4]	10.4	Lane	3.9	Umatilla	1.8
Douglas	4.6	Linn	6.0	Union	6.0
				Wallowa	4.9
				Wasco	7.3

[1] Based upon data for 1925 only.

[4] Population for 1925 not estimated. In place of it the estimated population for July 1, 1920, was used.

PENNSYLVANIA COUNTIES

Allegheny 8.1	Crawford 2.2	Luzerne 2.8
Armstrong 1.3	Dauphin 0.8	Lycoming 2.3
Beaver 9.0	Delaware 2.4	McKean 7.5
Bradford 1.9	Elk 1.4	Mercer 6.0
Bucks 3.4	Erie⁴ 1.7	Montgomery ... 2.9
Butler 4.6	Fayette 11.1	Northumberland. 5.7
Cambria 2.2	Greene 9.6	Potter 4.7
Cameron 15.9	Huntingdon ... 2.5	Schuylkill 5.5
Carbon 1.5	Indiana 9.4	Somerset 7.5
Centre 1.1	Jefferson 1.0	Susquehanna ... 2.9
Chester 4.4	Lackawanna ... 6.3	Venango 1.3
Clarion 4.2	Lancaster 0.5	Washington ... 11.0
Clearfield 2.7	Lawrence 5.9	Wayne 1.8
Clinton 2.9	Lebanon 2.5	Westmoreland .. 7.1
Columbia 4.3	Lehigh 1.7	York 0.5

SOUTH CAROLINA COUNTIES

Abbeville⁴ 29.5	Dillon 11.5	Lexington 9.5
Aiken 20.3	Dorchester 2.5	McCormick⁴ ... 24.3
Allendale⁴ 12.4	Edgefield⁴ 14.6	Marion 6.1
Anderson 7.4	Fairfield 7.4	Marlboro 14.8
Bamberg 13.8	Florence 7.0	Newberry 11.2
Barnwell⁴ 17.3	Georgetown ... 9.2	Oconee 4.8
Beaufort⁴ 31.4	Greenville 6.5	Orangeburg ... 14.8
Berkeley 11.1	Greenwood⁴ 14.0	Pickens 1.7
Calhoun 15.8	Hampton⁴ 17.9	Richland 7.7
Charleston 10.7	Horry 5.9	Saluda 13.4
Cherokee 10.7	Jasper⁴ 20.3	Spartanburg ... 9.5
Chester 11.6	Kershaw 18.3	Sumter 16.9
Chesterfield 10.4	Lancaster 10.3	Union 3.3
Clarendon 4.2	Laurens 14.0	Williamsburg .. 9.0
Colleton 3.3	Lee 7.3	York 7.8
Darlington 10.0		

TENNESSEE COUNTIES

Anderson 2.7	Chester 10.2	Dyer 6.5
Bedford 4.6	Claiborne 10.7	Fayette 14.1
Bledsoe 20.1	Clay 16.2	Fentress 4.4
Blount 6.4	Cocke 21.2	Franklin 16.9
Bradley 7.7	Coffee 14.0	Gibson 4.6
Campbell 14.0	Crockett 2.8	Giles 6.5
Cannon 14.7	Cumberland ... 4.9	Grainger 7.5
Carroll 8.2	Davidson 12.0	Greene 13.5
Carter 6.8	De Kalb 3.3	Grundy 4.9
Cheatham 5.0	Dickson 5.2	Hamblen 9.7

⁴ Population for 1925 not estimated. In place of it the estimated population for July 1, 1920, was used.

Hamilton	5.0	Lincoln	13.6	Rhea	14.5
Hardeman	11.2	Loudon	5.9	Roane	11.9
Hardin	11.6	McMinn	15.2	Robertson	5.8
Hawkins	2.2	McNairy	2.6	Rutherford	9.1
Haywood	17.7	Madison	11.7	Scott	11.1
Henderson	5.3	Marion	11.5	Shelby	37.5
Henry	7.2	Marshall	2.9	Stewart	3.4
Hickman	3.1	Maury	7.1	Sullivan	7.7
Houston	8.1	Meigs	8.2	Sumner	7.1
Jackson	6.7	Monroe	15.6	Tipton	11.5
Jefferson	2.8	Montgomery	14.0	Unicoi	4.5
Johnson	4.1	Morgan	14.5	Union	4.3
Knox	1.6	Obion	10.6	Warren	11.4
Lake	27.2	Overton	5.5	Washington	2.3
Lauderdale	34.7	Perry	6.4	White	15.8
Lawrence	7.9	Pickett	19.0	Williamson	6.4
Lewis	26.3	Polk	17.5	Wilson	7.6
		Putnam	4.4		

UTAH COUNTIES

Box Elder	7.4	Grand	53.8	Uintah[4]	5.9
Carbon	34.1	Rich	26.4	Utah	3.2
Davis	4.2	Salt Lake	4.7	Weber	4.5
Duchesne[4]	11.0				

VERMONT COUNTIES

Bennington	2.3	Franklin	1.7	Windsor	1.3
Caledonia	5.8	Orleans	2.1		
Chittenden	2.4	Washington	3.5		

VIRGINIA COUNTIES

Accomac	7.2	(city)	31.8	Greensville	30.2
Albemarle	15.4	Culpeper	11.3	Halifax	6.0
Alleghany	6.4	Cumberland	5.5	Hanover	2.7
Arlington	8.2	Dickenson	13.4	Harrisonburg	
Augusta	4.2	Elizabeth City	13.5	(city)	8.1
Bedford	6.5	Essex	17.6	Henrico	9.1
Botetourt	9.1	Fairfax	2.2	Henry	16.9
Bristol (city)	7.3	Floyd	3.8	Isle of Wight	10.4
Brunswick	16.2	Fluvanna	5.8	James City	8.2
Buchanan	27.4	Franklin	13.3	King William	11.4
Campbell	7.2	Fredericksburg		Lancaster	10.2
Carroll	2.3	(city)	8.5	Lee	7.8
Charles City	20.9	Giles	4.2	Louisa	2.9
Charlotte	2.8	Gloucester	4.2	Lunenburg	6.2
Chesterfield	2.4	Grayson	5.1	Madison	5.2
Clifton Forge		Greene	7.9	Matthews	5.9

[4] Population for 1925 not estimated. In place of it the estimated population for July 1, 1920, was used.

Mecklenburg	7.8	Prince Edward	3.4	Southampton	1.8
Montgomery	2.6	Prince George		Suffolk (city)	26.0
Nansemond	7.3	Hopewell		Surry	16.1
Nelson	5.8	(city)	12.4	Sussex	3.9
Norfolk	12.0	Prince William	7.1	Tazewell	10.4
Northampton	8.2	Princess Anne	17.5	Warren	5.6
Northumberland	8.5	Pulaski	8.8	Warwick	28.8
Nottoway	7.0	Roanoke	4.1	Washington	6.2
Orange	11.3	Rockbridge	7.3	Winchester	
Patrick	11.9	Russell	7.2	(city)	13.6
Pittsylvania	5.2	Scott	16.0	Wise	36.8
Powhatan	15.0	Shenandoah	4.8	York	12.3

WASHINGTON COUNTIES

Benton	4.2	Kitsap	2.6	Skagit	5.8
Chelan	4.4	Kittitas	8.5	Snohomish	6.0
Clallam	3.9	Lewis	6.5	Spokane	2.8
Clarke	2.4	Lincoln	3.3	Thurston	4.2
Cowlitz	17.0	Pacific	19.2	Walla Walla	12.5
Gray's Harbor	14.2	Pend Oreille[4]	7.9	Whatcom	2.0
King[4]	6.0	Pierce	7.0		

WEST VIRGINIA COUNTIES

Barbour[1]	10.4	Kanawha[1]	4.3	Morgan[1]	11.6
Berkeley[1]	8.0	Lincoln[1]	5.2	Nicholas[1]	4.5
Boone[1]	5.5	Logan[1]	33.9	Pendleton[1]	10.2
Braxton[1]	12.2	McDowell[1]	36.1	Raleigh[1]	15.4
Brooke[1]	5.1	Marion[1]	5.0	Randolph[1]	18.4
Cabell[1]	7.6	Marshall[1]	30.7	Roane[1]	5.0
Fayette[1]	13.8	Mason[1]	4.7	Summers[1]	15.4
Gilmer[1]	9.4	Mercer[1]	13.6	Taylor[1]	10.0
Grant[1]	10.4	Mineral[1]	4.6	Wayne[1]	11.1
Greenbrier[1]	14.8	Mingo[1]	49.5	Wirt[1]	13.3
Hancock[1]	3.9	Monongalia[1]	23.9	Wyoming[1]	11.2
Harrison[1]	5.1	Monroe[1]	7.6		

WISCONSIN COUNTIES

Barron	1.4	Langlade	4.4	Polk	1.8
Bayfield	5.7	Marathon	1.0	Portage	2.2
Dodge	1.0	Marinette	2.4	Price	2.5
Douglas	9.3	Milwaukee	3.5	Racine	2.3
Dunn	1.8	Monroe	3.5	Sauk	1.5
Grant	1.3	Oconto	1.8	Taylor	2.6
Iron	4.6	Oneida	6.8	Washburn	8.1
Kenosha	9.2	Ozaukee	3.1	Winnebago	1.6
Lafayette	2.5	Pierce	2.3	Wood	5.6

[1] Based upon data for 1925 only.

[4] Population for 1925 not estimated. In place of it the estimated population for July 1, 1920, was used.

WYOMING COUNTIES

Albany[1]	.... 21.5	Fremont[6]	...... 16.9	Sweetwater[1]	... 33.8
Carbon[1]	.... 31.5	Hot Springs[6]	... 19.4	Uinta[6]	.... 15.1
Converse[6]	..... 12.7	Sheridan[1]	...... 10.4		

TABLE XIII

In Table XIII are presented the monthly distributions of homicides in the states of the registration area for the years 1923-1927. These totals have not, however, been corrected to equalize the length of the months. All data are for the five year period except that for the states named below the totals are only for the years mentioned: Alabama 1925, 1926, 1927; Arizona 1926, 1927; Arkansas 1927; Georgia 1923, 1924; North Dakota 1924, 1925, 1926, 1927; and West Virginia 1925, 1926, 1927. This table has been discussed at length in Chapter IX.

[1] Based upon data for 1925 only.

[6] Homicide data for 1925 only. Estimated population for 1925 not available. In place of it the population for 1920 was used.

TABLE XIII. MONTHLY DISTRIBUTION OF HOMICIDES, U. S. REGISTRATION
STATES, 1923-1927

STATES	Jan.	Feb.	Mar.	April	May	June	July	Aug.	Sept.	Oct.	Nov.	Dec.	Total	Range
Connecticut..........	17	19	18	22	27	20	22	20	20	17	16	13	231	13-27
Maine...............	9	1	2	5	7	4	6	8	8	7	0	9	66	0-9
Massachusetts........	43	37	39	30	46	42	45	50	40	54	35	38	499	30-54
New Hampshire.......	0	4	1	4	3	2	4	5	1	4	2	2	32	0-5
Rhode Island........	10	9	9	7	4	6	12	4	4	8	6	7	86	4-12
Vermont.............	1	2	1	0	4	2	1	3	0	3	2	1	20	0-4
NEW ENGLAND........	80	72	70	68	91	76	90	90	73	93	61	70	934	61-93
New Jersey..........	60	64	74	70	80	56	98	72	76	82	75	57	864	56-98
New York...........	213	205	202	231	233	238	278	285	233	246	234	219	2,817	202-285
Pennsylvania........	242	208	236	228	222	222	247	243	263	239	245	262	2,857	208-263
MIDDLE ATLANTIC.....	515	477	512	529	535	516	623	600	572	567	554	538	6,538	477-623
Illinois..............	264	273	294	313	265	302	345	300	310	342	281	343	3,632	264-345
Indiana.............	82	70	84	84	87	69	93	98	92	74	76	84	993	69-98
Michigan............	127	104	137	122	177	139	159	188	152	137	126	132	1,700	104-188
Ohio................	196	170	204	209	183	232	217	243	209	210	212	207	2,492	170-243
Wisconsin...........	13	22	24	21	27	26	18	32	35	40	37	25	320	13-40
EAST NORTH CENTRAL .	682	639	743	749	739	768	832	861	798	803	732	791	9,137	639-861
Iowa................	23	17	19	20	22	21	32	39	28	21	26	32	300	17-39
Kansas..............	41	26	52	39	33	33	59	53	38	36	51	38	499	26-59
Minnesota...........	21	26	34	36	27	27	38	43	31	35	17	30	365	17-43
Missouri.............	169	166	193	148	184	158	175	200	199	153	152	192	2,089	148-200
Nebraska............	26	23	20	21	18	11	30	30	22	17	16	16	250	11-30
North Dakota........	6	5	2	3	7	3	2	9	3	3	4	3	50	2-9
WEST NORTH CENTRAL.	286	263	320	267	291	253	336	374	321	265	266	311	3,553	253-374
Arizona	2	9	6	13	13	13	7	6	7	14	5	16	111	2-16
Colorado............	35	26	30	30	35	38	37	39	32	26	37	39	404	26-39
Idaho...............	4	4	7	8	10	13	9	5	3	13	7	7	90	3-13
Montana............	18	8	19	18	14	11	15	16	23	20	14	20	196	8-23
Utah................	7	17	11	7	8	6	12	10	14	9	8	6	115	6-17
Wyoming............	12	8	10	10	14	9	14	15	8	11	14	10	135	8-15
MOUNTAIN............	78	72	83	86	94	90	94	91	87	93	85	98	1,051	72-98
California............	168	128	144	141	147	159	147	154	174	141	145	165	1,813	128-174
Oregon..............	16	11	7	12	10	7	14	16	19	25	17	14	168	7-25
Washington..........	29	34	35	32	22	32	40	24	30	30	28	22	358	22-40
PACIFIC..............	213	173	186	185	179	198	201	194	223	196	190	201	2,339	173-223
Delaware............	6	3	5	8	14	6	5	6	6	4	8	8	79	3-14
District of Columbia...	16	23	27	16	20	21	19	24	17	19	32	28	262	16-32
Florida..............	186	194	208	195	191	198	178	189	180	168	141	238	2,266	141-238
Georgia.............	79	76	99	75	77	88	98	102	80	90	84	121	1,069	75-121
Maryland............	48	37	37	40	46	60	45	45	57	45	51	42	553	37-60
North Carolina.......	98	109	125	120	117	110	113	123	111	110	114	128	1,378	98-128

TABLE XIII (*Continued*)

STATES	*Jan.*	*Feb.*	*Mar.*	*April*	*May*	*June*	*July*	*Aug.*	*Sept.*	*Oct.*	*Nov.*	*Dec.*	*Total*	*Range*
South Carolina........	94	65	78	79	71	80	96	97	93	89	95	119	1,056	65-119
Virginia..............	75	108	99	105	91	82	97	116	108	111	113	117	1,222	75-117
West Virginia.........	46	52	33	50	58	51	51	57	53	58	53	69	631	33-69
SOUTH ATLANTIC......	648	667	711	688	685	696	702	759	705	694	691	870	8,516	648-870
Alabama.............	112	89	115	126	127	108	134	136	134	123	128	132	1,464	89-136
Kentucky............	106	145	163	148	164	145	163	197	162	144	165	188	1,890	106-197
Mississippi...........	135	126	153	173	174	151	195	181	133	144	163	165	1,893	126-195
Tennessee...........	140	144	168	177	165	168	243	214	183	185	161	211	2,159	140-243
EAST SOUTH CENTRAL..	493	504	599	624	630	572	735	728	612	596	617	696	7,406	493-735
Arkansas.............	24	23	24	17	35	25	28	30	13	28	28	40	315	13-40
Louisiana............	148	183	151	155	187	155	152	190	160	152	152	174	1,959	148-190
WEST SOUTH CENTRAL.	172	206	175	172	222	180	180	220	173	180	180	214	2,274	172-222
TOTALS.........	3,167	3,073	3,399	3,368	3,466	3,349	3,793	3,917	3,564	3,487	3,376	3,789	41,748	3,073-3,917

SELECTED BIBLIOGRAPHY

Adamic, Louis. "Racketeers and Organized Labor." *Harper's Magazine,* CLXL, 404-16 (September, 1930).

"Alcohol." *Encyclopaedia of the Social Sciences* I, 626. New York: Macmillan, 1930.

Aschaffenburg, Gustav. *Crime and Its Repression.* Boston: Little, Brown, 1913.

Ayres, L. P. *An Index Number for State School Systems.* New York: Russell Sage Foundation, 1920.

Baker, O. E. "Agricultural Regions of North America, Part II." *Economic Geography,* III, 50-86 (January, 1927).

Banks, William. "Canada's Effective Criminal Law System." *Current History,* XXVIII, 405-07 (June, 1928).

Bettman, Alfred. "What the Criminal Justice Surveys Show." *Proceedings of the National Conference of Social Work 1927,* 50-60.

Bierstadt, E. H. "Our Permanent Crime Wave." *Harper's Magazine,* CLVI, 61-70 (December, 1927).

Bjerre, Andreas. *The Psychology of Murder.* London: Longmans, Green, 1927.

Black, Jack. "What's Wrong With the Right People?" *Harper's Magazine,* CLIX, 75-82 (June, 1929).

Blanchard, Phyllis. *The Child and Society.* New York: Longmans, Green, 1928.

Borden, Mary. "A Defense of the English Climate." *Harper's Magazine,* CLXI, 28-33 (June, 1930).

Brasol, Boris. *The Elements of Crime.* New York: Oxford Press, 1927.

Burling, L. D. "Stages of Evolution and Relation to Crime." *Scientific Monthly,* XXIV, 431-9 (May, 1927).

Calvert, R. E. "Murder and the Death Penalty." *Nation,* CXXIX, 405-07 (October 16, 1929).

Case, C. M. "Social Imbecility and Social Age." *Sociology and Social Research,* XII, 218-42 (January-February, 1928).

"Confessions of a Dean: Sons of Divorce." *Saturday Evening Post,* CCII, 25 (January 11, 1930).

Cooper, C. R. "The Worst of Us." *Collier's Weekly,* LXXVII, 19 + (February 28, 1931).

Criminal Justice in Cleveland. Cleveland: Cleveland Foundation, 1922.

Dashiell, J. F. *Fundamentals of Objective Psychology.* Boston: Houghton, Mifflin, 1928.

Davis, Barnes, and Others. *Introduction to Sociology.* Boston: Heath, 1927.

Davis, H. B. "A Substitute for Lynching." *Nation,* CXXX, 12-14 (January 1, 1930).

Dexter, E. G. *Weather Influences.* New York: Macmillan, 1904.

Di Tullio, Benigno. "Biological Factors in Criminology." *Social Science Abstracts,* II, 946 (May, 1930).

Dodd, W. E. "Our Ingrowing Habit of Lawlessness." *Century,* CXVI, 691-8 (October, 1928).

Drever, James. *The Psychology of Industry.* London: Methuen, 1927.

Durrett, J. J., and Stromquist, W. G. "Preventing Violent Death." *Survey,* LIV, 435-8 (July 15, 1925).

Ellwood, C. A. *Sociology and Modern Social Problems.* New ed. rev. New York: American Book Co., 1924.

Ferri, Enrico. *Criminal Sociology.* Boston: Little, Brown, 1917.

Frenkel, Helene. "The Murderer Who is Not Motivated by Personal Gain." *Social Science Abstracts,* II, 947 (May, 1930).

Furfey, P. H. "Developmental Age." *American Journal of Psychiatry,* VIII, 149-57 (July, 1928).

Garrett, H. E. *Statistics in Psychology and Education.* New York: Longmans, Green, 1926.

Gillin, J. L. *Criminology and Penology.* New York: Century, 1926.

Gordon, R. G. "Certain Personality Problems in Relation to Mental Illness, With Special Reference to Suicide and Homicide." *Social Science Abstracts* I, 1546 (December, 1929).

Gorki, Maxim. "About Murderers." *Dial,* LXXXV, 201-10 (September, 1928).

Gunther, John. "The High Cost of Hoodlums." *Harper's Magazine,* CLIX, 529-40 (October, 1929).

Hartshorne, Hugh. "Sociological Implications of the Character Education Inquiry." *American Journal of Sociology,* XXVI, 251-62 (September, 1930).

Haynes, F. E. *Criminology.* New York: McGraw-Hill, 1930.

Healy, William, and Bronner, Augusta. *Delinquents and Criminals: Their Making and Unmaking.* New York: Macmillan, 1926.

Hoffman, F. L. "Murder and the Death Penalty." *Current History,* XXVIII, 408-10 (June, 1928).

——— *The Homicide Problem.* Newark: Prudential Press, 1925.

——— "The Homicide Record for 1929." Reprinted from the *Spectator,* March 22, 1930.

Holmes, F. L. "Making Criminals Out of Soldiers." *Nation,* CXXI, 114-5 (July 22, 1925).

Holmes, J. L. "Crime and the Press." Reprinted from the *Journal of Criminal Law and Criminology,* XX, Nos. 1 and 2 (May and August, 1929).

Huntington, Ellsworth. *Civilization and Climate.* 3rd ed. New Haven: Yale University Press, 1924.

——— "Temperature and the Fate of Nations." *Harper's Magazine,* CLVII, 361-8 (August, 1928).

Huxley, Julian. "Mice and Men." *Harper's Magazine,* CLVI, 42-50 (December, 1927).

Illinois Crime Survey. Chicago: Illinois Association for Criminal Justice, 1929.

Jesse, F. T. *Murder and Its Motives.* New York: Knopf, 1924.

Johnson, C. S., and Others. *The Negro in American Civilization.* New York: Holt, 1930.

Koller, A. H. *The Theory of Environment.* Part I. Menasha: Banta, 1918.

Laski, H. J. "The Dangers of Obedience." *Harper's Magazine,* CLIX, 1-10 (June, 1929).

Leffingwell, Albert. *Illegitimacy and the Influence of the Seasons Upon Conduct.* New York: Scribner's, 1892.

Lichtenberger, J. P. *The Development of Social Theory.* New York: Century, 1923.

Lombroso, Cesare. *Crime: Its Causes and Its Remedies.* Boston: Little, Brown, 1918.

McAdoo, William. "Causes and Mechanisms of Prevalent Crimes." *Scientific Monthly,* XXIV, 415-20 (May, 1927).

Mackaye, Milton. "Youthful Killers." *Outlook,* CLI, 3-6 (January 2, 1929).

Maynard, L. M. "Murder in the Making." *American Mercury,* XVII, 129-35 (June, 1929).

Merz, Charles. "Bigger and Better Murders." *Harper's Magazine,* CLV, 338-43 (August, 1927).

Miller, R. S. "Divorce and Child Crime." *Ladies' Home Journal,* XLIV, 26 (March, 1927).

Miner, J. R. "Church Membership and the Homicide Rate." *Social Science Abstracts,* II, 947-8 (May, 1930).

Missouri Crime Survey. New York: Macmillan, 1926.

"Modern Crime: Its Prevention and Punishment." *Annals* of the American Academy of Political and Social Science, CXXV, 1-286 (May, 1926).

"More Murders." *Literary Digest,* CV, 13 (April 5, 1930).

Murchison, Carl. "Criminal Intelligence," *Journal of the American Institute of Criminal Law and Criminology,* XV, 239-316 and 435-94.

"Murderous America." *Literary Digest,* XCVIII, 17 (July 21, 1928).

National Commission on Law Observance and Enforcement. *Reports.* Washington: Government Printing Office, 1931.

Nock, A. J. "Officialism and Lawlessness." *Harper's Magazine,* CLX, 11-19 (December, 1929).

Odum, H. W. *An American Epoch.* New York: Holt, 1930.
——— *Man's Quest for Social Guidance.* New York: Holt, 1927.
Odum, H. W., and Jocher, Katharine. *Introduction to Social Research.* New York: Holt, 1929.
Ogburn, W. F., and Winston, Ellen. "The Frequency and Probability of Insanity." *American Journal of Sociology,* XXXIV, 822-31 (March, 1929).
Oliver, J. R. *Foursquare.* New York: Macmillan, 1929.
"Our 12,000 Killings in 1926." *Literary Digest,* XCIV, 12-13 (July 2, 1927).
Parmelee, Maurice. *Criminology.* New York: Macmillan, 1918.
Phelps, H. A. "Rhode Island's Threat Against Murder." *Journal of the American Institute of Criminal Law and Criminology,* XV, 552-67 (February, 1925).
Poffenberger, A. T. *Applied Psychology.* New York: Appleton, 1927.
Pound, Arthur. "The Iron Man and the Mind." *Atlantic Monthly,* CXXIX, 179-89 (February, 1922).
——— "The Sunny Side of Crime." *Independent,* CXVI, 708-10 (June 19, 1926).
Quiros, Bernaldo de. *Modern Theories of Criminality.* Boston: Little, Brown, 1911.
Reforming America With a Shotgun. Washington: Association Against the Prohibition Amendment, 1929.
Reuter, E. B. *American Race Problems.* New York: Crowell, 1927.
Robinson, L. N. *Criminal Statistics.* Boston: Houghton, Mifflin, 1911.
Sands, Irving, and Blanchard, Phyllis. *Abnormal Behavior.* New York: Moffat, Yard, 1923.
Schlapp, M. G., and Smith, E. H. *The New Criminology.* New York: Boni and Liveright, 1928.
Schmidt, C. F. "A Study of Homicides in Seattle, 1914-24." *Social Forces,* IV, 745-56 (June, 1926).

Shaw, C. R. "Correlation of Rate of Juvenile Delinquency with Certain Indices of Community Organization and Disorganization." *Proceedings* of the American Sociological Society, XXII, 174-9 (1928).

Shaw, C. R., and Others. *Delinquency Areas.* Chicago: University of Chicago Press, 1929.

Sherrill, G. R. *Criminal Proceedings in North Carolina.* Chapel Hill: University of North Carolina Press, 1930.

Sockman, Ralph. "Morals in a Machine Age." *Harper's Magazine,* CLXII, 365-74 (February, 1931).

Sorokin, P. A. *Contemporary Sociological Theories.* New York: Harper, 1928.

South Carolina. *Annual Report of the Attorney General.* Columbia: State Printers, 1920-1926.

——— *Code of Laws.* Volume II. Columbia: State Printers, 1922.

Statistical Bulletin of the Metropolitan Life Insurance Co., VII, 1-4 (December, 1926).

Sutherland, E. H. *Criminology.* Philadelphia: Lippincott, 1924.

——— "Murder and the Death Penalty." *Journal of the American Institute of Criminal Law and Criminology,* XV, 522-9 (February, 1925).

Tallack, William. *Penological and Preventive Principles.* London: Wertheimer, Lea, 1896.

Tersiev, N. "The Evaluation of Their Deeds on the Part of Condemned Murderers." *Social Science Abstracts,* II, 1661-2 (October, 1930).

Thomas, D. S. *Social Aspects of the Business Cycle.* London: Routledge, 1925.

Thomas, Franklin. *The Environmental Basis of Society.* New York: Century, 1925.

United States Bureau of the Census. *Fourteenth Census of the United States.* Volumes I, II, III, IV, and *Abstract.* Washington: Government Printing Office.

——— *Mortality Statistics 1916-1928* (Inclusive.) Washington: Government Printing Office.

———— *Prisoners 1923, 1926, 1927*. Washington: Government Printing Office.

———— *The Prisoner's Antecedents*. Washington: Government Printing Office, 1929.

United States Department of Agriculture. *Census of Agriculture, 1925*. Washington: Government Printing Office.

———— *Seedtime and Harvest*. Circular 183. Washington: Government Printing Office, 1922.

United States Department of Commerce. *Statistical Abstract of the United States, 1929*. Washington: Government Printing Office.

United States Department of Justice. *Uniform Crime Reports*, I, No. 5. December, 1930.

"U. S. Redder Than Russia." *Literary Digest*, XCVII, 12 (April 21, 1928).

United States Weather Bureau. *Climatological Data*, XXIV-XXIX, No. 13. South Carolina Section. Columbia, 1921-1926.

———— *Summary of Climatological Data for the United States, by Sections*. Sections 87 and 88. Washington.

Venn, F. E. "Murder." *Independent*, CXIII, 361-2 (November 8, 1924).

Villard, O. G. "Official Lawlessness." *Harper's Magazine*, CLV, 605-14 (October, 1927).

Waite, J. B. "Control of Crime." *Atlantic Monthly*, CXXXVII, 214-9. (February, 1926).

Wines, F. H. *Punishment and Reformation*. (Revised edition by Lane.) New York: Crowell, 1919.

World's Almanac. New York: World Publishing Co., 1922 and 1930.

INDEX

ABBE, Cleveland, 198.
Adaptation to climate, 197.
Agar, W. E., 194.
Age of homicide victims, 78-80.
Agricultural activities and homicide, 198-9.
Alcohol and homicide, 46-7, 58-61, 89, 180-1, 195. *See also* Prohibition.
All-Ukrainian Cabinet for Research in Criminality and the Criminal, 88-9.
Alpha intelligence test, 83-4.
Arrest: of slayers, 132-4; statistics of, 200-1.
Aschaffenburg, G., 152, 164, 182.
Assault and battery, monthly variation in, 169-71, 182.
Assault with intent to kill. *See* Attempted homicide.
Association Against the Prohibition Amendment, 46-7.
Atlanta, Georgia, 66.
Attempted homicide, punishment of, 139-40.
Aubrey, Paul, 9.
Australia, 27, 50, 68.
Ayres, L. P., 44-5.

BABSON, R. W., 32-3.
Baker County, Florida, 105.
Baker, O. E., 199.
Banks, William, 75-6, 123-4.
Baptists, 160.
Barometric pressure and homicide, 171.
Berlin, 27.
Bettman, Alfred, 120, 137-8, 142.
Binet-Simon intelligence test, 84.
Birmingham, Alabama, 49, 66.
Bjerre, Andreas, 9-10, 89.
Biological defects. *See* Degeneracy.
Blackstone, William, 138.
Blanchard, Phyllis, 33, 165.
Bodin, Jean, 161.

Borden, Mary, 192-4.
Boston, Massachusetts, 154, 193.
Brill, A. A., 31.
Bronner, Augusta, 33.
Burglary and homicide. *See* Robbery.
Burling, L. D., 140.
Burt, Cyril, 33.
Business cycles and homicide, 160.

CALABRIA, 28.
California, 153.
Calvert, R. E., 59, 81, 108, 122-3, 131-2.
Canada, 8, 27-8, 50, 75-6, 123-4, 132.
Canadian police, 132.
Capital punishment: value of, 126-9; of Negroes, 110; "death watch" in, 129-31; absence of, 139.
Case, C. M., 96 n.
Cases: Hickman, 37-8; Hotelling, 38; S., 51-2; Colonel C., 52; P., 52-4; Welch, 54-5; C. H., 55-6; Ev and Amati, 90; Loeb-Leopold, 91-2, 118; Mr. A., 93; Harry K. Thaw, 117-8; Gray-Snider, 118; Hall-Mills, 118; Birger, 135.
Catholics, Roman, and homicide, 159-60.
Causes of homicide. *See* Explanations and Inciting causes.
Certainty of punishment, effect of, 137-9.
Chicago, Illinois, 5, 8, 58, 63, 66, 67, 97, 101-2, 112-3, 119-20, 127, 132, 149.
Chain gangs, 87.
Chinese and homicide, 97-8.
Christmas and homicide, 179-81, 187.
Church membership and homicide, 159-60.
Cities, homicide rates of, 207-19.
City. *See* Urban.
Civilization defined, 55.

[243]

Venn, F. E., 50, 72.
Vice and homicide, 157.
Vicksburg, Mississippi, 105.
Victims of homicide, 78-82.
Villard, O. G., 67.

W AR and homicide, 31-2.
Washington, D. C., 63, 101.

Weaklings and homicide, 89-91, 96.
Wealth and homicide, 29-30.
Weather and homicide, 161-99.
Williams, G. C., 110.
Winds and homicide, 171-2.
Winston, Ellen, 42-3.

"Y ELLOW journalism," 35-40.

www.ingramcontent.com/pod-product-compliance
Lightning Source LLC
Chambersburg PA
CBHW021812270326
41932CB00007B/160